# Defending the Faith

D. G. Hart

# DEFENDING THE FAITH

## J. Gresham Machen and the

## Crisis of Conservative Protestantism

## in Modern America

 Baker Books

A Division of Baker Book House Co
Grand Rapids, Michigan 49516

©1994 by The Johns Hopkins University Press

First published by The Johns Hopkins University Press
2715 North Charles Street, Baltimore, MD 21218-4319
The Johns Hopkins Press Ltd., London

First paperback edition published in 1995 by Baker Books
a division of Baker Book House Company
P.O. Box 6287, Grand Rapids, MI 49516-6287

Printed in the United States of America

**Library of Congress Cataloging-in-Publication Data**

Hart, D. G. (Darryl G.)
    Defending the faith: J. Gresham Machen and the crisis of conservative Protestantism in modern America / D. G. Hart.
       p.    cm.
    Originally published: Baltimore : Johns Hopkins University Press, c 1994.
    Includes bibliographical references and index.
    ISBN 0-8010-2023-9 (paper)
    1. Machen, J. Gresham (John Gresham), 1881–1937. 2. Presbyterian Church—United States—Clergy—Biography. 3. Presbyterian Church in the U.S.A.—Clergy—Biography. 4. Orthodox Presbyterian Church—Clergy—Biography. 5. Modernist-fundamentalist controversy. I. Title.
[BX9225.M24H37    1995]
285′.1′092—dc20
[B]                                         95-15099

A catalog record for the original cloth edition of this book is available from the British Library.

# CONTENTS

This book is about J. Gresham Machen (1881–1937), the scion of a prominent and genteel Baltimore family, who studied at the finest American and European universities and, while teaching at Princeton Seminary, went on to become one of the United States's leading authorities in New Testament studies. This side of Machen's life is not as well known as his involvement in the fundamentalist controversy of the 1920s. A devout Presbyterian, Machen railed against the infidelities of theological modernists and eventually left the Protestant establishment to found a new seminary and denomination. ← What is the name of the Seminary?

This capsule summary of Machen's career highlights a number of anomalies that make him an interesting object for study. (He was known as a gentleman and a scholar, two traits not associated with the militancy, stridency, and populism of fundamentalism even in recent revisionist accounts of the movement.) ← interesting

Westminister Seminary in Philly

Explaining how a privileged and learned Protestant became embroiled in the religious disputes of the 1920s is one purpose of this book. To understand Machen's involvement in the fundamentalist-modernist controversy, we need to locate the religious conflict over America's churches and schools in the broader intellectual and cultural climate of the 1920s, a climate that cultivated dissatisfaction with the white Anglo-Saxon Protestant ethos of American culture generally and the tenor of Protestant church life specifically. A variety of conservative intellectuals, from the New Humanists to the Southern Agrarians, denounced the modernizing drift of mainstream Protestantism. Machen's criticism of liberal Protestantism echoed many of these complaints. To be sure, he attracted a following within fundamentalist circles—one that had all but dried up by the time of his premature death in 1937. But his attraction for fundamentalists should not obscure Machen's identity as a conservative intellectual who opposed religious modernism for reasons having as much to do with his academic training and social background as with his Presbyterian convictions. Nor should it conceal his identity as a Presbyterian traditionalist who championed Calvinistic creeds and Reformed patterns of church government against the innovations of fundamentalists and modernists alike.

 A further anomaly about Machen was the way his critique of mainstream Protestantism was received by secular intellectuals. The support he garnered from prominent members of the liberal intelligentsia, a surprising twist in the fundamentalist controversy, reveals a puzzling and limited but nonetheless genuine alliance during the 1920s between  orthodox belief and secularism. Machen was by no means representative on this score, but his critique of liberal Protestantism was a religious expression of the post–World War I attack upon America's religious and cultural establishment, what one historian has called "the rebellion against Victorianism."[1] Of course, Machen's reasons for opposing the Protestant establishment differed from those of secularists. Nevertheless, unlike fundamentalist and modernist Protestants, Machen fully rejected the hope of building a Christian civilization in America and so found himself on the same side with other secular intellectuals in many of the cultural conflicts of the 1920s.

A study of Machen's thought and career, therefore, has much to tell us not just about the issues that unsettled—some would say unseated—mainstream Protestantism's hold on American intellectual and cultural life. But it also offers a distinctive and revealing perspective on the way we have come to assess and locate religion, science, and modernity in the early twentieth century.

# ACKNOWLEDGMENTS

I began this book in 1985. Since that time my dear wife, Ann, has been a constant source of support, encouragement, and good sense. Her affection has tempered the disappointments and enriched the satisfactions of academic life. As a partial payment I dedicate this to her.

I am also grateful for assistance, both financial and intellectual, from the department of history at the Johns Hopkins University, where this project started. Wheaton College and the Pew Charitable Trusts provided generous support to the Institute for the Study of American Evangelicals which allowed me to complete revisions. An additional grant from Wheaton College's Aldeen Faculty Development Fund subsidized the completion of the index. Timothy L. Smith deserves special mention for his careful reading, astute criticism, and his wise counsel both as advisor in graduate school and friend since. Mark Noll's guidance, encouragement, and example have been indispensable to this book and my understanding of American Protestantism. Among the other readers who provided many helpful comments along the way were Ronald G. Walters, John Higham, George M. Marsden, Harry Stout, William R. Hutchison, Richard B. Gaffin, Jeffrey A. Charles, and David Watt. For virtually unlimited access to the Machen papers at the Montgomery Library of Westminster Seminary and for their friendship many thanks go to John R. Muether, Grace Mullen, and Jane Patete. Thanks also go to the Johns Hopkins University Press and especially to Robert J. Brugger for much patience and steadying advice in seeing this project through to publication. Finally, Therese D. Boyd deserves recognition for her attentive and conscientious work as copyeditor.

# Religion and Cultural Modernism

# in America

By most accounts, the post–World War I era in American history witnessed the splintering of religion from cultural and intellectual life. According to one recent assessment, intellectuals in the 1920s came to regard religion as "alien to their endeavors" because the prevailing outlook among intellectuals was "cosmopolitan and irreligious." This verdict only repeats what contemporaries believed. More than sixty years ago, in 1931, describing the "revolt of the highbrows," Frederick Lewis Allen summarized the credo of the country's writers, artists, and intellectuals. These restless souls promoted sexual freedom, defied propriety, opposed Prohibition, took pleasure in overturning popular idols, and in general were "religious skeptics." "Never before," Allen wrote, "had so many books addressed to the thinking public assumed at the outset that their readers had rejected the old theology." The "chief tomtom beater" of this cultural offensive, in Allen's judgment, was the Baltimore journalist and editor H. L. Mencken, for whom rebellion was the breath of life. Mencken derided almost every convention of America's middle class, from "the religion of Coolidge Prosperity" to the sentimentality and idealism of polite literature. According to Walter Lippmann, himself an important member of America's secular intelligentsia, Mencken was "the most powerful personal influence" on a whole generation of educated people.[1]

What Allen failed to recognize was that, despite the highbrows' antipathy toward religion, the void created by the lapsing of belief still absorbed the attention of many intellectuals, including Mencken and Lippmann. Just before the appearance of Allen's *Only Yesterday*, for instance, Lippmann published *A Preface to Morals* (1929) and Mencken followed with *A Treatise on the Gods* (1930). To be sure, neither Lippmann nor Mencken embraced the Protestant values that theretofore had dominated American culture and institutions. Yet both authors confronted directly what they considered a central problem in modern American society, namely, the loss of traditional beliefs in the face of widespread cultural change. For Lippmann, the problem of modern unbelief was without precedent. "This is the first age," he wrote, "when the circumstances of life have conspired with the intellectual habits of the time to render any fixed and authoritative belief incredible to large masses of men." This predicament haunted Lippmann for it meant that "whirl [was] king" and that modern men and women no longer possessed certain foundations for moral and spiritual ideals. Debunker that he was, Mencken was less troubled than Lippmann by the loss of religious certainty and more eager to mock the superstitions still prevalent in rural America. Nevertheless, even Mencken sounded at least a trifle concerned about the skepticism embraced by the educated. "What survives under the name of Christianity, above the stratum of the mob, is no more than a sort of Humanism with little more supernaturalism in it than you will find in mathematics or political economy."[2]

Such words, though betraying anxiety about the loss of religion, were hardly consoling to the leaders of America's Protestant churches. For almost a half century theologians and clergy of various denominations had been overhauling Protestant beliefs, hoping to appropriate new directions in the intellectual world in order to preserve the allegiance of the very people for whom Mencken and Lippmann professed to speak. Now they were being told that the whole project of refashioning Christianity in modern garb had failed. Reactions to Mencken and Lippmann from prominent Protestants were predictable. Reinhold Niebuhr dismissed Mencken for telling "little more than how one fanatic feels about other fanatics of a different type." Lippmann provoked a deeper response. George A. Gordon, a prominent Boston Congregationalist, complained that Lippmann had "everywhere overdone" the modern loss of certainty. Meanwhile, the popular preacher Harry Emerson Fosdick was irritated enough by Lippmann to accuse him of being a closet fundamentalist. The only religion Lippmann could understand, Fosdick snapped, was "the most naive and medieval sort"; Lippmann was not "at home with any intelligent religion since the Deism of the eighteenth century went to pieces."[3]

Fosdick's rejoinder to Lippmann touched a little noticed irony that accompanied the breach between religious leaders and intellectuals during the 1920s. One stimulus to books such as Lippmann's and Mencken's was their perception that modern Protestantism was intellectually bankrupt. According to Lippmann, the faith of mainstream Protestants was incapable of supplying the certainty modern culture needed. "Something quite fundamental is left out of the modernist creeds," he wrote. They reject revelation, the authority of any particular church, and the inspiration of the Bible. In sum, modern Protestants had lost the conviction "that religion comes from God." Mencken spoke in similar terms. The effort to reconcile Protestantism and modern learning had reduced Christianity to "a vague sort of good will to men" with little more clout in the wider world than abstract notions such as "justice" or nostalgic claims about the love of God. The irony in such criticisms, as Fosdick perceived, was that Lippmann and Mencken, themselves resolutely modern, were echoing the opinions of Protestant fundamentalists. By faulting the leaders of Protestant churches for abandoning the traditional, if unfashionable, tenets of Christianity, secular intellectuals were in fact advancing the fundamentalist argument that Protestant modernism compared poorly with historic, doctrinal Christianity.[4]

The possibility that America's secular intelligentsia might join Protestant fundamentalists in a wartime alliance against mainstream Protestantism now sounds farfetched. At the time, however, it was not, for in mounting their attack on modernizing Protestantism Lippmann and Mencken both cited with approval the opinions of the fervent fundamentalist J. Gresham Machen. Machen, a respected New Testament scholar and professor since 1906 at the "West Point of Presbyterian orthodoxy," Princeton Theological Seminary, had come to the attention of these cultural savants because of his outspoken opposition to Protestant liberalism. To Lippmann and Mencken, Machen, though he spoke from the opposite end of the religious spectrum, had yet made criticisms of liberal Protestantism that they found cogent. Machen had become something of a celebrity with the publication in 1923 of his book *Christianity and Liberalism.* There he argued that by denying the supernatural character of Christianity liberal Protestants had actually created an entirely new religion. It was precisely this argument that Lippmann praised in *A Preface to Morals* for its "acumen," "saliency," and "wit." For Lippmann, Machen had provided a "cool and stringent" defense of traditional Protestantism, "the best popular argument" produced by either fundamentalists or liberals in a decade of religious turmoil. Mencken was no less impressed. To readers of the *American Mercury* he introduced the person he would later dub "Doctor Fundamentalis" as "a man of great learning and dignity—a former student at European universities, the author of various valuable books, . . . and a member of several societies of savants."[5]

In this instance, at least, Mencken had abandoned hyperbole for

straight journalism, for Machen was decidedly not a typical fundamentalist. He had trained at Johns Hopkins University, Princeton Seminary, Princeton University, and the German universities of Marburg
and Göttingen. Through his involvement in Presbyterian controversies
of the 1920s he had earned a reputation as the nation's most learned
and articulate defender of traditional Protestantism. But Mencken's respect went beyond Machen's credentials to his argument, which the
journalist judged was "completely impregnable." "If he is wrong,"
Mencken wrote, "then the science of logic is a hollow vanity, signifying
nothing."[6]

The way in which both Lippmann and Mencken exempted Machen
from their otherwise dismissive critique of twentieth-century Protestantism poses an important question. How could Machen's religious
and cultural convictions serve both as ammunition for "modernists"
to criticize the mainstream church and as a foundation from which to
defend Protestant orthodoxy? The lengthy parade of anomalies in Mach-
en's career makes this question even more pressing. These quirks may
even extend so far as to suggest that religion and modern culture in the
early twentieth century were more complicated than has been assumed.

.

In the Presbyterian Church Machen wanted to enforce strictly the details of Calvinist orthodoxy, yet in society he was an ardent libertarian
who opposed the efforts of government to impose anything.

.

His published writings defended the historical reliability of the New
Testament, yet Machen also championed the methods of modern biblical scholarship.

.

He opposed the secularization of life in America, yet did not oppose
the teaching of evolution.

.

He railed against the biblical scholarship of mainstream Protestantism,
yet published with an established New York firm a grammar of New
Testament Greek that was used widely at the institutions of his religious foes.

.

Like conventional fundamentalists, Machen opposed the growth of the
federal government, but very much unlike his fellow fundamentalists
he attacked Prohibition.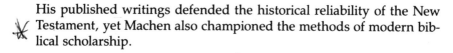

Like later fundamentalists Machen advocated private Christian schools,
yet unlike many later fundamentalists he opposed Bible reading and
prayer in public schools.

•

Machen, like other Southern Protestants, was a segregationist who opposed the admission of black students to Princeton Seminary, yet as a  proponent of cultural pluralism he championed bilingual primary and secondary school education in ethnic communities.

•

Like other fundamentalists, he opposed women's suffrage, but at the same time, unlike Northern Protestants, Machen was a life-long member of the Democratic party; and in 1928 he was one of the few Protestants, Northern or Southern, to vote for the first Roman Catholic presidential candidate, Al Smith.

In sum, while Machen stood with other fundamentalists in reprobating many features of modern society, on a surprising number of questions his views allied him more closely with modernist intellectuals such as Lippmann and Mencken who scorned the vapidity of mainstream Protestantism in American culture and who otherwise were far removed from Machen's theology. To observe the selected affinities between Machen and particular secular intellectuals is, in the first place, to gain a better understanding of the thought and career of fundamentalism's lone scholar. It is also a way to see more clearly the meaning of the "modernism" that came to prevail among American intellectuals in the 1920s.

To be sure, standard evaluations of Machen in surveys of American religion are not entirely misguided when they feature his reactionary character as a fundamentalist. Machen's theological strictures against liberal Protestantism, though informed by rigorous scholarship, were in many ways only learned variations of fundamentalist biblical literalism. With other fundamentalists, he condemned liberal Protestant efforts to adapt traditional interpretations of holy writ to the broader intellectual and cultural changes that had transformed America from a rural, agricultural, and religiously oriented society to one dominated by cities, industrialization, and science. Machen's long association with Princeton Seminary, the institution whose theologians provided fundamentalists with reasoned arguments for the historical reliability of scripture, makes it natural to regard him simply as a fundamentalist distinguished only by academic polish. Perceived in these terms, it seems entirely appropriate to fit Machen neatly into one of the standard categories for early twentieth-century Protestantism. He seems to belong securely with "the party of the past" that stoutly defended traditional Protestant verities against all comers, whether academic innovations of German higher critics or popular adjustments to the old faith from Protestant pulpiteers.

In such a view, Machen's religious convictions pose no difficulty for standard treatments of the relationship between fundamentalism and modern American culture. Although definitions of cultural modernism abound, most of them stress an inherent antagonism between religion and modernity, an intellectual conflict where the certitudes of faith give way to the uncertainties of modern existence. The modern outlook of the early twentieth century, most historians and literary scholars concede, featured a frank recognition that the world and our experience of it are never fixed or complete but forever haunted by flux and uncertainty. According to Daniel Joseph Singal, the modernist worldview begins with the premise of "an unpredictable universe" where nothing is stable and human knowledge is "partial and transient at best." In such a universe, absolute systems must make way for values that adapt continuously to "changing historical circumstances." In sum, modernists wanted "to know 'reality' in all its depth and complexity," even as they recognized that such knowledge ended in paradox or pain.[7]

While modernism of this sort found vivid expression in literature and art that plumbed the depths of uncertainty, it did not develop independently of academic or scientific pursuits. In fact, literary and artistic modernism resonated with the biology of Charles Darwin, the philosophy of William James and John Dewey, the anthropology of Franz Boas, the "new" history of James Harvey Robinson and Charles Beard, the physics of Albert Einstein, and the religious historicism of the University of Chicago's Shirley Jackson Case and Shailer Mathews, all of which expressed reservations about the abstract certainties of Victorian intellectual life.[8]

In this reading, cultural modernism and its intellectual antecedents clashed with traditional religious faith. And of all traditionalist faiths, Protestant fundamentalism collided most directly with the new way of understanding the world. Fundamentalist protests against Darwinism as well as conservative notions about the Bible could not have been more contrary to modernist notions about historical development and metaphysical uncertainty. One of the reasons, then, why fundamentalists were, in the words of one historian, "losing a battle of prestige . . . in America's best known centers of learning" was because their mental habits were becoming marginal within a "modern" academy and a broader culture shaped by the "modernist" outlook.[9]

This simple (and not entirely unfounded) picture of religion and "modernity" in the early twentieth century becomes more complicated, however, when we examine the relationship between liberal Protestantism and the concerns of modernist writers and intellectuals. On the one hand, specific liberal Protestant notions, such as the conviction that the truth of religious beliefs was relative to time and place, or the desire to adapt Christian faith to modern science, did reflect features of cultural modernism. Thus, it came about that the term *modernism* was applied to theological liberals even before it was used in artistic and literary circles because these Protestants seemed to be clearing the same path that cultural modernists later followed. On the other hand, the use of a common adjective to describe both "modernist" Protestants and "modernist" intellectuals creates confusion. Except for the most radical fringe of Protestant "modernists," mainstream and liberal Protestants only sought adjustments to traditional Christianity. They wanted to preserve historic Protestant certainties and the privileged position of Protestantism in American culture. They thought they could reach this goal with tactical adaptations of the historic faith. Cultural modernism, by contrast, according to David Hollinger, was "resoundingly post-Biblical" and rejected inherited religious authority. Liberal Protestantism's confidence in a benevolent God and its optimism about finding a lasting solution to the problems of modern society were "distant" from the intents of modernist writers and intellectuals. In this latter understanding, if modernist sensibilities about the recalcitrant nature of the universe became as dominant within intellectual circles as some argue, liberal Protestantism was just as marginal as fundamentalism to modernist culture in America. More recently, religious historians have suggested as much when they describe the 1920s as a time of Protestantism's "second disestablishment," a period when the old-line denominations' efforts to maintain their hold on American life and thought collapsed.[10]

Even though "cultural modernism" may have in the 1920s passed "Protestant modernism" by, the liberal Protestant denominations that comprised the Federal Council of Churches were still firmly entrenched in powerful institutions and organizations. To be sure, their establishment was no longer complete; they did not speak for several large groups of other Protestants, and their actual authority did unravel as the century progressed. Nonetheless, mainstream Protestantism, the wing of American Christianity that adjusted its faith in a "modern" direction (though stopping far short of cultural "modernism"), continued to enjoy considerable religious and cultural authority. Against religious critics and cultural modernists, the Protestant mainstream still strove to define American society's moral outlook, articulate the religious content of national ideals, and perform many humanitarian services not supported by the state. At the end of the twentieth century, scholars can now look back and recognize the failure of mainline Protestants to maintain cultural prominence. Yet, at the time the strength of Protestant efforts—from Prohibition to character education in public schools—as well as the possibility that those efforts might succeed, loomed much larger than their eventual decline. In fact, the resurgence of Protestant moralism combined with the mainline churches' attempt to "modernize" Christianity to shape the two prominent conflicts of the 1920s, Allen's "revolt of the highbrows" outside of the churches, and the fundamentalist-modernist controversy within the churches.[11]

Only by viewing "modern" Protestantism in this second sense—as a movement every bit as alien to cultural "modernism" as fundamentalism was—and by noting the lingering vitality and moral authority of the mainline churches can we begin to see the significance of the apparent anomalies in the career of J. Gresham Machen. Machen was indeed concerned about the dangers that "cultural modernism" posed to traditional faith. But he was even more worried about the "modernism" of American Protestantism and the cultural outlook upon which Protestant reconstructions of Christianity rested. For Machen, the moves by Protestants to "modernize" the faith—and not the efforts of "cultural modernists" to move beyond Christianity—comprised the greatest danger to Christianity. For by refashioning Christianity mainline Protestants hoped to maintain the churches' role as cultural guardian. But in the process, Machen believed, they had confused influence with faithfulness. In fact, he held that theological integrity and cultural authority were inversely related: a theology eager for public influence invariably compromised the Christian faith, while a principled theology could at best benefit society indirectly.

Machen's cultural concerns, thus, made him in the 1920s a reluctant ally of secular intellectuals but in the 1930s would cost him the support of fundamentalists. Like Machen, though for different reasons, cultural modernists also bristled under mainstream Protestantism's moral code, rejected its cheery estimate of human nature and the universe, and opposed its bid to Christianize American society. The subtext of Machen's theological critique of Protestant modernism—that the churches had no business meddling in society—was good news to secularists who thought that America's Protestant ethos impeded intellectual and cultural life. Fundamentalists, in contrast, were virtually deaf to Machen's ideas about the relationship between Christianity and culture. To most conservatives throughout the 1920s, Machen was a champion of orthodoxy who had reestablished the theological foundations for Christian civilization in America. By the 1930s, however, his understanding of the church's limited role in public life began to alienate fundamentalists. When Machen's efforts to reform the Presbyterian Church were finally thwarted and he withdrew in 1936 to form a new denomination, his new church attracted few fundamentalists. They stayed away at least in part because they, unlike Machen, shared with modernizing Protestants the belief that Christian values constituted the bedrock of American society.

An examination of Machen's life is imperative, then, not because he is representative of fundamentalism or because he exercised enormous influence. Rather, he merits attention because his criticism of mainstream Protestantism's lukewarm faith yields a fresh, and startling, perspective on the encounter between religious conservatism and modern culture. For Machen, although he was very conservative in religion, the threat of cultural modernism—pitting modern relevance against old-fashioned dogma, scientific verification against an implausible faith, and metaphysical skepticism against religious certainty—was not as great as the danger posed by Protestant hegemony in a free and diverse society. As great as the challenges of modern science and philosophy were, in the end they were not as profound as the peril of a religion that tailored its faith and practice to fit the prevailing temper of the age. It was no accident, then, that when Machen faulted Protestant churches for abandoning their proper tasks he used language that with surprising regularity echoed secular intellectuals.

In his only published autobiographical reflection Machen wrote that his life deserved attention only because, "not being remarkable," it revealed "in a concrete way the experience of a considerable body of men." He was wrong, for what makes Machen interesting and deserving of more careful study was his unconventional dedication to both an old Protestant orthodoxy and a new (even "modern") standard of religious pluralism. To understand how these apparently contradictory impulses could coexist in J. Gresham Machen enlightens cultural dimensions of the fundamentalist controversy in a new way and, more generally, redefines our knowledge of the relationships among religion, science, and modernism in the early twentieth century.[12]

# Between Culture and Piety

The religion of the sensible American is, therefore, not one of
creed or ceremony or emotion, not one primarily of the intellect,
but a religion of faith and love and action—a confidence that
the universe of matter and of spirit is reality, that its functions are
in wise hands, . . . and that our part is to help our brother
organisms to more abounding lives.   *David Starr Jordan (1908)*

J. Gresham Machen grew up in an era when a career in the ministry no longer held the appeal or status that it had for previous generations. By the late nineteenth century many Americans who in earlier decades would have entered the ministry chose alternatives from a wide variety of professions. When the choice regarding the ministry was complicated by religious doubts, the decision making was often traumatic. For some, the encounter with Darwinism or biblical criticism made it intellectually impossible to pursue a career as a traditional minister. For others, ambivalence about an ecclesiastical career stemmed from an uncommon dread of the cultural restrictions placed upon the clergy. Especially for undergraduates at America's new universities, who relished intellectual freedom and who believed that an academic career represented a calling as high and serious as the ministry, serving the church might seem tantamount to giving up the life of the mind as well as the refinements and amusements of genteel culture.[1]

An article in *World's Work* published in 1904 gives some perspective on the depreciating fortunes of a clerical vocation. Entitled "The Decline of the Ministry," it showed that many church and college leaders were worried about the obstacles facing prospective ministers and documented an "unprecedented reluctance" to choose the ministry as a profession. The author found that fewer undergraduates were preparing to be clerics, that those undertaking such preparation tended to be poor students, and that the number of seminarians with degrees from Eastern colleges was declining. Varied explanations for these developments included the comparative poverty of ministers, the falling status of clergy, the rise of opportunities to accomplish social good outside the church, and the narrowness of denominational creeds. One student voiced the problem that worried many of Machen's generation. "If a thing is right it's right, and that's all there is to it, but if I'm a minister, I can't do a great many things the church people will do, just because I am a minister." He concluded that he was willing to do his best, but he would not be "labeled and tagged and put off from the rest of the world."[2]

Such opinions were very much a part of J. Gresham Machen's early life. Indeed, his emergence in the 1920s as the country's foremost conservative New Testament scholar and academic spokesman for the fundamentalist movement could not have been predicted by the religious and vocational doubts he experienced as a young man. Not until 1913, at the age of 32 and after lengthy turmoil, did he decide to seek ordination. The steps leading up to that decision go a long way toward understanding the contours of his career as a scholar and ecclesiastical reformer. They also provide an unusually sharp instance of the intellectual tensions within Victorian Protestantism and the effort by some believers to find ways to reconcile the competing claims of religion and the intellectual life encouraged by America's new universities.

In 1920 H. L. Mencken, though often regarded as a debunker of Southern life, paused to celebrate the South as a once-civilized land "with men of delicate fancy, urbane instinct and aristocratic manner—in brief, superior men." Even after Southern Agrarians had revealed to him less appealing aspects of Southern culture, Mencken still cited the civilization of "Virginia gentlemen" among his reasons for residing in Baltimore. Although he now distinguished between the "Classical Age" of the South and the industrialized New South, Mencken always idealized the good manners and aristocratic air of Southern culture.[3]

The home into which John Gresham Machen was born on July 28, 1881, embodied the gentility that charmed Mencken. The second of three sons, Machen came from a prominent and affluent family of ancient English stock whose sympathies and outlook were distinctively Southern. Machen's father, Arthur Webster Machen (1827–1915), was the son of Lewis Machen, a Principle Clerk in the U.S. Senate's Secretary's office, and Caroline Webster, a native of New Hampshire. Arthur grew up on the family's farm in Fairfax County, Virginia, attended Columbian College (later George Washington University), and then studied law at Harvard. He settled in Baltimore in 1853 and established a legal practice that eventually placed him in the top rank of Maryland's lawyers. During Arthur's fifty-three-year career, only two Maryland lawyers argued more cases before the Baltimore bar than his total of 204.[4]

Arthur Machen's tastes and interests, rooted in the classical tradition of the Old South, were decisive in defining his sons' interests. He read the works of Horace, Thucydides, and Caesar with pleasure and found personal inspiration in the Septuagint version of the Old Testament and in the Greek New Testament. Classical training provided attorneys with rhetorical skills and gave them legal and political guidance from the examples of Greek and Roman republics. It also nourished the hallmark of the legal mind, precise and logically consistent reasoning—a trait on which Arthur's sons would later rely whether opposing Prohibition in Maryland politics or theological liberalism in the Presbyterian Church. Arthur put this training to use by writing essays and book reviews on legal topics. Moreover, he was a bibliophile whose library contained a wide array of books, including fifteenth-century editions of classical authors.[5]

The senior Machen's interests demonstrate the division between serious and amusing literature typical of Southern professional men before the era of specialized education. On the lighter side, Arthur Machen read French and English authors. He dabbled in writing, publishing several detective stories and short novels, some of them prize winners, in order to put himself through law school. His fiction was penned under a pseudonym, however, in order to avoid any suspicion of being a *litterateur* and so hindering his legal career. When 80 years old, he taught himself Italian "for the fun of it," as his son wrote. Arthur showed a well-informed interest in biblical criticism, following his son Gresham's academic interests and demonstrating a knowledge of German scholarship that impressed the younger Machen. It was no exaggeration when the *Baltimore Sun* eulogized the older Machen's "wider claim to ordinary human interest and sympathy than his professional achievements." The newspaper also praised "his intense and critical literary taste and the broad culture by which he strengthened and rounded his professional studies." He was one of the last representatives of a profession "which was once the center of literary arts and graces."[6]

Machen's mother, Mary Gresham (1849–1931), also known as Minnie, grew up in Macon, Georgia, the daughter of John Jones Gresham (1818–91), a prominent public and commercial figure in that Southern town and Machen's namesake. Although Machen would inherit money from his father, who profited from land sold in the nation's capital, much of his wealth came from his maternal grandfather who, in addition to practicing law and serving as mayor of Macon, owned a cotton mill and directed two railroads. Mary Gresham Machen was educated in her home town at Wesleyan College and numbered among her college friends Gertrude Lanier, the sister of Sidney Lanier, and also Mary Day, the woman who would become Lanier's wife. Minnie met her husband during a visit to an aunt, Mrs. Edgeworth Bird, a prominent member of Baltimore's Southern gentry. After their marriage in 1873, the Machens settled a few blocks from Mary Gresham's aunt in the Mount Vernon neighborhood, an area that was home to many affluent Baltimore families.[7]

Like her husband, Mary Gresham Machen was well read, but her tastes and routine were more typically Victorian. She displayed a marked interest in literature and read widely in French and English fiction and prose. Her greatest love was Victorian poetry, and she wrote *The Bible in Browning*, published in 1903, a work that defended the poet's faith and indexed his use of biblical allusions and King James English. The Presbyterian faith that she nurtured in her sons was not, however, the sentimental variety commonly associated with Victorian Protestantism. For religious instruction Minnie relied upon older forms of Protestant piety—the Bible, the Westminster Catechism, and *Pilgrim's Progress*—which acquainted her boys more with the intellectual content than with the emotional and moral demands of Christianity. She even required her sons to memorize the catechism and all the Kings of Israel. In addition to her literary interests and domestic duties, she regularly attended the theater and opera in Baltimore and entertained prominent guests at the Machen home, including Woodrow Wilson, Daniel Coit Gilman, president of Johns Hopkins University, and Francis L. Patton, president of Princeton University. Patton, who was also an ordained Presbyterian minister, was said to have welcomed his trips to the Machens' home because he could enjoy some "spirituous refreshment" without raising suspicions about his orthodoxy.[8]

Regular visits to relatives in Virginia and Georgia encouraged in Gresham (as he was called) a strong identification with the South. Until 1891, when Minnie Gresham Machen's father died, each winter she took her sons to her Macon home for several weeks. During those holidays, while his mother continued his education, Gresham grew to appreciate the charm of Southern gentility. He later recalled that his grandfather's home in Macon provided a glimpse of a "courtlier, richer life, and a broader culture" than that dominating the "metallic" culture of modern cities. Machen's affection for the South also included sympathy for that region's political sensibilities. Not only did Machen believe that whites and blacks should not mix socially, but he also held that the Civil War was primarily a struggle over states' rights.

For all their rootage in the South, the Machen family had interests elsewhere as well. Summer heat and humidity drove the elder Machens to vacation occasionally in New Hampshire's White Mountains (where Gresham developed an interest in mountain climbing), and to rent a summer cottage each year in Seal Harbor, Maine. In his teens, Machen also went to Dwight L. Moody's summer camp in Northfield, Massachusetts, and as an adult took advantage of New York City's charms as often as possible.[9]

The Machen household appears to have maintained an uneasy alliance between Victorianism and Southern classicism. That combination was not, however, the culture of the New South that Allen Tate described as "a superficial Victorian veneer pasted over what was still an eighteenth-century way of living." Although Mrs. Machen inculcated Victorian norms of domesticity, spirituality, and restraint, and while she nurtured an appreciation for refinement, the male culture of the Virginia gentleman still survived in her home. The Machens' sons, Arthur, Jr., Gresham, and Thomas, grew up resisting the stuffy manners and dress expected of them when in the company of women. They reveled in the pranks and male camaraderie of college fraternities while avidly following the athletic exploits of the teams from Johns Hopkins as well as the Baltimore Orioles, then a minor-league team. Sometimes their behavior bordered on crudeness, but it was typical of a patrician outlook that both cultivated good manners and promoted manifestly virile forms of behavior. This perspective informed Machen's advice to his younger brother, Tom, regarding a fraternity brawl, that "roughhousing is one of those inherent rights—regardless of group—residing in anyone who has succeeded in bucking into the second stage of his education." During his graduate education Machen especially enjoyed club life. As a member of Princeton's Benham Club, where diners were prohibited from talking about religion or women, Machen gained a reputation as one of the greatest "stunters" (relating a humorous tale in an exaggerated and boisterous manner). While a student in Germany, he was also an active member of the Burschenschaft *Germania* which, according to his estimate, required six hours of activity each day. Members, as he explained to his brother, ate large quantities of food, drank beer, played tennis, fenced, and, when women were present, danced.[10]

The Machen boys' literary tastes mirrored their father's, encompassing both serious study (classics, history, and political philosophy) and reading for pleasure (poetry, romance, and detective stories). While he enjoyed poetry, Gresham thought that it lacked the seriousness of other kinds of writing. The publication of *The Bible in Browning* caught him with little knowledge of the poet and forced him to cram some Browning into Sunday reading in order to sound informed when commenting on his mother's work. Overall, the Machen household managed to avoid the extremes of Victorian sentimentality and genteel formality thanks largely to the father's classicist roots. Their home embodied what Mencken called the Southern gentleman's "art of living," which went "beyond and above the state of a mere infliction" and became "an exhilarating experience."[11]

The tensions between classicism and Victorianism, however, were not so easily resolved in the university world that Machen entered as a young man. Gresham's primary and secondary education had reinforced his interests in the classics. His parents supervised his early schooling before enrolling him at age 11 in Marston's University School for Boys, a private high school in Baltimore. Machen's instruction in Greek and Latin there stood him in good stead for the classical curriculum he chose at Johns Hopkins University, one of Baltimore's prize institutions, only a few blocks from the family home. Machen's undergraduate course in Latin and Greek was not modeled strictly on the ideal of mental discipline, as had been the case at antebellum colleges. Johns Hopkins, although a path-breaking institution in graduate education and advanced research, still offered a three-year undergraduate course in the classics, a program crowned by the presence of the renowned classicist and Southern gentleman, Basil L. Gildersleeve (1831–1923). During the university's infancy, President Daniel Coit Gilman had recruited Gildersleeve from the University of Virginia, put him in an empty lecture room, and told him to "radiate," something that, by most students' accounts, he did. To Machen, Gildersleeve's rapid-fire classical allusions and his knowledge of world literature were as captivating as his precision in philology was exacting. In Gildersleeve's Greek seminar, the translation and interpretation of original texts formed the basis of instruction. Meanwhile, the scientific methods of the German *seminarium* put a premium on specificity and prohibited ambiguity, thereby reinforcing in Machen attention to careful argumentation.[12]

Gildersleeve's teaching furthered the distinction between lighthearted literature and the study of ancient languages, or, in the professor's terms, between aesthetics and grammar. Indeed, the philologist represented a tradition within American learning which promoted philological investigation as the surest means to a correct understanding of ancient texts, an approach that comported well with the university's scientific atmosphere. While Machen was an undergraduate, philology also governed Hopkins's instruction in English literature where courses in Anglo-Saxon and Middle English were prerequisite to advanced courses. Nevertheless, Gildersleeve, who in 1853 received a Ph.D. from Göttingen, thought the focus of German philology on translation, rather than interpretation, had created an "unbecoming controversy" between poets and philologists. So while encouraging specialization, he also defended the traditional undergraduate arts curriculum for its mental discipline and historical perspective, hoping to reconcile philology and aesthetic appreciation. Gildersleeve believed that the love of art required intensive study of grammar. Machen's later concern for precise doctrinal expression and fidelity to the original meaning of scripture during the religious controversies of the 1920s can be traced in part to his studies with Gildersleeve. Meanwhile, his defense of the intellectual aspects of faith also paralleled Gildersleeve's rationale for grammar. In fact, several classicists would later make criticisms of liberal Protestantism similar to Machen's.[13]

As much as Gildersleeve tried to reconcile the scientific and aesthetic aspects of the study of language, the classicist orientation that Machen learned at Hopkins ran counter to the approach that dominated the study of literature in some universities and in polite society. "New Humanists," such as Paul Elmer More of Princeton University and Irving Babbitt of Harvard University, were critical of the university's stress upon science but their moral didacticism set them apart from "custodians of culture" commonly associated with the Genteel Tradition. Individuals such as Harvard's Barrett Wendell and Princeton's Henry Van Dyke deplored the specialization of modern learning, dispensed with pedagogical theory, and maintained that literature's spiritual essence would teach itself. For them, literature should be beautiful and uplifting, "presenting life in its broad human interest" and revealing the ethical, the spiritual, and the immortal as the "chief factors in the divine drama of man." Their eclectic methods relied on intuition and lacked the systematic analysis that Gildersleeve advocated. According to one of Wendell's students, after reading a poem in class the Harvard professor would meditate for a moment and then exclaim, "Isn't it beautiful?" The student explained that Wendell never "dissected a piece of literature" because he knew that "to dissect [was] too often to kill."[14]

In many respects Machen's ambivalence about entering the ministry was rooted in the classicist perspective (both old and new) that he had learned at home and at university. The sentimentality and didacticism of Victorian culture also permeated mainstream Protestantism. In the late nineteenth century many well-educated Americans had come to believe that religious experience was intimately tied to poetic expression. Thus, the sharp distinctions that Victorian culture made between the intellect and the emotions, materialism and idealism, and science and faith prompted Protestants to defend Christianity on idealist grounds. Romantic and evangelical influences furthered the affinity between Protestantism and aesthetic feeling by placing a premium on experience and heartfelt religion. Although they valued rationality and order in the workplace, Victorians loved preachers who could move their souls. Henry Ward Beecher and Phillips Brooks, two of the most popular preachers of the era, clothed religious truth in the "language of a poem." At the same time, the revivalist Dwight L. Moody, whose sermons rarely relied on poetic images, used sentimental stories to win souls and further his crusade against vice in urban centers. The message contained in such preaching was a highly optimistic one that assured the middle class that changes and uncertainty in the spheres of science, politics, and business would be ultimately resolved through faith in a benevolent God and adherence to a strict moral code.[15]

The same emotional appeals of Victorian preaching surprisingly made their way into Franklin Street Presbyterian Church, where the Machens were members. This church had been one of the most influential congregations within the Old School Presbyterian denomination, a wing of American Presbyterianism known primarily for its dogged allegiance to Calvinism in theology and its insistence upon uniformity in administrative matters. Harris E. Kirk, who came to the church in 1891, seemed at times to embody the Old School spirit. He prided himself on appealing to "men's intelligence" and refusing to preach "the pretty, polite, rosewater sermon delivered with kid gloves on." Yet sentimentality permeated Kirk's conception of Christianity and crept into his sermons. He thought Christianity a religion of "invitations," "inclusions," and "affirmations" that penetrated civilization with the ideal of "the Divine kingdom." For Kirk, religion was primarily concerned with the "unseen world" and required "periods of quiet, and private spiritual cultivation." By mystical, spiritual communion with God individuals could "command . . . the highways of the soul."[16]

Henry Van Dyke, pastor at New York's Old Brick Church prior to taking up the teaching of literature at Princeton, showed Machen another side of sentimental idealism in the pulpit. A distant relative of the Machens whom the sons called "Uncle Henry," and host to Machen at Princeton on many social occasions, Van Dyke fused Victorian aesthetics and Christian spirituality even more intentionally than Kirk. In a sermon on the Bible's truthfulness, for example, he asserted that the best way to verify scripture was through "spiritual life," not the detailed scholarship that professors at Princeton Seminary were still recommending. This religious spirit alone brought "strength and beauty and fragrance as of the springtide into the soul," so that despite the cares and burdens of life in this world, the inward man could be "renewed day by day." Van Dyke also spoke in idealistic terms when preaching on the role that religion should play in the "purifying, preserving, and sweetening of society." The true test of faith lay "in its power to cleanse life and make it worth living" and "to save the things that are most precious in our existence from corruption and decay." Faith lent "a new luster to our ideals" and fed human aspirations "with inextinguishable light."[17]

The cultural and intellectual instincts of J. Gresham Machen did not rest easily with the moralism and sentimentality of Victorian Protestantism. His reaction to such piety was probably similar to his older brother's assessment of Van Dyke's literary criticism. After listening to the professor's lectures on poetry at Johns Hopkins, Arthur Jr. wrote to his brother in 1906 that the addresses were "commonplace to a degree . . . wholly unworthy of delivery in a university," and suitable only "for the entertainment of a crowd of women at an afternoon tea." Church leaders in the early decades of the twentieth century also sensed the inadequacy of a faith that seemed to be limited to the world of ideals and the human spirit, wholly removed from everyday concerns of business, politics, and academics. In turn, they tried through a variety of programs to bring men back to the churches by recognizing the religious significance of work, sports, and practical affairs. No doubt Machen's prolonged and at times meandering search for a career after his undergraduate education reflected the problems that Protestants were trying to correct. But his difficulties went beyond the seeming irrelevance of Christianity to a deep ambivalence about the intellectual shallowness of the churches. His distaste for Victorian spirituality and accompanying reluctance to become a clergyman would be overcome only when he found a way to use in the church the critical thinking he learned in the university.[18]

After a distinguished undergraduate career at Johns Hopkins, from which he was graduated in 1901 with the highest honors and elected to Phi Beta Kappa, Machen searched for a professional niche. As a reward for his achievements, his parents sent him for a summer in Europe with his older brother and cousin. After returning to Baltimore, he enrolled in Basil L. Gildersleeve's graduate seminar in the classics. Despite his success under Gildersleeve, an academic career in classics held no immediate appeal. He then spent the summer of 1902 at the University of Chicago taking courses in banking and international law. A letter to his father, who was long on patience, encouragement, and financial resources, reveals that Machen actually considered studying economics at Columbia the following school year. "The ministry," he wrote, "I am afraid I can't think of."[19]

Throughout these years of indecision Machen exhibited an inability to accept a routine existence. The success of his father and older brother haunted his thoughts about a career. He would later confess that his own talents seemed "utterly puny" next to the broad cultural and professional attainments of his family. As a result, fear of failure compounded religious anxiety. Even if Machen had pursued a career in law or banking he would have wanted the assurance that his work was of vital and lasting importance. Although his parents were always supportive, Machen's hesitancy about a religious vocation stemmed from a deep urge to show a family quite successful in the legal world that his own work was not, at best, commonplace, or, at worst, a failure. Nevertheless, no matter how indecisive Gresham might be about a career, he usually managed to have a good time. While studying at the University of Chicago with its theaters, bookstores, and its flat terrain for bike rides, he remarked that he had found "the best summer resort."[20]

A stop in Baltimore before the fall semester of 1902 provided the maturing student with some advice from the family's minister, Harris E. Kirk. Kirk counseled Machen to attend Princeton Seminary for one year. Machen reluctantly heeded his minister, with the understanding that such a move would not commit him to the ministry. "With many serious misgivings," he wrote his mother, "I have decided to go to Princeton for the year's work and I only wish I could go into it with more faith and more assurance that it is the right thing." At Princeton, Machen showed little interest in the course of instruction. Fresh from the independence of Gildersleeve's seminar, he complained at once of being required to attend all classes. Princeton Seminary, he wrote, "is run like a boarding school." He abhorred afternoon classes, "that evil invention," because they impeded fun and relaxation. The surface of the seminary's tennis courts was so uneven that he compared it to the Swiss Alps. (Years later as a faculty member, Machen eventually financed and supervised the construction of new tennis courts, complete with an irrigation system, but was less successful in convincing the seminary's groundskeeper to maintain them.)[21]

Since the seminary's basic courses in homiletics and Old Testament could hardly compare with the riches of Princeton University—Woodrow Wilson's lectures on American constitutional history, Henry Van Dyke's class in English poetry, Alexander T. Ormund's seminar in German philosophy, and Francis L. Patton's instruction in British ethics—Machen took advantage of the seminary's proximity to the university and enrolled as an M.A. candidate in philosophy. Yet he did not let formal instruction interfere with an insatiable desire for amusement. Trips to New York for its plays and bookstores, bike rides to Swarthmore to watch Johns Hopkins's lacrosse and football teams, and ice skating on the Delaware Canal were constant distractions. On one occasion, when confronted with a choice between a Princeton football game and a late afternoon Hebrew class, the decision was an easy one. Football, his "chief pleasure," won easily.[22]

During his first year at Princeton, Machen showed no inclination toward the ministry. In one letter to his mother he reported, as if boasting, that he had flunked an Old Testament test, even though he eventually learned he had passed. He protested of being "chiefly afflicted by the boredom of the thing" and looked forward to the "happy day when the last of the nauseating series has been left behind forever." Even intensive work in New Testament exegesis, for which he won a $100 fellowship, was to Machen no more than "a trifling matter." When he discovered that only two students had entered the contest, he considered refusing the prize. Of a homiletics exam Machen wrote that he hoped he had "hot-aired as much as the subject required." The only subject that interested him was the university's seminar in philosophy and he was comforted by the professor's reputation for never having failed anyone.[23]

Despite Machen's pose of lassitude, both William Park Armstrong, professor of New Testament, and Francis L. Patton, president of the seminary, were impressed by his abilities. At the end of his second year Patton recommended that Machen remain at the seminary after finishing his degree to teach New Testament Greek and related topics. During Machen's senior year, he began what would become a book-length study of the birth narratives in the New Testament. The first fruits of this work were good enough to merit the seminary's New

Testament fellowship, the Maitland Prize, and to be published in the *Princeton Theological Review.* Despite such encouragement, Machen still remained unclear about his future. He eventually decided to pursue further study in Germany, but with no clear end in view. Although he could have used his fellowship from Princeton to finance part of this trip, he refused, fearing that acceptance would obligate him to return to teach at the seminary.[24]

At Marburg, where Machen studied first in the fall of 1905, the main attraction was Adolf Jülicher, well known for his *Introduction to the New Testament* and *The Parables of Jesus.* But the teacher who most captivated Machen was Wilhelm Herrmann, professor of theology and a disciple of Albrecht Ritschl, the magisterial ethicist whose chief accomplishment was to redefine Christian faith as a moral, not dogmatic, system. It was Herrmann who forced the young American to reexamine his understanding of piety, a process that in the end made it possible for Machen to enter the ministry.

Like Protestant preachers in America who viewed Christianity in idealistic terms, Herrmann made a sharp distinction between the competing methods of science and theology. He relied upon Ritschl's disdain for Hegelian metaphysics to break all ties between religion and philosophy, maintaining that correct metaphysics had nothing to do with moral behavior. Indeed, for Herrmann, Christianity was primarily moral and active. In contrast to philosophy's stress upon the world of science, religion concerned the highest good and how it might be achieved. Hermann premised his theology upon the recognition that liberal Protestant efforts to ground Christian faith on the historical Jesus would always be subject to the shifting sands of biblical scholarship. Consequently, Herrmann argued that the significance of Jesus did not rest upon the accuracy of historical inquiry and he stressed the ethical demands of the gospel, conceiving of Christian life as one of service. He still insisted upon the importance of Christianity's historical origins to theology and tried to avoid reducing theology to ethics. But Herrmann's effort to liberate theology from historical investigation, no doubt, explains the profound impact he had upon Machen and Karl Barth, both of whom would sharply criticize liberal Protestantism for making Christianity independent of biblical history.[25]

The spirituality of which Herrmann wrote, however, provided an immediate benefit to the struggling Machen. As a student of Ritschl, Herrmann stressed the active life demanded by Christian faith and thus broke significantly with the tradition of Protestant liberalism inaugurated by Friedrich Schleiermacher who early in the nineteenth century had made a feeling of dependence the essence of religious experience. More important for Machen than the apparent strenuousness of Herrmann's piety was his status as a university professor. Unlike America, where preachers and academics seemed to be drifting apart, the German university continued to recognize theology as an important discipline. For Machen, Herrmann represented a model for reconciling the seemingly divergent worlds of religion and academic rigor.[26]

Machen described his first encounter with Herrmann as "an epoch" in his life. "Such an overpowering personality I think I almost never before encountered"—overpowering, he explained, in the sincerity of his religious devotion. Not only did Machen find Herrmann's theology alive, in comparison to New England's "corpse cold liberalism," but the theologian's Christocentric teaching aided Machen's own faith. "He is a Christian not because he follows Christ as a moral teacher; but because his trust in Christ is unbounded." Machen confessed that Herrmann's "revolutionary" views had confused him. Still, he rated the theologian's *The Communion of the Christian with God* as "one of the greatest religious books" he had read.[27]

Some have interpreted the religious doubts that appeared in Machen's letters from Germany as a sign that the acids of higher criticism had begun to eat away at his inherited faith in a historically reliable Bible. Yet Machen's worries clearly preceded his study in Europe. As he later wrote about this period, "It was not Germany . . . that first brought doubts into my soul." Years before his German student days, he admitted, he had been forced to face the problem of "hold[ing] on with the heart to something that one has rejected with the head." Machen's training at Johns Hopkins, a university that had no faculty of theology or ecclesiastical ties, was probably more overtly secular than what he encountered in Germany. Moreover, his flippant behavior while attending Princeton Seminary, a citadel of Protestant orthodoxy, confirms that he was by no means a model of conservative convictions before studying in Germany.[28]

Herrmann's vigorous presentation of Christian ethics had actually heightened the sense of religious inadequacy that Machen had begun to experience at Princeton. By the time he moved from Marburg to Göttingen during the winter of 1906 he began to reassess his faith. In February he admitted to his father that the religious atmosphere at Princeton had seemed insincere. "I had so long kept up the form of piety, and even engaged in active church work," he wrote, "when the whole thing was hypocrisy." What he needed was to start out fresh, as he had done in Germany, to break all connections with a "false life." To choose the ministry now, he thought, "would be simply to fall back into the old rut." He planned to finish the year and then go directly into "some line of work where I at least know that I am doing no harm." Without a sense of moral worth Machen thought he was unfit for the ministry. As he prepared for his studies in Göttingen in the spring of 1906, Machen wrote to his brother that he had little enthusiasm for what awaited him. "I am too much troubled with problems of various kinds—there is not a solid enough bottom under my whole course of life." Because of the expectations he and his family placed upon the ministry, Machen felt that moral as well as intellectual certitude was required before making such a decision. "I wish I could live over the last five years of my life," he lamented to his brother, "so that I could get into something where every stroke of work surely tells."[29]

At Göttingen, as Machen immersed himself in New Testament studies, his apprehensions shifted more narrowly to intellectual grounds. These doubts concerned the truthfulness of Christianity. Still, he rarely discussed these matters in letters to his family. And despite his earlier enthusiasm for Herrmann's teaching, he did not think that liberal Protestant efforts to make Christ's teachings independent of the supernatural were convincing. Throughout his stay in Germany, in fact, Machen demonstrated a firm grasp of the distinctions between liberal and traditional Protestantism, always siding with the latter. In one letter to his brother he expressed surprise that Herrmann had been so appealing. In another he informed his mother that he would be sorry if German liberalism were true. Machen was even prepared to give up his highly esteemed membership in Burschenschaft *Germania* if it meant that he could not wear the society's uniform into the conservative Baptist congregation where he often worshiped. Only after a chat with Prof. Wilhelm Heitmueller of Göttingen about the religious views of the *Germania,* which blossomed into a debate over liberal theology, did Machen decide that he could stay in the society in good conscience. He thought that liberals in Germany, though suspect on doctrinal grounds, were properly concerned about Christian morality and reforming society. Moreover, the earnestness of liberal Protestants and their desire not to divide the church were "grounds for the utmost caution in our manner of opposing them."[30]

During his stay at Göttingen Machen began to be troubled by the absence of conservative scholarship that could match the impressive attainments of German liberals. From Marburg he had complained that insufficient knowledge of New Testament criticism left him unable to rebut the views of his professors. As he studied the *religionsgeschichtlich* method of biblical criticism with Wilhelm Bousset, Wilhelm Schuerer, and Wilhelm Heitmueller, feelings of inadequacy grew. This school of study strove to understand the New Testament in relation to its surrounding cultures. Unlike American theological liberalism, which Machen believed was cut off from the university, here was impressive scholarship that rooted liberal religion in demanding academic training. "In the field of N. T. there is no place for the weakling," he wrote. "Decisiveness, moral and intellectual, is absolutely required."[31]

The intellectual challenges of New Testament criticism gradually resolved Machen's doubts about both his faith and the choice of a career. The emphasis of Bousset's research on the historical origins of Christianity in particular offered Machen an outlet for both his religious and academic interests, and a way to reject what he believed was the sentimental anti-intellectualism of American Protestantism. It began to dawn on Machen that a career might be built by using his training in philology and the classics to ground orthodox belief in sound scholarship. Machen's sense of intellectual mission was manifest in his growing appreciation for Princeton Seminary, particularly New Testament scholar William Park Armstrong. As he listened to Bousset's lectures Machen was reminded of Armstrong's thorough lectures on the history of New Testament criticism. He wrote home that Princeton differed from other conservative institutions because it did not "hide from the real state of affairs in biblical study." It made an honest effort to understand "the ruling tendency." While still in Germany, Machen was offered a teaching job by the Winonia Bible School in New York. Machen's response indicated the problems he saw in the work promoted by such institutions. "That kind of semi-popular and devotional semi-scientific work is no doubt a good thing—but it is the last thing I could do." Besides, he explained, "a little learning is a dangerous thing." What was needed was "real *university* work." Now from Germany he could see that his own training at Johns Hopkins was modeled on the demanding regimen of German graduate study. That realization, in turn, prompted him to rethink his opinion of Princeton Seminary, which now he praised as "imbued with 'university' spirit in its best form."[32]

Machen's new admiration for Princeton Seminary turned out to be well timed. Armstrong was eager to hire Machen as a junior colleague. On July 14, 1906, Armstrong wrote to Machen at Göttingen, offering him the position of instructor in New Testament. The older man was well aware of Machen's recent ambivalence about a career and so presented the offer without strings attached. Machen would not have to be licensed or ordained as a Presbyterian minister, or even take the preliminary steps toward ordination. His duties would include instruction in elementary Greek, a class in exegesis, and a survey course on the content of the New Testament. Machen felt that he could not put Armstrong off any longer and accepted the position, worrying that he would have to bluff his way on unfamiliar subjects but relieved that he would not have to be ordained.[33]

Machen's rising estimate of Princeton's intellectual respectability was accompanied by a growing identification with the institution's theological traditions. Founded in 1812 to combat skepticism and Deism, the seminary through its leading theologians, Archibald Alexander (1772–1851), Charles Hodge (1797–1878), Archibald Alexander Hodge (1823–1886), and Benjamin Breckinridge Warfield (1851–1921), had become well known for its defense of the rational and objective nature of Christianity. These Presbyterian theologians made regular, if selective, use of the Scottish philosophy of Common Sense to frame their apologetics. This included the adoption of Francis Bacon's inductive method and the complementary belief in the basic reliability of ordinary human perception. That philosophy was rooted in the notion that ordinary people, not just philosophers, could truly understand the physical universe and human experience through careful observation. The apparent contradiction between Princeton's trust in Common Sense and its adherence to the doctrine of universal human sinfulness had little effect on these professors' assertions about the scientific character of theology. In his introduction to *Systematic Theology* (1872), Charles Hodge had argued that the theologian should strive to be just as scientific as the chemist or astronomer. "The Bible is to the theologian what nature is to the man of science," he wrote. "It is his store-house of facts." In similar terms, Warfield, who like Hodge before him was the chief name at Princeton, claimed that the theologian needed to think through and organize Christian teaching not merely in order to defend it but to attack opposing views. Christianity, he argued, "has been placed in the world to *reason* its way to the dominion of the world."[34]

The Princeton theological tradition that others at the time and since have criticized for overintellectualizing Christianity became even more attractive to Machen. Francis Patton's teaching about the objective, factual truthfulness of Christianity proved especially influential in helping the junior scholar resolve his religious doubts. Why Machen failed to appreciate the seminary's instruction while a student remains a mystery. To be sure, Machen's frivolous attitude and lackadaisical approach to the seminary curriculum contrasted with his earlier seriousness in Gildersleeve's seminars. Another distraction was his preference for his courses in the master's program at Princeton University over those at the seminary. Whatever the reason, his time in Germany had given him the chance to see Princeton in a different light and to regard employment there as a way of pursuing first-rate scholarship while avoiding the sentimental hazards of an ecclesiastical career.[35]

To imply that the transition to Machen's new perspective was smooth, however, would be misleading. Immediately upon return to Princeton he complained that his first faculty meeting was "long and stupid." He found the students ill-prepared and threatened to flunk 75 percent of an early class on the Pauline epistles. The possibility of entering the ministry also seemed as remote as it had in Germany. Machen decided, consequently, to teach for only one year at Princeton, out of respect for Armstrong, and then return to Germany to pursue a Ph.D. in classics. He wrote to his mother that if his sole hopes for a career were confined to the ministry he would be in despair. Still, he believed that his studies in classics would contribute "something to our knowledge of the New Testament." This secondary purpose, he confessed, was his "secret reliance" because it gave him "something to fall back on" should he not be able to resolve his religious and professional doubts.[36]

Rather than bringing relief to his family for at least making up his mind, Machen's decision alarmed his mother. She interpreted his talk of hypocrisy and plans to study in Germany as a sign of rejecting Christianity. As an antidote to what she perceived as spiritual decline, Mrs. Machen appealed to the faith of Gresham's youth, one which "though not contrary to reason, does transcend reason." She admitted that this was strictly an emotional appeal, "a clinging to that faith for myself and for you." But she had misjudged not only her son's intention but also his predilections. Machen's sharp rebuke reasserted his discomfort with the Victorian habit of overcoming intellectual doubts by appealing to experience. He conceded to his mother that "your own religious experience" and "the clear way in which you see [its] many grounds . . . are legitimate arguments." But he objected to their being used to stifle other kinds of arguments and to restrict his own intellectual development. Then he asked her, "Don't you see, that however right your action is from your point of view—however loyal and admirable even—if I should follow you I should be guilty of simple old-fashioned intellectual dishonesty?" This, he said, was "a sin greater than disbelief."[37]

Machen never returned to Germany to pursue a Ph.D. Instead, a close friendship with Armstrong and the steadying advice of Patton gradually won him over to the seminary. Doubts about abilities as a teacher and tortured thoughts about entering the ministry still riddled the letters he wrote during his first years as an instructor. But once Machen grew more comfortable with teaching he also began to discover a spirituality fitting his intellectual concerns. No dramatic breakthrough occurred, but a letter to his mother in the fall of 1908 was revealing. He complained that none of the students were enrolling in his elective courses (which were intended as rigorous encounters with modern scholarship) and few showed any real interest in New Testament Greek. These were signs, he wrote, of "the extremely low intellectual standard among the future ministers of the Presbyterian Church." For them, "true piety, high motives," but also "deep ignorance" were the rule. Despite his discouragement at the students' lack of intellectual convictions, he supposed he ought to reconcile himself to this state of affairs for the situation differed little from the early church. Still, he believed that there should be at least one place in the church for scholars who could address the problems of modern life and "make modern culture subservient to the gospel." This letter, which defends intellectual life as a religious calling, was the closest Machen came to a formal declaration for the ministry. But despite the absence of a well-defined turning point, this letter's line of reasoning became pivotal for his later opposition to liberal Protestantism. That opposition would grow, to be sure, from a concern for defending traditional theology, but its sting would come from an expectation that other Presbyterian clergy and educators would display the same intellectual honesty that he demanded from himself.[38]

An incident in 1909 during his third year as an instructor demonstrated how rapidly Machen's resolve had solidified. In February of that year, first- and second-year students staged a pocket rebellion by complaining to the seminary's board of directors about the institution's curriculum and its teaching. Specifically, the students criticized the course of instruction for being too academic and far removed from the demands that clergy faced in the parish. They wanted more electives and more instruction in the English Bible rather than having to master Greek and Hebrew. Although this revolt was mild compared to the student riots occurring at other American colleges and universities in these years, the seminary's troubles did attract a good deal of coverage in the major newspapers of New York, Philadelphia, and Baltimore. The *Baltimore News*, for example, sided with the students and opined that the school needed a "modern and more scientific and practical course of instruction." Princeton Seminary's "sister Presbyterian institution," Union Seminary in New York, the paper added, was "among the foremost in all departments" and represented the "broader spirit of the Presbyterian Church." According to the *News*, the "old order" was gone and ministers needed instruction in practices that accorded with "the nature and the spirit and the laws of life," rather than a formal education that forced students into the tight categories of particular religious doctrines.[39]

Machen's first letter home about the incident confirmed the newspaper report. What the students wanted were more courses in English Bible and practical theology. Machen considered this compelling evidence of anti-intellectualism. The students "want to be pumped full of material which, without any real assimilation or any intellectual work of any kind, they can pump out again upon their unfortunate congregations." Machen believed that concessions to the students would extinguish whatever "spark of learning" still existed in the Presbyterian Church. He also believed the students' demands were completely out of step with the sort of academic standards he had come to appreciate at Johns Hopkins and in Germany. To him Princeton's curriculum, emphasizing systematic theology and the study of scripture in the original languages, perpetuated the precision and clarity he had learned to value while doing advanced studies in the classics and the New Testament. What especially angered him was that the students had singled out Armstrong, who lectured brilliantly but in a soft-spoken monotone voice on the history of biblical criticism, when they complained that some professors were oblivious to the practical considerations of future ministers. This criticism sprang, Machen said, from a "revolt against modern university methods rather than against theological conservatism." Professors at the university were wondering why "the only gleam of light in the general darkness of the seminary should have been one of those singled out for attack." In the end, the student uprising did not result in any significant curricular reforms but did reveal the seeds of dissatisfaction at Princeton Seminary that twenty years later would blossom into a major crisis in which Machen would be the key defender of conservative ways.[40]

Machen's support for senior faculty suggests that he was forgetting his own seminary days. At that time he had complained about the poor quality of the lectures and the monotony of the curriculum. As a professor, Machen tried to enliven his classes with comic and at times eccentric behavior. His students, for instance, recalled his habit of reading the morning mail while catching their errors as they declined Greek nouns or parsed verbs. One student remembered an incident when a particularly befuddled classmate could not readily explain a grammatical construction. Machen leaned over the student and gradually inserted his fist into his own mouth until the perplexed pupil gave the correct response. While lecturing, Machen would also sometimes bump his head gently against the wall, balance a book on his head, or write an entire conjugation backwards on the blackboard. Such unorthodox teaching techniques, however, were only matters of form. On issues of substance, Machen believed that revising the seminary's older curriculum would compromise the institution's theological and academic distinction.[41]

Further evidence of Machen's growing identification with Princeton's traditions came again in 1909 when the seminary's board of directors considered his own pastor, Harris E. Kirk, for the vacant chair of homiletics. As one of the Southern church's most popular preachers, Kirk spoke frequently at both Princeton University and the seminary and was a natural choice for the position. Yet Kirk refused the offer because be believed that the seminary was isolated from the university and because he felt he would be too aggressive for the seminary's good. Machen was relieved to hear of Kirk's decision, but not because he thought that Kirk would be too aggressive. Rather, from Machen's perspective, Kirk was too much beholden to the standard pieties of Victorian Protestantism and not aware of the issues that were dividing the American churches. Machen wrote to his mother and father, who were among the minister's biggest supporters at Franklin Street Church, that Kirk was scared off by the "biggest fight" facing Presbyterians in many years. Moreover, because the seminary affirmed two doctrines, "the incarnation and the necessity of a new birth," that were becoming increasingly suspect in fashionable circles, Machen believed it would always suffer from a "certain degree of isolation" from the university. He speculated that Kirk's refusal in fact stemmed from the seminary's isolation from the more popular and sentimental elements in the Presbyterian Church. The reason for this isolation was the seminary's belief that "scientific work is an absolute necessity for a religion that pretends to be based on facts." The seminary had to convince the church's evangelical wing that scholarship was just as important as evangelism. If Kirk was unaware that such battle lines were being drawn, Machen reasoned, then it was just as well that he turned Princeton down. This incident did not result in an open breach between the young man and his family's pastor. Kirk knew nothing of Machen's reaction and later agreed to preach at Machen's ordination as Presbyterian minister. But Machen's belief that Kirk was not suited for Princeton Seminary underscored his hardening conviction that a tradition that always yoked the intellectual and spiritual aspects of Christianity was the only one he could embrace. After having reached this conclusion, Machen found that his earlier reluctance to seek ordination disappeared.[42]

Although he was not licensed until 1914, Machen showed no further signs of spiritual or professional doubt. Beginning in 1911, he began to preach more regularly in the seminary chapel and accepted invitations to preach at nearby churches in New Jersey and Pennsylvania, despite worries that his delivery was putting worshipers to sleep. In 1912 he also began to teach Sunday school courses for teenagers at First Presbyterian Church, Princeton. About the same time he also agreed to become Sunday school superintendent provided he would not have to lead singing. Machen grew so comfortable in his position at the seminary, in fact, that in letters to his family he mentioned only in passing what earlier had loomed as a traumatic decision to seek ordination.[43]

An address that the young professor delivered to the Philadelphia Ministers' Association in the spring of 1912 revealed his maturing thoughts on the ministry. The address was to be a defense of "scientific theological study" that he repeated at the seminary's opening exercises in the fall of that year. A forthright declaration of the aims of theological education at Princeton, the lecture also contained Machen's personal confession of faith. It was published a year later in the *Princeton Theological Review* under the title "Christianity and Culture."[44]

As Machen saw it, the central problem facing the church was the strain between knowledge and piety, between "culture and Christianity." Within the church this tension was evident in the growing rift between evangelists and theologians, between "practical" and "scientific" tendencies. It was also apparent in the prevalent notion that religion had to do only with the emotions and the will, while intellectual life concerned knowledge and culture. At the seminary, however, these airtight compartments were unacceptable. Princeton prided itself in applying the same methods of study to religion "as were formerly reserved for natural science and history." The Bible at the seminary, moreover, was not studied for moral and spiritual improvement alone but also for the sake of knowledge. Machen described the confrontation between culture and piety not as a clash over the truth or falsity of Christianity but rather as a divide between competing methods, the "scientific spirit" *versus* the "old spirit of simple faith." In short, theological study brought students and faculty "face to face" with the problem of the relationship between knowledge and piety.[45]

Machen went on to say that to this conflict three solutions were possible. The first, and most popular in the modern university, was the subordination of the Christian message to science by eliminating the supernatural. Although Machen would later argue that Protestant liberals pursued this course, in 1912 he focused upon the prevailing idea of religion which identified belief with the emotions and the will. Such a conception subordinated Christianity to culture by driving a wedge between religion and science and left Christians to take their intellectual cues from the secular culture. The second solution, which prevailed in the young Bible institutes and would eventually spawn fundamentalism, went to the opposite extreme. In its effort to preserve the supernatural authority of the gospel, this approach destroyed culture or, at best, regarded it as a matter of indifference. Although Machen preferred the consistency of this solution to the first, he nonetheless argued that it was "illogical and unbiblical"—illogical because Christianity could not be separated from truths discovered by the intellect, and unbiblical because God had intended humans to exercise their powers of mind. The fully legitimate solution in Machen's view was the consecration of culture to religious endeavor. Instead of destroying or being indifferent to the arts and sciences, instead of "stifling the pleasures afforded by the acquisition of knowledge or by the appreciation of what is beautiful," he thought Christians should "cultivate them with all the enthusiasm of the veriest humanist" while at the same time consecrating them to the service of God. This solution resolved the clash of Christianity and culture by affirming them both. The other approaches, no matter how attractive, left the tension unresolved.[46]

Machen's proposal from 1912 may be seen as part of the widespread effort in the early twentieth century to overturn the dichotomies of fact and spirit that defined Victorian culture. George Santayana, the Harvard philosopher, summarized this endeavor in his essay "The Genteel Tradition and American Philosophy." Santayana blamed the idealism of the Genteel Tradition for the unusual doubleness of American culture. He thought that it separated unnaturally the higher things of the mind (religion, literature, and morals) from the practical concerns of the will (business, technology, and science). His criticisms challenged a host of younger intellectuals to restore unity to American life, usually by trying to make ideals conform to reality. In literature, Van Wyck Brooks expressed the belief that the only hope for modern writers lay in striking a balance between society's "transcendent theories" and its "catch-penny realities." In philosophy, pragmatists demanded that ideas be rooted in everyday life and that philosophy appropriate the implications of Darwinian science. The same impulse affected history and politics. James Harvey Robinson's "New History" strove to incorporate socioeconomic factors into a discipline that hitherto had been dominated by political abstractions. At the same time, Walter Lippmann and Herbert Croly were rejecting the doctrines of individualism and laissez faire for a corporate liberalism that yoked the interests of both big business and labor to social reform.[47]

Because Machen defended traditional Protestantism his religious views have rarely been linked to critics of the Victorian order. Yet Machen shared much of the critics' vision. To be sure, his foundational concerns were explicitly religious while the younger intellectuals who broke with the Genteel Tradition were often antagonistic to or uninterested in religion. Yet the Calvinistic theology with which Machen had come to identify could also be a source for criticizing the sentimentality and moralism of Victorian culture.

Machen expressed discomfort with Victorian Protestantism in the sermon he preached at his ordination to the Presbyterian ministry on June 23, 1914. His text, "Rejoice with trembling" (Psalm 2:11), yielded a definition of Christian joy that broke with the optimism that then prevailed widely in American Protestantism. Machen conceded that most Christians were joyful, but contended that theirs was a joy stemming almost entirely from membership in the "happy, contented, respectable classes." This kind of joy was merely the happiness of "social adjustment" and material comfort. It was not, however, the joy of which the text spoke. The source of the problem, Machen believed, lay in the faulty idea of God as a gentle and loving father. To restore a proper sense of joy, Machen recommended the "horrors of the old theology." Men and women needed only to look at human suffering and natural catastrophes, along with a clearer-eyed view of biblical teaching, to see that the humane God of modern Christianity was "one-sided" and not a "real God." Only the God of traditional theology, Machen insisted, could restore the mystery and the sense of guilt that modern preaching lacked, and thus proclaim the forgiveness and mercy that enabled Christians to rejoice with trembling.[48]

It made perfect sense, then, that Machen, who articulated this sterner theology after coming through years of doubt and distress, would find at Princeton Seminary a welcome environment in which to work and live. Even at this early stage in his career Machen sensed that Princeton provided a sobering theology and an academic rigor that made it possible for him to yoke his religious sensibilities and his scholarly interests. This union of piety and culture was the essential argument of his essay "Christianity and Culture" and, in fact, echoed a point that the seminary's leading theologian, Benjamin Breckinridge Warfield, had made at the opening of the 1903 seminary year. Had Machen not been so distracted then by uncertainty over his career he might have heard Warfield also affirm the necessity for ministers to receive both "intellectual training" and "spiritual culture." On that occasion Warfield even equated intellectual attainment with piety by describing systematic theology as a means of grace and recommending Protestant orthodoxy as a guide to practical religion. For Warfield, as for Princeton theologians before him, the connection between the head and the heart was intimate. If forced to choose between intellect and piety, Warfield replied, "Why of course give us life!" But the alternative did not have to be so sharp. Rather than choosing one or the other, Warfield held that the proper Christian response was to affirm both intellectual cultivation and practical devotion. In his eyes the daily routine of seminary study should be both highly cerebral and deeply spiritual.[49]

But there was a difference between Machen's and Warfield's addresses that reflected the dissimilar trajectories of their careers. Warfield, also a product of the Southern Presbyterian Church and at first a professor of New Testament before coming in 1887 to Princeton as professor of theology, devoted most of his energies to scholarship, teaching, and nursing an invalid wife. He had little time for church councils. Perhaps owing to these circumstances, his address stressed the cloistered life of seminary life. Machen may have missed the substance of Warfield's address because the professor's message seemed to reinforce the student's impression that religion was an musty affair, cut off from the strenuous life of the scholar. Had Machen listened carefully, however, he would have heard what was to become the theme of his own later address and the theme that defined his career. As Warfield saw it, the task of the minister demanded more, not less, intellectual rigor. Because Christianity depended upon public proclamation, ministers needed intellectual training of the first order.[50]

For Machen, the growing rift between church and academy made Warfield's conception of the ministry all the more urgent. The minister, according to Machen, must transform "the unwieldy, resisting mass of human thought until it becomes subservient to the gospel." Certainly, this task would require the service of Christian scholars. But ministers were not exempted. "What we need first of all," he said, especially in our intellectually flaccid age "is a more general interest in the problems

# CHAPTER TWO

# The Double-edged Sword of
# Biblical Criticism

Textual criticism confirms our general confidence, but slays our
hope of absolute precision. And historical criticism . . . tells us that
we are less certain than we thought of the very words that
[Jesus] did utter . . . But his revelation has been raised to a height
in history and experience where historical criticism upon the gospels
cannot destroy it . . . It is changing them in our hands, but will
not silence their testimony to Christ.  *William Newton Clarke (1907)*

When Theodore Roosevelt bolted from the Republican party in 1912 to
run as the presidential candidate of the Progressive party he included
many planks in his platform to garner the support he would need as
a third-party nominee. His program, which advocated presidential pri-
maries, women's suffrage, popular elections of United States senators,
and a comprehensive social-welfare program, was a charter for progressive reform. But Roosevelt added another element to his campaign
that must have troubled his Democratic and Republican rivals. That
element was religion.

Religious fervor pervaded the Progressive party's 1912 convention.
On their way to the convention Massachusetts delegates held religious
services, praying "for the success for the new party in the same Spirit
that their Pilgrim ancestors appealed for divine help." At the convention, as he outlined the Progressive platform, former senator Albert J.
Beveridge told delegates that without these reforms American government was, in the words of the apostle Paul, "as a sounding brass and
tinkling cymbal." He added that "we are indeed a nation whose God
is the Lord" and closed by leading in the singing of "The Battle Hymn

of the Republic." Roosevelt also assured his followers that the party's plans were "based on the eternal principles of righteousness." "We stand at Armageddon," he concluded, "and we battle for the Lord."[1]

Questions about Roosevelt's sincerity or success in the 1912 campaign are not as germane as what the Progressive party's convention reveals about the importance of religion to American politics and culture during the early twentieth century. The winner of the 1912 election, Woodrow Wilson, was equally convinced of the righteousness of his program and readily appealed to biblical ideals in his campaign. As one contemporary would later comment, "The people were ready to cry 'God wills it' and set out for world peace, prohibition, the Progressive Party, the 'New Freedom' or 'the World for Christ in this Generation.'" As the election of 1912 makes clear, Protestant convictions continued to be central to American ideals and institutions.[2]

The religious and moral rhetoric used in the 1912 presidential campaign is often overlooked as the context in which Machen began his serious work as a New Testament scholar. Histories of fundamentalism have generally interpreted his conservative scholarship as a response to the increasing secularization of American culture and to growing skepticism about the Bible. According to this view, the rise of biblical scholarship during the late nineteenth century undermined older Protestant beliefs and precipitated an "intellectual earthquake" that shook the "foundations of Western social thought." The only alternative left for conservatives such as Machen was to circle the wagons and insist upon the Bible's inerrancy.[3]

Machen's own remarks during his inaugural address in the spring of 1915 as assistant professor of New Testament at Princeton Seminary would seem to support the view that the aim of his scholarship was to defend the Bible as the only source of religious and moral truth. In this lecture he asserted that the "centre and core of all the Bible is history," it is "primarily a record of events." Machen went on to contrast the "Bible account" of Jesus as a "heavenly being" and "Saviour" with the modern portrait of Jesus as "the fairest flower of humanity," and throughout the address displayed an eagerness to do battle with higher critics, which must have delighted conservatives.[4]

Yet the conventional understanding of biblical criticism's impact and Machen's response to it overlooks the widespread confidence that many Americans still had in the Bible and in their ability to know what it taught. In fact, issues that would divide Protestants during the fundamentalist controversy—the truthfulness of the Bible and the propriety of critical methods in biblical study—were not readily apparent in the churches or in the wider culture during the years prior to World

War I. Mainstream Protestantism was remarkably fluid; general commitments to Jesus and the Bible united the churches and still undergirded hopes for a Christian civilization in America. Finding a consensus was especially urgent if the oldest denominations were to maintain dominance at a time when immigration and the growth of cities and industry threatened cultural homogeneity.[5]

Thus Machen's scholarship should not be read strictly as a rejoinder to liberal infidelities or secularization but also as a critique of the Protestant ethos that still dominated American culture. Again his inaugural address is revealing. Machen did not just censure liberal critics but also went after what he considered the conventional and unthoughtful piety of American Protestantism. From his perspective, establishmentarian impulses had prevented the churches from confronting difficult intellectual issues that went to the core of the Christian faith. Historical criticism had brought to the surface two rival conceptions of Christianity. "Is Christianity a means to an end, or an end in itself . . . Is communion with God a help toward the betterment of humanity, or itself the one great ultimate goal of human life?" Yet, in a spirit of compromise, the church continued to read the Bible for moral uplift or to "scale the dizzy height of Christian experience," all the while ignoring the issues raised by higher criticism. "She is saying peace, peace, when there is no peace."[6]

Ten years later many fundamentalists would agree with Machen's assessment, which in 1915 seemed to be largely inflated. To be sure, his own scholarship did not singlehandedly alert conservatives to the intellectual challenges confronting the American churches. But Machen's early research on the virgin birth of Christ and his book on the apostle Paul did lay the foundation for arguments he would use during the fundamentalist controversy. Rather than eschewing the methods and findings of higher criticism, as many conservatives did, Machen used the new learning both to defend historic Christianity and to attack the complacency of mainstream Protestantism.

Critical scholarship on biblical writings had emerged in German universities as early as the late eighteenth century but did not make their way into American Protestant discourse until the second half of the nineteenth century when, with increasing regularity, American students pursued graduate study in Germany. Discoveries of documents from the biblical era as well as advances in philology, archaeology, and the study of non-Christian religions called traditional conceptions of the Bible into question. Whether debating the accuracy of Old Testament historical narratives or the uniqueness of biblical writings, many scholars concluded that rather than providing direct revelation from God the Bible was more accurately a record of Jewish and Christian religious experience. Some of the resulting changes concerned relatively minor matters of translation. Still, as debates about the revision of the King James Version of the Bible showed, even minor matters such as modern-language translation could result in acrimony. When scholars turned from linguistic considerations to challenge older interpretations, the possibility of controversy loomed even larger. According to one historian, "the claims of the new scholarship" were "the most serious social and intellectual challenge faced by the American Protestant establishment."[7]

The growth of universities and the professionalization of higher education on the German model was critical for the reception of the new scholarship. The lure of German research hastened the acceptance of many critical conclusions. Perhaps more significantly, German ideals of following truth wherever it would lead reinforced the authority of science among American Protestants who already put a premium on reason and inductive methods. Whenever they sensed resistance from nonacademics to controversial views, biblical scholars readily defended their enterprise with the claim that they were not "bigots" but "scientists." Their task was indeed a demanding one, requiring proficiency in ancient languages, textual criticism, lexicography, history, and hermeneutics. While intensifying investigation of the phenomena of scripture, scientific methods freed biblical scholars from theological considerations, a job that academic specialization increasingly left solely to theologians. Theology was suspect also because it ran counter to scientific ideals that valued empirical observation and avoided metaphysical questions.[8]

Nevertheless, conservative scholars fared well and in some cases thrived from 1880 to 1900, the initial phase of the reception of biblical criticism. The high-water mark for American conservative biblical scholarship came in the decade of Machen's birth. Leading the conservatives were Princeton Seminary professors such as Benjamin Breckinridge Warfield, who spelled out a sophisticated understanding of biblical inspiration and inerrancy, and William Henry Green (1825–1900), who defended the Mosaic authorship of the Pentateuch on philological, theological, and philosophical grounds. They debated the merits of higher criticism with moderate evangelicals such as Charles A. Briggs (1841–1913) of Union Seminary (New York) and William Rainey Harper (1856–1906) of the University of Chicago. Briggs and Harper were more willing than Princetonians to follow the conclusions of German scholarship. Still, until 1900 conservatives participated fully in the academic study of scripture. Their dignified debates appeared in the pages of *Hebraica* and the *Presbyterian Review,* they were important members of the newly formed Society of Biblical Literature, and they sat on the American committees responsible for the revision of the English Bible.[9]

To be sure, critical views of the Bible provoked some controversy and many denominations took steps to insure sound theological instruction at their seminaries. Conservative Congregationalists ousted E. C. Smyth from Andover Seminary in 1885 for his use of the new scholarship, even though the eventual victory of "Andover liberals" meant the reinstatement of Smyth only seven years later. Within Northern Baptist circles, Newton Theological Institution dismissed Ezra P. Gould in 1882 for advocating critical views in his lectures even while Colgate Seminary and the University of Chicago Divinity School offered outlets for those with less conservative conclusions. Methodists also experienced their share of controversy when in 1905 Boston University School of Theology removed Hinckley G. Mitchell from his position for questioning the Mosaic authorship of the Pentateuch. Meanwhile, Northern Presbyterians proved to be particularly sensitive to departures from conventional views. During the 1890s, Charles Briggs, Henry Preserved Smith of Lane Seminary (Cincinnati), and A. C. McGiffert of Union Seminary (New York) were either brought to trial or forced to resign for promoting critical ideas. In fact, during the Briggs proceedings, the Presbyterian Church declared in its famous "Portland Deliverance" that the "inspired Word, as it comes from God, is without error, and the assertion to the contrary cannot but shake the confidence of the people." So adamant was the denomination that it reaffirmed biblical inerrancy at its 1910 General Assembly as an essential article of faith.[10]

Nevertheless, only in those few cases where criticism was tied to an aggressive effort to overturn older notions did students of the Bible encounter hostility. In many instances, the issues that plagued biblical scholars went beyond the Bible or the implications of critical views. The Briggs case, for example, took place in the midst of debates over revision of the Westminster Confession and reflected older struggles between Old and New School Presbyterians. At the same time, the McGiffert and Smith episodes involved questions about the meaning and scope of Presbyterian ministers' ordination vows. In sum, most scholars could advocate the newer views so long as they respected traditional concerns.[11]

Biblical criticism in America, therefore, despite some hostility from the churches, remained moderate into the early twentieth century, affirming the Bible's uncommon worth as a source of religious truth. This was a position well in keeping with what most American Protestants believed. Devotion to Jesus insured relevance for scripture as the foundation of knowledge about his life and teachings. In fact, the Old Testament generated more controversy than the New in part because scholars as well as the clergy and laity were loath to subject Christ to criticism. Professional students of scripture continued to affirm the Bible as the supreme fountain of Christian faith and practice even while carving out a scholarly niche for the new learning. Daniel Coit Gilman's remarks in 1903 while vice-president of the American Bible Society were representative of those in the academic community. Biblical criticism, the former president of Johns Hopkins University declared, had revealed the Bible's unparalleled role in the "development of personal character, and . . . in purifying and elevating human society wherever its precepts have been read and accepted."[12]

Gilman's esteem for the Bible was also shared by those who may have appeared to be the book's toughest critics. William Newton Clarke, whose popular *Sixty Years with the Bible* (1909) mediated critical scholarship to Protestant laity, concluded his book with a stirring affirmation that diligent scrutiny of the Bible actually sustained faith. "Our sacred book is thus our guide to Jesus, to God and to life divine." "This fact," Clarke concluded, "has been established in long human experience . . . It will stand." No less optimistic was Shirley Jackson Case, New Testament scholar at the University of Chicago and an influential advocate of critical views. Even though Case encouraged methods that questioned scripture's divine qualities, he could still profess in 1912 that critical study of the Bible yielded the "content of [Jesus'] own personal religious life," which was the "foundation" for modern faith. Lyman Abbott, the editor of the *Outlook*, who also made the scholarly consensus accessible to the American reading public, reiterated the conviction that modern Christians had nothing to fear from biblical criticism. According to him, the new understanding of the Bible was "more sacred" than older views because rather than presenting a "message from God to a godless world" it unveiled "God in human experience, that all human experience may be full of God." Critical views could easily become popular as long as they were conventionally pious.[13]

When Machen began to publish on the New Testament, then, the field was not clearly divided between progressives and traditionalists. To be sure Princeton Seminary's specific defense of the Bible had been repudiated by most scholars, but this did not mean that barriers existed that prevented Machen or other conservatives from participating in the academic world. In fact, his first articles on the virgin birth of Christ deviated little from the prevailing scholarly standards. Whereas his first published writings, two articles in the *Princeton Theological Review* of 1906 based upon his senior thesis as a seminarian, reflected a classroom context, the three pieces that appeared in 1912 demonstrated his growing maturity as a scholar. In the latter publications, Machen made little effort to defend the trustworthiness of scripture or to show the inadequacies of higher criticism. He wrote with exceptional detachment for one who would become the principle scholarly spokesman for fundamentalism.[14]

Machen's aim in the first two of these articles was to account for the stylistic differences between Luke's birth narrative and the remainder of the gospel. When he marked the German critic Adolf von Harnack the foil for his study, Machen appeared to be employing a standard conservative tactic. But unlike other conservatives who often used liberal scholars as strawmen, Machen avoided questions about biblical inerrancy and infallibility. This omission was particularly noteworthy since Machen conceded that Luke may have relied on oral traditions or nonbiblical texts. This view departed from the fundamentalist understanding of inspiration, which restricted divine influence to the canon and regarded noncanonical sources as human creations and, therefore, prone to error. Neither did Machen concern himself with the truthfulness of Luke's narrative. The only sure conclusion was that Luke's first two chapters, in contrast to the views of Harnack, were "genuinely primitive and Palestinian." Later on, these findings would aid Machen in his defense of the virgin birth. But for conservatives wanting to hear that their Bibles were trustworthy, his early scholarship offered little reassurance, much less an easy read. Machen himself was aware of the difficulty that his articles presented. He wrote to his mother, "If you succeed in reading my article out of love for the writer I shall have a new proof of what an affectionate mother I have."[15]

Machen's third article in the series, "The Virgin Birth in the Second Century," was a historical inquiry into the origins of the church's beliefs about Christ's birth. This topic took on added significance in light of the Presbyterian Church's 1910 affirmation that the virgin birth was an essential article of faith. Still, Machen must have disappointed conservative readers again. His study gave no compelling reason for believing that Luke's account was factual. He concluded only that a firm and well-formulated belief in the virgin birth extended back to the early years of the second century and that denials of the doctrine in the early church were rooted in philosophical presuppositions rather than historical tradition. The same lack of conviction that Machen had displayed in his linguistic studies reappeared in his historical analysis. His impartiality may have been a sign of lingering religious doubts but may have also reflected a scholarly demeanor. On this score his articles were a success. In Harnack's review of the articles, which Machen had bound as a unit and sent to the German scholar, he complimented Machen for his objectivity and candor and declared that the Princetonian's scholarship deserved careful attention.[16]

Machen's work was well received in part because he employed the same methods used by other students of ancient texts. Although philosophical and theological convictions separated Machen from his professional peers, questions about the sources for Matthew's or Luke's gospel, the date of a particular manuscript, or the meaning of a specific passage required more or less identical techniques. Both liberals and conservatives assumed that they were studying the phenomena of scripture in an objective manner, that their conclusions were reliable if not certain, and that the author's intent should determine the meaning of the text.[17]

Where Princeton scholars did seem to depart from the mainstream of American New Testament studies was in their preference for textual analysis. Benjamin Breckinridge Warfield established Princeton's orientation in New Testament studies with his *Introduction to the Textual Criticism of the New Testament* (1886), a work informed by recent European scholarship which set forth the procedures for close attention to the text's original meaning. Machen's mentor and colleague, William Park Armstrong, also gave priority to textual analysis and in 1913 outlined the methods guiding Princeton's scholarship. The critic's first task, sometimes called lower criticism, according to Armstrong who followed Warfield, was to establish a text that approximated "as closely as possible" that of the autographs. Next came higher criticism, which involved literary and historical considerations. Then followed literary criticism, which looked for the text's sources, and finally historical criticism, which placed the Bible in its social and cultural environment and ultimately judged its "historical trustworthiness." Armstrong admitted that this last concern went beyond the scientific method into the sphere of religious and philosophical values but believed that as long as scholars were aware of their assumptions they would be able to discount the influence of "a priori" commitments.[18]

As incongruous as it seems, Princeton Seminary's doctrine of biblical inerrancy prompted its scholars to intensify rather than shy away from critical study. The seminary appeared to have a policy, unsaid but understood, that its biblical instructors would study overseas, usually in Germany, before assuming their teaching duties. Of the professors who taught in the Old Testament department during Machen's tenure, John D. Davis (1854–1926) studied at several German universities, while his colleagues Robert Dick Wilson (1856–1930) and Oswald T. Allis (1880–1973) undertook advanced study at the University of Berlin. In New Testament, Armstrong, Machen's older colleague, had studied at Marburg and Erlangen. Although they approached the Bible from a Calvinistic perspective, their findings benefited from detailed exegetical, historical, and philological study. Meanwhile, Princeton theologians used critical methods to argue that inspiration and advanced scholarship were compatible. They did not regard inspiration merely as a mechanical process of dictation, but rather as a special instance of providence. Divine inspiration concurred with the writer's literary style, selection of sources, family background, and cultural and religious perspectives in the composition of scripture. Rather than imposing limits, this doctrine allowed Princeton scholars to explore fully the human aspects of the Bible's formation and reception.[19]

Machen's early publications continued this practice. His studies of Luke showed a familiarity with German, English, and American scholarship. His literary and historical analysis also demonstrated Princeton's willingness to grapple with the Bible's human qualities. Thus, his silence on the inspiration and infallibility of scripture said a good deal about Princeton's attitude toward the newer learning. Rather than studying scripture merely to show where liberal critics had erred and thereby confirm conservative beliefs, Princetonians engaged in critical scholarship because they thought such study would lead to a fuller understanding of the Bible.

Until the time of his promotion to assistant professor Machen was content for the most part with his duties at Princeton and his place in the academic world. On the eve of World War I conservative scholars like those at Princeton could still participate in the professional study of scripture while at the same time taking part in a variety of ecclesiastical duties. The weighty influence of mainstream Protestantism insured cooperation between church and academy. Thanks to Princeton Seminary's position in the mainstream, Machen enjoyed a wider audience for his work than if he had been a religious or cultural outsider. He could not, however, bear such good fortune for long. Soon after his promotion Machen again began to show signs of restlessness with his routine at the seminary. This uneasiness would prompt him to consider service in the Great War.[20]

In the years after his ordination in 1914 Machen experienced a letdown that sapped his scholarly interests. In 1915 he undertook a one-year course of Sunday school lessons for the Presbyterian Board of Education entitled "A Rapid Survey of the Literature and History of New Testament Times." This was his first exposure to church bureaucracy and raised suspicions about the Presbyterian leadership's indifference to intellectual matters. The Board of Education's editor, John T. Faris, often "punched up" Machen's style and revised the lessons in order to make them more practical. Faris wanted to convince young adults that the New Testament contained "living messages . . . full of vital things for their life today" whereas Machen wanted to deal with substantive issues in New Testament studies. When Faris began to make changes in the galleys without Machen's knowledge or consent, the latter took offense. Machen overreacted when he wrote to his mother, "I do not suppose anyone has submitted to much more blatant injustice and humiliation than I have been during this year." But he confined such remarks to his family, accommodated Faris's changes, and was eventually praised by Faris for his gracious attitude.[21]

Meanwhile, teaching at the seminary became drudgery, partly because students showed little interest in his seminars and partly because some of his closest friends moved away from Princeton. As early as the spring of 1916 Machen felt as if he might be "getting into a rut." He contemplated moving away from Princeton, he wrote to his mother, "to enter into entirely new associations." Here Machen's concerns went far beyond academic and ecclesiastical to deeply personal matters. When students failed to show interest in his courses he admitted that he had lost his "youthful illusions." "There was a time," he explained, "when I thought I was going to be an exception to the general lot of humanity." The only aspect of his life that he found gratifying was preaching and he began to accept more invitations.[22]

Even his friendships with senior colleagues Armstrong and Caspar Wistar Hodge, professor of theology, offered little consolation. Machen was hurt when he learned secondhand that Armstrong, a dinner companion and bridge partner whom Machen considered an intimate friend, had been awarded an honorary doctorate from Philadelphia's Temple College. Machen's discontent was compounded by his father's death in 1915. Although he may have been closer to his mother, Machen held his father in high regard and had always hoped to impress the elder Machen. His grief is difficult to monitor since he spent several weeks with his family in Baltimore and his correspondence involved little more than formal letters of gratitude or acknowledgment. But his father's death, coupled with growing discontent in his professional life, may help to explain Machen's decision in 1917 to serve as a Young Men's Christian Association (YMCA) secretary in World

War I. Apparently unable to make a substantial impression on seminary students, and with research and writing on hold, Machen hoped to make a difference outside academia.[23]

In the spring of 1917, when the United States appeared to be headed for war, Machen jumped at the chance to get involved. "To remain behind in an easy life, and loaf as I am now doing," he wrote to his mother, "would throw me into the depths of skepticism." He ruled out serving as a soldier because he thought it wrong for ministers to be combatants. Chaplaincy was also out of the question because he would feel inadequate preaching to men who were making a greater sacrifice than he. He also thought a chaplain's status as an officer would prevent friendship with enlisted men. He preferred service in the American Ambulance Field Service but was discouraged to discover that if he volunteered for this work he might be transferred to munitions transport. That left the YMCA, which had the advantage, according to Machen, of being "at the front right with the men." Though "very cool toward the Y.M.C.A." in general and concerned about having to work on Sundays, Machen volunteered for service in late 1917 and in January 1918 left for France.[24]

Machen's political dispositions highlight the fact that this decision was influenced more by personal struggles than patriotism. He backed Woodrow Wilson's initial policy of neutrality. Because of his studies in Germany and friendships he had made there, Machen was more willing than many Americans of English descent to sympathize with Germany. Not only did Machen dissent from his family's attitude toward the war but he also lamented Princeton's "patriotic enthusiasm and military ardor," which made him "feel like a man without a country." When Germans invaded France, Machen was "wild against them." But the alliance of Britain, Japan, and Russia provoked fierce opposition. He thought Germany's military might was understandable given "the countless barbarian hordes of Russia within easy striking distance." He also surmised that the Allies were out merely "to crush the life out of a progressive commercial rival." Talk of a war in the interest of democracy was particularly hypocritical. "Great Britain," Machen observed, "seems to me the least democratic of all the civilized nations . . . with a land-system that makes great masses of the people practically serfs." He believed the underlying cause of the war was the "British attitude towards Germany's just effort at a place in ocean trade." When President Wilson began to prepare the country for war, Machen criticized compulsory military service as a "permanent policy," thereby giving the first signs of his libertarian views. While tolerable as an emergency measure, conscription seemed a "brutal in-

terference of the state with the life of the individual and of the family."
Conscription, as he wrote to his congressmen, was a greater danger
than Germany to "American liberty and the whole American ideal of
life." Only when he saw the brutality of the war did he side with the
Allies "in the interests of peace."[25]

As YMCA secretary Machen's assignments included supervising a
canteen for French soldiers and then an American post exchange. Of
the many YMCA services during the war, the sale of cigarettes, hot
chocolate, candy, razor blades, and stamps were probably the best
known. The association operated almost 1,500 canteens among American troops alone which were staffed by over one-third of its overseas
workers. By performing this service, which had traditionally been conducted by military personnel, the YMCA freed American soldiers for
fighting and, according to Gen. John J. Pershing, was a "large factor
in the final great accomplishment of the American Army."[26]

Machen first ran a canteen in the town of St. Mard, which though
still inhabited by civilians had been desolated by German artillery. In
a damp, rat-infested house, the roof of which had been almost entirely
blown off but whose first-floor ceiling still offered some shelter,
Machen set up the canteen and his own living quarters. His duties
consisted largely of mixing and selling hot chocolate to soldiers and
village residents although he also tried to organize games. In one letter
home Machen grumbled that the YMCA secretary was a "grocery clerk
and nothing else." He had hoped for more opportunities for religious
service. The chaplain of his regiment was a priest and so a Catholic
mass was celebrated each Sunday. Machen himself tried to hold services during the week but the attendance was small. He had more success leading a Bible study.[27]

Machen's next post took him closer to the fighting. He was limited
to one uniform and unable to bathe regularly. Moreover, he slept fit-
fully because of the constant noise of explosions and airplanes. Still,
the sufferings caused by the war rather than his personal discomfort
made the deepest impression. As he walked to secure supplies,
Machen was struck by the scene of desolation "so abominable" that
photographs could not capture it. The countryside had been reduced
"to a few straggling stumps" and along the road lay many dead. He
was also moved by many scenes of human misery. On one occasion,
as Machen along with soldiers fled their encampment which was being
bombed, Machen could not help but notice the steady stream of ref-
ugees. "The roads for miles and miles," he wrote, "were crowded with
wagons containing household effects piled on in direst confusion." The
effects of the war on the French people was the "saddest part of all."[28]

After the Armistice Machen continued to work under the YMCA's auspices at various camps in the Paris area for about three months before returning to the United States. He preached at weeknight services sponsored by company chaplains and conducted afternoon Bible studies informally. He also used his time in Paris to his own advantage. He read Voltaire's history, sampled the plays of Racine and Molière, studied Gothic architecture, and attended lectures at the Sorbonne. Machen's extra duties after the war required a longer stay than he had expected but his cultural pursuits in Paris more than made up for the inconvenience.[29]

Machen returned to the United States in early 1919 with a renewed commitment to his duties at the seminary. But it would not be business as usual. His desire for a sense of purpose and usefulness which had led to his wartime activities spilled over into his professional life. As he began to prepare lectures on the apostle Paul which would lead to his first major book, Machen staked out a scholarly position that confronted the major assumptions of mainstream American Protestantism and at the same time edged him closer toward ecclesiastical controversy.

Machen's first book resulted primarily from an invitation by W. W. Moore, the president of Union Theological Seminary (Richmond) and longtime friend of the Machen family, to give that institution's annual James Sprunt Lectures for 1921. Interestingly enough, this invitation came in 1915, well before Machen volunteered for YMCA service. He knew full well of the commitment when he left for France. Even so, Machen returned worried about his long separation from a "theological supply." As his deadline of January 1921 approached, Machen repeatedly fretted that his rapid "digestion" of recent scholarship was insufficient. He complained to his mother after one particularly grueling session of writing, "I suffered intensely, I paced the floor in agony; I dawdled because nothing would come to me . . . The product, I am afraid is miserably poor."[30]

Nevertheless, Machen was not unfamiliar with the chosen topic for his lectures—a historical exploration of the apostle Paul's religion—and so did not have to prepare entirely from scratch. He had contributed an article on Paul to a volume of essays commemorating Princeton Seminary's centennial in 1912 and had offered several seminars on the Pauline epistles and apostolic history. Machen's background in the classics also prepared him well to investigate the Acts of the Apostles and the apostle's letters, the primary sources necessary for this study. Personal factors, moreover, predisposed Machen to identify with his subject. As he pointed out, Paul was born and reared in a university city and his parents, as Roman citizens, enjoyed a privileged social position, two characteristics that were also true of Machen. He saw in Paul a man of principle who sacrificed expediency and personal considerations for the sake of correct doctrine. Dedication to principle irrespective of consequences was certainly a trait that Machen admired and one by which he would justify his efforts during the fundamentalist controversy. Moreover, Machen's reading of Paulinism provided the theological basis for his own critique of liberal Protestantism and a model for settling church disputes.[31]

Despite Machen's worries about the lectures, they passed without a hitch and, according to W. W. Moore, were "an unqualified success." What Moore considered a success the students at Union must have considered a nightmare. Machen was informed that students were required to attend the lectures and would be examined on them. Mastering his presentation was indeed a formidable task, especially since previous Sprunt lectures had been more homiletic in character. Machen prepared his lectures with publication rather than public delivery in mind. He surveyed recent trends in German criticism and advanced arguments that required extensive knowledge of Greek, Greco-Roman culture, Judaism, and the text of the New Testament. Machen's eight nights of lectures did not even include question-and-answer sessions for befuddled students. In fact, one reviewer of the book wondered how it could have been delivered as lectures since it deserved "leisurely reading and careful appreciation."[32]

Machen's careful attention to detail was necessary to explain why he departed from the dominant trends in Pauline studies. The apostle Paul presented an important problem for biblical scholars. The spread of critical views concerning the Bible had rarely resulted in outright skepticism or agnosticism. Rather, the consensus of new scholarship was that Jesus' ethical teachings constituted the essence of early Christianity. Jesus' ideas and example, according to Protestant scholars in Europe and the United States, had not been blemished by higher criticism and were still the norm for Christian faith and practice. Paul's teachings were not easily reconciled with this view, however. The apostle conceived of Jesus not as a prophet and teacher but rather as messiah and redeemer. Paul deified Jesus, said that Christ's death was central to his role as messiah, and made the resurrection the basis for Christian faith. Not only did Paulinism collide with the reigning conceptions of Christianity but Paul's epistles outnumbered Jesus' teachings by a wide margin and raised the possibility that the early church had been more interested in the apostle's theology than in Jesus' practical guidance. As discrepancies between Paul and Christ became more evident, some scholars began to suggest that Paul had diverted the church from Jesus' teaching, and that while historic Christianity could be traced to Paul, the modern church needed to return to Jesus in order to recover genuine Christianity.[33]

Scholars also devised a number of strategies for distancing Jesus from Paul and for restoring Jesus' moral and spiritual guidance as the core of Christian faith. An older approach typical of the liberal Protestantism associated with Adolf von Harnack distinguished between the kernel and husk of Christianity. From this perspective, Paul and Jesus were united by their common religious experience. As a child of his time, Paul could only express his faith in language that was alien to the experience of Jesus. In the early twentieth century, especially in German scholarship, this explanation received sharp criticism. Some argued that the effort to distinguish between Paul's faith and theology was too facile and that these two elements of Paulinism were inextricably linked. For this reason, some claimed that Paul was the second founder of Christianity and two schools of scholarship emerged that tried to account for the apostle's divergence from Jesus. Although stressing different aspects of Paul's background, each reflected the growing influence of comparative religion on New Testament studies. Some scholars explained Paul's ideas as a reflection of his Jewish background while others traced the apostle's beliefs to Hellenic religions of the first century. Whatever the explanation, neither view threatened the centrality of Jesus' teaching and experience to prevailing Protestant conceptions of Christianity. According to Johannes Weiss, a proponent of the new Pauline research, although the faith of modern Christians might "lose the mystical background of Paulinism," Jesus' experience would continue to be the "highest expression of Christianity."[34]

Machen acknowledged at the outset of his study that he was departing from the general trend in Pauline studies which rejected supernaturalism and explained Paulinism "as a phenomenon which emerged in the course of history under the operation of natural causes." For his part, Machen was most comfortable with the traditional explanation, which accepted "at face value" what Paul believed about Jesus. According to this view, Jesus was a heavenly being, who redeemed sinners through his death and resurrection. If this interpretation was correct, Machen reasoned, then nothing was left to explain because Paul had not apotheosized a man but had merely recognized Jesus' true character and significance.[35]

Although he advanced a simple explanation—some would call it no explanation at all—Machen's analysis did not lack historical awareness. In addition to questioning the dominant position in New Testament studies, Machen thought that a study of Paul would resolve several problems surrounding Christianity's emergence as a world religion. One concerned the Bible's enormous influence on Western society. How could a "thoroughly Semitic book," Machen wondered, come to a place of prominence even greater "than the glories of Greek literature" in a civilization shaped by the language, literature, and philosophy of Greece and Rome? The intrinsic value of the Bible could not explain this phenomenon since "the race from which the Bible came" had been despised throughout Western history. Christianity's influence upon the West was also worthy of historical investigation because this religion originated among a "very peculiar people." In A.D. 35 Christianity appeared to be nothing more than "a Jewish sect" but within thirty years was "plainly a world religion." Such questions gave *The Origin of Paul's Religion* a tone that clearly separated his criticisms of liberal scholars from fundamentalist diatribes against higher criticism. To be sure, Machen clearly had theological motives for his argument but was also striving to make a positive scholarly contribution.[36]

The academic style of Machen's study was also evident in his effort to solve these historical problems. Even though he believed that Christianity's origins were supernatural and that Paul's views were best understood as a reflection of that reality, Machen was not content with providential history to explain the early Christian movement. Rather than simply relying upon acts of God to account for the spread of the church, Machen advanced explanations that acknowledged the natural and human components of historical process. For instance, he argued that the spread of Christianity depended upon Paul as a historical actor. The establishment of Christianity as a world religion, he wrote, "to almost as great an extent as any great historical movement can be ascribed to one man," was the work of Paul. This proposition must have startled some conservatives who would normally have explained Christianity's origins as the work of God in Christ. Machen backed up this claim by pointing out the importance of Paul's missionary activity. Paul extended Christianity "in the geographical sphere . . . far more abundantly than any other man." "Despite the labors of others," Paul "planted the gospel in a real chain of the great cities," and "conceived most clearly the thought of a mighty Church universal which should embrace both Jew and Gentile." This position led to a claim even more astonishing to conservatives, that Jesus' teaching was not sufficient for the spread of Christianity but rather depended upon the supplementary efforts of Paul. To be sure, Machen did not intend to deny traditional Protestant beliefs that made Christ's ministry the basis for the work of the apostles. But Machen's historical instincts made him sensitive to what he called Paul's genius "in the hidden realm of thought." Jesus, Machen explained, had only implied but not made explicit the universal mission of the church and had not clarified how Gentiles were to be admitted into the church. These limitations made necessary "the epoch-making work of Paul" who "for the first time" viewed the death of Christ "in its full historical and logical relations," and established the principles of the Christian movement.[37]

Machen's sensitivity to historical explanation, however, did not make him any less critical of liberal scholars. Most of the book concerned the inadequacies of naturalistic explanations that attributed Paul's beliefs to historical development and cultural conditioning. Machen offered an extended critique of the history of religions school and a number of the scholars with whom he had studied in Germany. He countered interpretations that traced the apostle's faith to Jewish apocalyptic expectations by arguing that this branch of Judaism did not recognize the messiah as a divine being or as the creator of the universe, an important difference with Paul's conception of Jesus. Moreover, Machen believed that if Paul had been an advocate of Jewish apocalypticism he would never have elevated to the exalted figure of messiah a man who had died a shameful death on the cross. Machen also pointed out the flaws in accounts that attributed Paul's religion to pagan sources, an argument that required detailed historical and philological arguments. But these considerations were secondary to what Machen thought to be the overriding difference between Paulinism and Hellenistic religions. The particularism of Paul's religion invalidated efforts to explain Christianity solely by its first-century religious environment. The apostle, Machen wrote, demanded an "absolutely exclusive devotion" from his converts. While "oriental religions were tolerant of other faiths," individuals admitted into the early church on the basis of Paul's preaching had to forsake all other religions.[38]

Christian particularism, thus, raised the principle issue separating Machen and other New Testament scholars. What distinguished Paul's beliefs from all other first-century religions, Machen declared, "was the historical character" of Paul's message. "The religion of Paul was rooted in an event, . . . the redemptive work of Christ in His death and resurrection." Everywhere in his writings, according to Machen, Paul staked his life upon the truth of what he wrote about the miraculous events surrounding Jesus' death. The gospel of Paul was not founded upon a complex of ideas derived from Judaism or paganism but was "an account of something that had happened." In the end, this was the point of Machen's book. If Paul's account of Jesus' death and resurrection were true, then, Machen concluded, "the origin of Paulinism is explained; if it was not true, the Church is based upon an inexplicable error."[39]

Historians of American religion have argued that Machen's notions about historical facts and truth were typical of fundamentalism. His ahistorical outlook, like that of other conservatives, so the argument runs, rejected the historicist premise that held that religious beliefs and values were conditioned and shaped by the culture in which they developed. Thus, divergent conceptions of history were responsible for the conflicts between liberal and conservative Protestants during the fundamentalist controversy. Conservatives viewed history in static terms while liberals applied developmental categories.[40]

To explain the fundamentalist outlook many cite the persistence of Scottish Common Sense Philosophy and Baconian hermeneutics. Conservatives were the intellectual heirs of a naive empiricism that presupposed that truth could be established a priori by means of observation and induction. They maintained that the mind could perceive the real world truly, independent of personal, historical, or subjective factors. The truth of Christianity, fundamentalists said, depended upon examining the facts without prejudice, classifying those facts, and developing a reasonable hypothesis to explain them. This view of truth stood in direct contrast to the historicist epistemology that came to dominate American social thought and liberal Protestantism in the twentieth century. The "historical consciousness," as one historian calls it, embodied three closely related assumptions: that all knowledge is culturally determined, that particular ideas can be explained by reference to their historical context, and that these ideas are directed by functional laws of social process.[41]

The differences between liberal and conservative attitudes toward history were apparent even in Machen's day. In a review of a volume of essays commemorating Princeton's one-hundred-year anniversary in 1912, scholars at the University of Chicago Divinity School and advocates of the new historical awareness criticized their peers at Princeton for being insensitive to history. While conceding that Princeton had produced the "best conservative scholarship of the country," Chicago's faculty thought their Presbyterian colleagues were sadly behind the times. Anyone who was aware of the "intimate relations between Christian doctrine and the historical development of humanity," one Chicago scholar wrote, "is struck with the absence" of the feeling for this relationship in Princeton's discussions. Another thought Princetonians had concentrated so much on Christianity as a "system of revealed truth" that they ignored the "story of the development of human aspirations under the stress of historical circumstances." Princeton's approach made Christianity too formal, treating systems of thought as "actual entities" existing almost independently of social and psychological contexts. Rather than regarding the Bible as the product of an age that thought supernaturalism the only adequate basis "for estimating the social and religious values of life," Princeton scholars dwelt "so exclusively in the realm of ideas-as-such" that they ran the risk of "discussing the problem *in vacuo*."[42]

Reviews of *The Origin of Paul's Religion* registered similar complaints. They criticized Machen for restricting his analysis strictly to religious ideas. Critics objected specifically to Machen's tactic of exposing the inadequacy of naturalistic explanations. Henry J. Cadbury, professor at Haverford College, faulted him for not describing at length the supernatural account of Paul's religion. "Attacking vulnerable alternatives," he warned, was not the best method of proof. The reviewer for *The Hibbert Journal* was more direct. He thought Machen had been so eager to demolish critical interpretations—"although in some cases it is slaying the slain"—that he had not proposed a satisfactory alternative. German critic Rudolf Bultmann echoed these assessments, noting that Machen had correctly pointed out many shortcomings in other theories but had not advanced his own. A related criticism concerned Machen's tendency to treat his material formally rather than historically. Bultmann, for instance, said Machen had gone too far in denying the influence of other religions and cultures on Paul and had decided complicated questions "by means of a logic which [looked] at things from the outside." British scholar James Moffatt also believed that to deny or ignore Jewish and Hellenic influences on Paul was "to leave the origin and development" of his theology "in the air." Cadbury concurred that Christian theology in the early church was "far less static" than Machen had implied. Furthermore, the reviewer for the *Biblical Review* restated his "long-cherished feeling" that Paul was able to "absorb some elements of world-thought without endangering the Gospel." In sum, by stressing the differences between Christianity and other religions, critics urged, Machen cut Paul off from history.[43]

Despite these criticisms and the book's conservative argument, Machen received praise from the same reviewers for his scholarly contribution. Lyman Abbott called it the "work of a careful, able, and conscientious scholar" with whom others would have to reckon. Prominent members of the Society of Biblical Literature also praised Machen. George A. Barton wrote that the Princeton professor had made "all Christians his debtors" and had written "with adequate learning and in an excellent spirit." Benjamin W. Bacon thought the book was "worthy of a high place among the products of American biblical scholarship." In fact, Bacon, who led American developments in New Testament criticism, praised Machen for his "sound" use of historical methods. Cadbury, another prominent New Testament scholar, also complimented Machen for his treatment of important historical questions, especially the relationship between Paul's epistles and the Acts of the Apostles. In similar fashion, Bultmann commended Machen for his fairness in representing liberal views and his analysis of Paulinism. A Presbyterian minister, Edgar Whitaker Work, while confusing his weapons, compared Machen's argument to David's battle with Goliath and rejoiced to see "mighty protagonists of criticism . . . being driven into a corner by an American blade."[44]

These reactions reveal that the lines between modernists and fundamentalists had not been clearly drawn in the academic community even as late as 1922 when these reviews appeared. These positive assessments also suggest that conservative conceptions of history were not alien in the world of professional biblical scholarship. Few, if any, faulted Machen for his methods. Indeed, the appeal of historical methods was sufficient to unite most biblical scholars no matter what their theological perspective. The real problem for conservatives was that their numbers in the academy were declining, a dilemma related to the growth of Bible institutes and the evangelical habit of putting evangelism and missions ahead of critical reflection and inquiry.[45]

Part of the reason why Machen's research did not elicit sharper criticism was that while historical methods had broad appeal they escaped precise definition. For instance, some scholars described them in static terms. Bacon, professor at Yale, described the historical method as the effort to disentangle the "text's primitive thread . . . from all the web of pious legend" in order that "we may know the plain, bald facts, just the events as they occurred, in their own inherent significance." University of Chicago theologian Gerald Birney Smith sounded as though under the spell of inductive science when he wrote that historians were "playing fast and loose with truth" unless they allowed the Bible to speak directly, even if its teaching conflicted with the preferences of "modern religious faith." Yet a new conception of historical methods was also emerging, one influenced by the social sciences. Commonly called the New History, this approach was advanced by such prominent historians as James Harvey Robinson and Carl Becker. They attacked the conservatism of their profession and called upon historians to use the past to reform the present, or as Robinson put it, "to turn on the past and exploit it in the interests of advance." The New History also influenced the study of religion. Scholars at the University of Chicago Divinity School applied the New History to religious studies and the change of the institution's quarterly in 1921 from the *American Journal of Theology* to the *Journal of Religion* was indicative of this development. In its first issue, the journal's editors declared that their purpose was to study the social origins of Christianity in order to promote reform. "Modern historical study," Shirley Jackson Case opined, should deliver humankind from "bondage to the past" and provide direction for the future by "the mandate of efficiency."[46]

While Machen did not follow the lead of the New History, the approach of Robinson and Becker in history or the University of Chicago in biblical studies by no means dominated the study of American or ancient history. New ideas about historical methods not only separated Protestants but also divided scholars who studied ancient literature and culture. Like other historians, classicists, philologists, and some literary scholars, Machen assumed a static or timeless view of the past which aimed at finding the author's original purpose. Although the passage of time might shed more light on the text, traditionalists in the humanities held that particular works had a fixed meaning. They also tended to presuppose the permanency of human nature and so looked to ancient texts for timeless truths about the human condition. These students of antiquity were no more predisposed to accept New Testament supernaturalism than were reform-minded humanistic scholars. But because of their attention to a text's original meaning and their assumptions about the static nature of ideas, they were more inclined to regard Christianity as a fixed body of beliefs established by the first Christians. In Machen's case this outlook meant that the writings of the apostles were authoritative and determined the meaning of the Christian religion for all time. To be a Christian meant holding to the same conceptions of God and Christ that the apostles held, just as to be a Platonist meant affirming certain theories of universals and mathematical objects. Such an outlook also implied that the ideas of first-century Christians were still relevant for twentieth-century audiences, in the same way that classicists thought the teachings of classical authors were applicable to modern life.[47]

This scholarly position came under attack from academics who suspected that ancient ideas about God and the cosmos were in themselves of little use for the problems confronting a modern, urban, industrial society. Progressive scholars often started with traditional methods but the need to address contemporary social ills prompted greater reliance upon social scientific methods in order to explore the social and political contexts of particular documents or ideas. This stress upon the social context rather than the original intent of the author was part of a shift from intellectual to social history within biblical scholarship. Christianity, according to this view, was not defined by the ideas that Paul or other apostles taught but instead was a movement that attracted people from different racial, ethnic, and social backgrounds. Paul may have taught certain doctrines but the people who filled the first churches heard and appropriated his message from their own religious, cultural, and socioeconomic perspectives. The New Testament was not simply a product of the apostles but reflected the diverse appeal of Christianity to the people of the Greco-Roman world. This approach gave the Bible added relevance for the modern church. The New Testament's connections to the social forces in which it was written showed that Christianity always had to be adapted to its cultural setting. The search for the social and cultural origins of the Bible, then, stemmed from the practical desire of progressive scholars to free the modern church from outmoded ideas and make it more responsive to the realities of twentieth-century life.[48]

Religious motives, therefore, shaped the research methods advocated by both conservatives and liberals. Machen was sensitive to the way that theological assumptions affected biblical criticism, having sat under and worked with Armstrong. Princeton's chairman of the New Testament department was best known for his ability to show, as Machen described it, the "connection between various schools of New Testament criticism and various schools of modern philosophy." Seminarians often faulted Armstrong for spending too much time lecturing on the history of German higher criticism and philosophy. But he did not point out the presuppositions of German critics merely to question their objectivity. He believed that conservatives and liberals were motivated by religious convictions; the former held that Christianity was a religion of grace that depended upon the miraculous events told in scripture, while the latter maintained that Christianity was a syncretistic faith bound together by Jesus' religious experience and ethical teaching.[49]

Differences in theological convictions meant that while Machen gained the respect of his peers in the academy he failed to check the trends within American biblical studies that he resisted. His methods, research, and argument were those of a scholar fully acquainted with the norms of academic discourse and specific issues within New Testament studies. Yet Machen's religious views were at odds with liberal Protestant beliefs that increasingly dominated his discipline. Furthermore, Machen's classicist orientation made him sensitive to the intellectual aspects of the New Testament at a time when the discipline was focusing more on the social dimensions of Christian origins. Twenty years later, when biblical theology dominated the study of scripture in the United States, Machen's scholarship may have made more of an impact. As one scholar wrote looking back from the post–World War II era, Machen's "contention that classic Christian theology is the necessary outcome of faithfulness to the New Testament" looked "far truer" than much of the "shallow theology which often marked the social gospel." For the rest of his career, however, Machen remained an intelligent curiosity within the academic community.[50]

Still, Machen's purpose in writing was not strictly academic. In his introduction he wrote that questions surrounding Christianity's origin were also important to modern believers. "There are many who maintain that Christianity is the same no matter what its origin was," that the issue was completely independent of "the present religious interests of the Church." This view, Machen argued, assumed that Christianity was "simply a manner of life." But many believed that Christianity was a "manner of life" founded upon a message about the founder of the Christian movement. Machen thought his research had direct bearing upon the church because it revealed the fundamental issue facing the modern church: was Christianity rooted in what Christ taught or in what he did?[51]

The practical implications of Christianity's origins surfaced throughout the book, but were evident with particular force in Machen's discussion of Paul's relation to Jesus. The Princeton professor held that recent conclusions of German scholars no longer regarded Paul as a follower of the "liberal Jesus." "If Jesus was what the liberal theologians represent Him as being—a teacher of righteousness, a religious genius," then Paulinism was a complete departure from Christ. But newer work had revealed, according to Machen, that supernaturalism was at the core of Jesus' faith and life. Paul's religion was not a departure from but fully in accord with Jesus' life and teachings. By contending that Paul was a faithful disciple of Jesus Machen was, of course, trying to subvert modern efforts to circumvent Paul. Machen also hoped to demonstrate that Christianity for the early church was not a system of ethical ideals but a religion of redemption. "If imitation of Jesus had been central in the life of Paul, as it is central, for example, in modern liberalism," Machen argued, "then the Epistles would be full of the words and deeds of Jesus." Instead, the Pauline epistles revealed an intimate union of religion and theology. "Jesus, according to Paul," Machen concluded, "came to earth not to say something, but to do something." Paul's writings did not "deal with general principles of love and grace, and fatherliness and brotherliness" but instead with the "thing most distasteful to the modern liberal Church," Jesus' death and resurrection. The clear implication was that Paul and Jesus were of a piece and the modern church could not reject Paul without also rejecting Jesus.[52]

As the reviews of his book indicated, Machen's scholarly demeanor helped to mute these criticisms of religious liberalism. Yet the ecclesiastical ramifications of his study were not lost on Presbyterian conservatives. By showing unanimity between Paul and Jesus and by making the apostle's teaching foundational for the spread of the early church, Machen had cleverly put traditional Presbyterian theology at the center of Christian developments. Paulinism, according to Machen, which ran from "Augustine through the Reformation to the Reformed Churches," was the "true foundation" of the Christian church. His forceful defense of Reformed theology had particular appeal to the editors at the *Presbyterian*, a staunchly conservative weekly published in Philadelphia. The editor, David S. Kennedy, was quick to rank Machen with the outstanding Calvinist theologians of the day. Samuel G. Craig, an associate editor who reviewed Machen's book for the *Presbyterian*, also heaped praise on the Princeton professor. Machen's chief significance, Craig wrote, was not his contribution to biblical scholarship but his discussion of the "real nature of Christianity." *The Origin of Paul's Religion* was a "powerful apologetic for Christianity," that would appeal to "an age in which the conflict between naturalism and supernaturalism" had become crucial. Ironically, a book that followed many of the conventions of modern scholarship also propelled Machen directly into the struggles beginning to emerge in the Presbyterian Church. Such a development may have squandered his scholarly abilities but kept at bay the monotony that often afflicted Machen while carrying out his academic duties.[53]

# CHAPTER THREE

# Highbrow Fundamentalism

Dr. Machen was to [William Jennings] Bryan as the Matterhorn is to a
wart. His Biblical Studies had been wide and deep, and he was familiar
with the almost interminable literature of the subject. Moreover, he
was an adept theologian, and had a wealth of professional knowledge
to support his ideas. Bryan could only bawl.   *H. L. Mencken (1937)*

During the 1920s Victorian religious and literary traditions came under
increasing attack for what many younger men and women considered
a hollow and reality-denying vision of society and art. The literary front
of that decade's so-called battle of the books is well documented. H. L.
Mencken provided critical cover for the novels of Theodore Dreiser and
Sinclair Lewis whose work attacked the idea that art should be didactic
and uplifting. Younger intellectuals insisted instead that literature
should depict realistic views of human nature and society.[1]

While fundamentalism has usually been regarded as a resurgence
of Victorian sensibilities, Machen's religious outlook bears striking
similarities to the broader cultural reaction against the Genteel Tradition. Indeed, his most popular book, *Christianity and Liberalism* (1923),
found mainstream American Protestantism inadequate in terms similar to those used by modernist literary critics and writers. Machen
accused liberal Protestants of promoting empty rhetoric and sentimental ideals at the expense of intellectual honesty and theological faithfulness. Although his argument would eventually send ripples all the
way to the highest governing bodies of the Northern Presbyterian
Church, its splash was immediately unsettling at Machen's local
church where his strictures antagonized one of Victorian culture's
most celebrated guardians.[2]

Despite Machen's growing popularity among fundamentalists, he was still sufficiently respectable to fill the pulpit for several months during late 1923 at First Presbyterian Church, Princeton, as the congregation looked for a new pastor. This church was the oldest Presbyterian body in town and the choice of many professors and local elites. So Machen accepted the church's invitation "with great trepidation." Still, First Church's genteel surroundings did not inhibit him from speaking his mind on the religious issues of the day. His sermon on December 30, "The Present Issue in the Church," proved to be particularly feisty. In it he accused Protestant liberals of dishonesty, that they were using Christian language to deny the gospel. "The plain fact is," Machen concluded, "disguised though it may be by the use of traditional language, that two mutually exclusive religions are contending for the control of the church today." The only legitimate solution was a division between the parties.[3]

Not surprisingly, some of First Church's members did not agree. Henry Van Dyke, former Presbyterian minister in Brooklyn, professor of English literature at Princeton University, and ambassador to the Netherlands and Luxembourg during the Wilson administration, especially objected to Machen's billingsgate. Despite personal ties to the preacher, Van Dyke informed First Church's elders on December 31, 1923, that he was giving up his pew as long as Machen occupied the pulpit. Machen had "spoiled" too many Sundays, Van Dyke complained, with "bitter, schismatic and unscriptural preaching." In the statement, which he also released to the press and which was reported throughout the country, Van Dyke added that the few Sabbaths he was free to spend at home were too precious to be wasted listening to "such a dismal, bilious travesty of the gospel." "We want to hear about Christ, not about Fundamentalists and Modernists."[4]

Van Dyke is not as well remembered for this outburst as for one that occurred several years later. In 1930 he took umbrage at the selection of Sinclair Lewis, the author of *Main Street* (1920) and *Babbitt* (1922), as the winner of the Nobel Prize for literature. Van Dyke thought it an insult to the United States for Lewis, a man who regularly ridiculed the nation's values, to be the first American author honored by the Swedish Academy. Van Dyke would later clarify that the Nobel Prize was not an "insult" but a "back handed compliment." What he objected to specifically was Lewis's "meanness" and "lopsided" pessimism. America was filled with generous men and women who deserved to be called "sons and daughters of God," people who made the country great. But there was "no trace of their existence" in Lewis's books. The novelist replied that by criticizing any writing that was not a "glorification of everything American," Van Dyke had poisoned national literature. The cultural establishment that Van Dyke represented had ignored the problems of modern society and continued to think of America as a "pale edition of an English cathedral town."[5]

Van Dyke's confrontations with Machen and Lewis illustrate the ways in which religious conservatives and cultural modernists opposed a common enemy during the disputes of the 1920s. In fact, the iconoclastic temper of that controversy-riddled decade gave Machen's criticism of religious liberalism a wider hearing and greater saliency. In the process he was forced to redirect his energies from the fine print of theological quarterlies to the op-ed page of metropolitan newspapers.

H. L. Mencken did as much as any other writer to identify fundamentalism with obscurantism and charlatanism. In 1925 he wrote that in regions "where Beelzebub is still as real as Babe Ruth," Protestants "plunge into an abyss of malignant imbecility, and declare a holy war upon every decency that civilized men cherish." What one mainly notices about fundamentalists, Mencken continued, "is their vast lack of sound information and sound sense." Mencken spoke for many intellectuals when he concluded that conservative Protestants constituted "the most ignorant class of teachers ever set up to guide a presumably civilized people . . . even more ignorant than the county superintendents of schools."[6]

Only a few years earlier, however, fundamentalism had enjoyed better press. In a series of articles for *World's Work*, Rollin Lynde Hartt, a Congregationalist minister before turning to journalism, surveyed the issues dividing Protestants as well as the strength of fundamentalism. He noted that Moody Bible Institute, a fundamentalist stronghold offering instruction in Bible, evangelism, and missions, had over 1,000 students and twenty-eight buildings in downtown Chicago, and distributed "ultra-orthodox books by the million." William Jennings Bryan's outdoor Bible class, carried by over 100 newspapers into the homes of 25 million people, was another sign of conservative vitality. Although liberal Protestants had won many colleges and divinity schools, Hartt believed that fundamentalists had "the people" on their side. He concluded that the fundamentalist-modernist controversy was a "clean-cut division, full of promise." "There are splendid men on both sides. There is magnificent devotion. There is candor."[7]

However respectable in its early stages, fundamentalism was not a natural outlet for Machen's talents. The first article in the *World's Work* series noted, for instance, the anomaly of Princeton Seminary, one of

America's oldest seminaries, and Moody Bible Institute, which only required a common-school education for admittance, joining sides against liberal Protestantism. According to Hartt, many liberals consoled themselves that "the enemy 'lacks brains.'" Some also viewed fundamentalism as an "old gentleman's movement" that drew heavily from the rural South. Furthermore, the most visible leader of the movement in its early stages was J. Frank Norris, "the Texas cyclone," a Baptist minister from Fort Worth who had a reputation for "toting a gun" and whose escapades eventually resulted in his shooting and killing a man in self-defense. As a well-educated gentleman from Baltimore in his early forties, Machen was by most accounts out of his element.[8]

Just as remarkable as Machen's eventual identification with fundamentalism was his ability to weather the storm of criticism that followed many conservatives as the controversy wore on. At a time when America's intellectuals were largely indifferent to Christianity or busy undermining religious verities, Machen gained the respect of many who read his books. Even after the disgrace fundamentalists suffered following the Scopes trial, Machen continued to be published by major New York houses, his books received favorable reviews, and editors of newspapers and magazines regularly solicited him for articles and book reviews.[9]

Fundamentalist leaders were equally impressed with Machen's abilities and by 1923 had embraced him as one of their own. That year, President James M. Gray of Moody Bible Institute invited Machen to speak at the institution's Founder's Week Conference and published Machen's address, "Christianity versus Modern Liberalism," in the Institute's monthly magazine. Moody's administrators also asked for contributions in the same issue, pointing out that Machen's address contained the message for which the school had stood throughout its thirty-six-year history. Meanwhile, Charles B. Trumbull, editor of the conservative *Sunday School Times,* introduced Machen to his readers, writing that "in training and exact scholarship" no one was better fit to speak on the "striking differences between Christianity and its chief modern substitute."[10]

What endeared Machen to many conservatives was his indictment of religious modernism, summed up in *Christianity and Liberalism,* published in February 1923. Even so, while fundamentalists were delighted to count an academic among their ranks, they knew little of Machen's scholarly work and may have been scared off by his use of modern methods. His forceful argument in *Christianity and Liberalism* was a different matter. It quickly caught the eye of observers on both sides of the controversy and made him a spokesman for fundamentalism. Recognized by historians as one of the ablest critiques of theological modernism produced during the 1920s, this book not only accounts for Machen's popularity but also explains the reason for his unlikely alliance with the fundamentalists.[11]

Machen himself did not like the term *fundamentalism* because it suggested "some strange new sect." Yet when forced to choose between fundamentalism and modernism, he admitted he was a fundamentalist "of the most pronounced type." True to his word, Machen accepted many invitations to present the conservative point of view. In 1924 he debated Union Seminary (New York) Old Testament scholar Charles F. Fagnani in *Survey Graphic* over the question "Does Fundamentalism Obstruct Social Progress?" In the same year Machen defended conservative beliefs before audiences at the Brooklyn Institute of Arts and Sciences and New York's Unitarian Laymen's League. One year later he published "What Fundamentalism Stands for Now" in the *New York Times*. In 1929 he also spoke at Columbia University's Symposium on Religion and lectured at Union Seminary (New York) to an audience that included Reinhold Niebuhr, Henry Sloane Coffin, the seminary's president, and Henry P. Van Dusen, Union's future president.[12]

Machen's ambivalence about fundamentalism combined with his activities on behalf of the movement highlight the difficulty in deciding who was a fundamentalist. In most historical accounts of the movement Machen is the one most difficult to pigeonhole. He was clearly not the rural and intellectually backward Protestant, unable to cope with modern urban society that many in his day associated with fundamentalism. But even when theological concerns are isolated from the social and cultural circumstances that gave rise to fundamentalism, Machen does not fit the mold. Recent scholarship has shown that fundamentalism was an alliance of conservatives who held that human history was on the verge of collapsing, that Christ's return was imminent, and that the Bible was inerrant in scientific and historical details as well as spiritual matters. During World War I the threat of German barbarism politicized many of these Protestants. In turn, they began to view evolutionary science, biblical criticism, and liberal Protestant theology as considerable threats to Christian civilization in America. The crisis generated by the war prompted Protestants with specific views about Christ's second coming (dispensational premillennialism) and about the truthfulness of the Bible to mount a campaign against evolution in the schools and religious modernism in the churches. Dispensationalism was crucial to this outlook because it taught that human sinfulness and divine judgment, not the progressive improvement of society, would be the final stage of human history before the thousand-year reign of Christ.[13]

William Bell Riley, a Baptist pastor in Minneapolis and an influential figure in premillennialist Bible and prophecy conferences, tapped this discontent to found the World's Christian Fundamentals Association (WCFA). This organization met for the first time in the spring of 1919, during a week of revivalistic meetings in Philadelphia that according to one estimate attracted 6,000 people. Although conservative Protestants formed other associations, the WCFA united the most influential fundamentalists. Its stated purpose was to fight the "Great Apostasy" that was spreading "like a plague" throughout Christendom. WCFA members committed themselves to support "fundamentally safe" seminaries, Bible schools, periodicals, and missionary societies, to establish Bible conferences in metropolitan areas, and to pray for "world-wide revival."[14]

Machen did not attend these meetings, however, and his absence said a good deal about his differences with mainstream fundamentalism. One of the chief differences was Machen's repudiation of dispensationalism. When Riley finally asked Machen to join the WCFA in 1929, Machen declined the invitation and wondered whether it would even be proper to address an organization where premillennialism was "not just important, but necessary." Riley followed with a request for Machen only to speak to the WCFA. Machen accepted but made sure people knew he was speaking as a guest rather than a member. He did not want his appearance to be construed as an endorsement of dispensationalism. Machen wrote in *Christianity and Liberalism* that the dispensationalist preoccupation with Christ's return gave him "serious concern" because it relied upon a "false method of interpreting Scripture." In similar fashion, in correspondence with J. W. Milton, editor of *The Fundamentalist* (Texas), Machen expressed regret that fundamentalism had made dispensationalism an essential belief. He thought Christians could not be exact about the "order of future events" and that fascination with the end of history obscured more important issues and gave modernists a way to discredit conservatives. By the end of his life Machen would vigorously oppose fundamentalist views of the millennium.[15]

Fundamentalists also held strong convictions about the inerrancy of the Bible. Since expositions of this doctrine by theologians at Princeton Seminary were crucial to the fundamentalist defense of scripture, the presumption has been that inerrancy was the issue that allowed Machen to align himself with a movement that otherwise gave him pause. To be sure, inerrancy was an important weapon against liberalism and Princeton theologians armed conservatives well. The first of the WCFA's nine-point doctrinal platform affirmed that the Bible was "verbally inspired of God, and inerrant in the original writings," a statement that closely followed the Princeton formula. Moreover, of the 100 articles in *The Fundamentals*, a series of twelve volumes published between 1910 and 1915 that became a reference point for fundamentalism, one-third defended the authority and truthfulness of scripture. *The Fundamentals*, it is said, cemented the alliance of Princeton theology and premillennialism, thus laying the foundation for fundamentalist theology.[16]

Nevertheless, while inerrancy united conservatives, it was not the source of Machen's opposition to religious modernism, nor was it as pivotal to the creation of the fundamentalist movement as dispensationalism. Machen's work on the apostle Paul and his rebuttal of German New Testament criticism, which ignored the doctrine of inerrancy, were virtually unknown to fundamentalists who were absorbed with the first chapters of Genesis and evolution. The only mention of the New Testament in *The Fundamentals* was a devotional study of John's gospel. Furthermore, fundamentalists rarely made inerrancy the cornerstone of their case against theological modernism. For most the task of distinguishing between liberal and fundamental Christianity was a relatively easy one even though conservatives could not agree on modernism's basic flaw. Some pointed to evolution and the acceptance of scientific naturalism. Others looked to higher criticism and noted affinities among evolution, postmillennialism, and critical theories about the Bible. Still another group stressed Christ's premillennial, miraculous, and cataclysmic return in contrast to modernist optimism about social progress.[17]

Perhaps *Christianity and Liberalism* met with such acclaim because fundamentalism lacked coherence. Machen's purpose was "to present the issue as sharply and clearly as possible." Yet he wrote this book specifically with the Presbyterian Church in mind. In fact, *Christianity and Liberalism* was not aimed at the rarefied liberalism to which Machen had been exposed in Germany but rather took issue with specific trends in American Protestantism.[18]

When Macmillan published *Christianity and Liberalism* in 1923 Machen was still a little-known professor of New Testament. To be sure, editors at the New York house were familiar with his work, having already published *The Origin of Paul's Religion* (1921) as part of a standing contract with Union (Richmond) Seminary's Sprunt Lectures. While sales for Machen's first book were slow, his second book, *New Testament*

*Greek for Beginners* (1922), also published by Macmillan, did better, filling a need at American seminaries for a textbook that introduced students without previous knowledge of Greek to the language of the New Testament. Undoubtedly, marketing was easier for a Greek grammar than for a specialized study of Paulinism. Nevertheless, even the polemical nature of Machen's third book with Macmillan did not guarantee a large market. In its first year in print *Christianity and Liberalism* sold about 1,000 copies and in early 1924 Machen wrote to his mother that it was being outsold by *The Origin of Paul's Religion*. Sales jumped to 4,000 in 1924, thanks in large part to the publicity surrounding Van Dyke's fulmination against Machen's preaching at Princeton's First Church. The national press coverage made him something of a celebrity. He initially complained that reporters "were as thick as flies" at his door but eventually saw the benefits of unsolicited publicity. Van Dyke had made him a "publicly recognized leader overnight" and had given the sales of *Christianity and Liberalism* a "big boost."[19]

Indeed, the sermon that so riled Van Dyke, "The Present Issue in the Church," repeated arguments from the book and became for conservatives what Harry Emerson Fosdick's "Shall the Fundamentalists Win?" had become for liberals. Although ordained a Baptist minister, Fosdick was on the staff of New York's First Presbyterian Church, and his famous sermon, which was printed and distributed church-wide and published in several periodicals, brought into the open divisions that had been festering in the Presbyterian Church. Fosdick angered conservatives by declaring that biblical inerrancy, the virgin birth, and the physical return of Christ were not essential doctrines. Furthermore, he depicted fundamentalism not as a benign movement but rather as a genuine threat. "Fundamentalists," he maintained, "are giving us one of the worst exhibitions of bitter intolerance that the churches of this country have ever seen." Like Fosdick's, Machen's sermon was distributed throughout the church and excerpted in several newspapers and religious weeklies, not because of a well-oiled conservative machine, but rather because of Van Dyke's reaction. Instead of defending the doctrines that Fosdick thought unessential, Machen accused liberals of intellectual dishonesty, of claiming to be Christian while denying traditional beliefs. He asserted that "plain old-fashioned honesty of speech" was absent in religious circles.[20]

Fosdick's sermon, although it attracted the most attention, was not the only incident that alerted conservative Presbyterians to irregularities in their denomination. Two years earlier Presbyterian traditionalists had begun to marshal forces in opposition to plans for a union of the largest American denominations. In fact, the ecumenical efforts of the early twentieth century have not been included among the factors leading up to the Presbyterian controversy. Yet, resistance to church union was critical for drawing Machen into denominational politics, for establishing the network of Presbyterian traditionalists that would be his chief base of support, and ultimately for his writing *Christianity and Liberalism*.[21]

The crusading spirit of the progressive era fueled a number of Protestant cooperative endeavors that sought to construct at home and around the world a society founded upon Christian principles broadly defined. At the institutional level, ecumenical impulses produced the Federal Council of Churches in 1908, a body that drew the largest denominations into systematic cooperation in a variety of activities. A less formal expression of Protestant collaboration was the Men and Religion Forward Movement, an association launched in 1912 by businessmen which raised money and recruited lay leaders for revivalistic meetings across the nation. The high moral aims of World War I spurred further cooperation among Protestants, such as the Federal Council's General War-Time Commission of the Churches, which recruited chaplains and provided educational programs for the soldiers. After the war, Protestants seized the momentum of the Allies' victory to establish even closer ties among the churches. Examples of these postwar efforts were the Interchurch World Movement, an agency that had international ecumenical aims, and the American Council on Organic Union, a body given the task of planning a federated union of Protestant denominations.[22]

The American Council on Organic Union drew immediate fire from conservatives at Princeton Seminary, including Machen, and from ministers and elders in southeastern Pennsylvania. Philadelphia would remain the regional center of conservative Presbyterian strength throughout the 1920s and 1930s. The plan for organic union also marked the beginning of Machen's outspoken criticism of liberalism. A first-time delegate to the 1920 General Assembly held in Philadelphia, Machen heard the report that recommended church union. While in Philadelphia he established ties with conservative ministers and elders in the vicinity, speaking before a ministerial association and warning about the dangers of this particular plan. During the following year Machen penned three articles for the conservative Philadelphia weekly, the *Presbyterian*. Over the next few years, he spoke to groups in the Philadelphia and nearby Chester presbyteries on themes he would develop in *Christianity and Liberalism*. The book itself stemmed from an informal address on November 3, 1921, before the Chester Presbytery Elders' Association. Members of the association were so impressed with

Machen's talk that they wanted to have it printed and distributed throughout the denomination. In an attempt to keep the cost of printing down, Machen had his remarks published in the *Princeton Theological Review* under the title "Liberalism or Christianity?" The expense of distributing the article as a pamphlet still proved too expensive so Machen developed the essay into a small book that in late 1922 Macmillan agreed to publish. Although identifying Machen as a fundamentalist, *Christianity and Liberalism* voiced a form of religious conservatism, Presbyterian traditionalism, that differed in significant respects from popular fundamentalism.[23]

Differences between traditionalists and fundamentalists were evident as early as the Presbyterian General Assembly of 1923, when Philadelphia conservatives presented an overture that called attention to Fosdick's inflammatory preaching, reminded the denomination of a 1916 ruling that made the virgin birth and biblical inerrancy essential doctrines, and asked the delegates to take necessary steps to insure sound preaching in the New York pulpit. After some debate the assembly ratified this overture. This conservative victory was fairly remarkable because the fundamentalism of William Jennings Bryan had dominated debates. At the 1923 assembly, true to his form in national elections, the statesman ran and lost as a candidate for moderator. Despite defeat, Bryan managed to bring two proposals to the floor. He won support for a resolution endorsing total abstinence from alcoholic beverages, but his motion to prohibit the teaching of evolution in Presbyterian schools yielded only a watered-down motion that instructed churches to withhold approval from institutions that taught a "materialistic evolutionary philosophy of life." Machen, whose views on prohibition and evolution differed from Bryan's, was not at all pleased by the populist's efforts, fearing they would sidetrack the assembly from the more important issue of Fosdick's preaching.[24]

Although Bryan and Machen were perceived to be on the same side, their concerns were distinct. Many of Bryan's efforts actually failed to win the support of Presbyterian traditionalists. Bryan, like fundamentalists more generally, believed America should be a Christian society and so worked to purge liberalism from the nation's schools and churches. In contrast, Machen, like Presbyterian traditionalists, sought to preserve Presbyterian theology and church practice, and limited his efforts against liberalism to the ecclesiastical sphere. Although Bryan was not a premillennialist, his desire to preserve Christian civilization resembled popular fundamentalism in that he thought the institutional church was at best indifferent and at worst detrimental to spreading of the gospel. Bryan minimized doctrinal and denominational differences and conceived of Christianity as a sure means to improve society. Fundamentalist concerns about secularism in American society ran counter to the narrowly ecclesiastical and confessional aims of Presbyterian traditionalists. Rather than linking Machen to Bryan, a better parallel to Presbyterian traditionalism was the contemporaneous effort in Canada by Presbyterian conservatives who in 1925 refused to join the United Church of Canada and formed their own denomination to preserve Presbyterian faith and practice.[25]

Machen's Presbyterian particularism was lost on many readers of *Christianity and Liberalism* who focused on the author's sweeping and acerbic indictment of religious modernism. According to Willard L. Sperry, dean of Harvard Divinity School, the book stood out for its "mixture of theological patronage and theological vitriol." Machen's thesis that liberalism was "un-Christian" infuriated many Protestant church leaders. He also charged that the greatest menace to the church is a "type of faith and practice that is anti-Christian to the core." Whether or not liberals were Christians, he said, it was perfectly clear that "liberalism is not Christianity." For good measure, Machen added that although the Church of Rome represented a "perversion" of the Christian religion, "naturalistic liberalism is not Christianity at all." Even without the publicity surrounding the Van Dyke incident or Bryan's crusades, *Christianity and Liberalism* was sufficiently controversial to arouse some interest.[26]

Nevertheless, the volume disappointed readers solely interested in polemics. It read more like a textbook in theology than a fundamentalist tract. Machen used material and arguments from *The Origin of Paul's Religion* to explain the basic tenets of "historic Christianity," devoting separate chapters to the doctrines of God, man, Christ, and salvation. He was virtually silent about biblical inerrancy. Even though most participants in and observers of the controversy agreed that the Bible was central to the struggle, Machen's chapter on scripture was the shortest. Instead, he attempted to show under traditional theological headings that Christianity was a religion of grace and redemption, and that liberalism, while using traditional Christian phrases, was a religion of morality and human goodness. *Christianity and Liberalism* was also a way for Machen to release some of his pent-up interest in theology. When Benjamin Breckinridge Warfield died in 1921, Princeton Seminary's directors chose Machen to fill the chair of dogmatic theology, thereby freeing another colleague, Caspar Wistar Hodge, to take Warfield's position. Machen called it a magnificent opportunity but could not accept because he felt unprepared in the philosophy and history of doctrine. Even so, Machen's book probably instructed more people in the rudiments of Presbyterian orthodoxy than he would have as a professor of theology.[27]

Machen started with doctrines concerning God and man and contrasted the liberal conception of God's universal fatherhood with the conservative notion of God's "awful transcendence." Liberalism came perilously close to pantheism, he argued, because it applied the term *God* to the ever-evolving world process. In Christian teaching, Machen wrote, a great gulf lay between God and man, and it was widened by human sinfulness. In contrast, the modern age had exhibited a "supreme confidence in human goodness," giving liberal ministers the impossible task of "calling the righteous to repentance." But Christianity, Machen said, began with the law of God and a conviction of sin.[28]

He next considered Christ's place in the Christian faith, asking whether Jesus was an "object of faith" or an "example for faith." Machen asserted that liberalism regarded Jesus of Nazareth as the first Christian and that Christianity involved emulating his religious experience. In contrast, Machen maintained that the early church did not have faith in God like Jesus had but instead had "faith in Jesus." The liberal refrain "Back to Jesus," therefore, had a hollow and deceitful ring, for the ethical teachings of Jesus and his moral example were not the essence of Christianity. Equally problematic for liberals were Christ's claims to be the messiah. These claims, if not true, placed a "moral stain" upon his character. Was Jesus really a great moral teacher, as liberals believed, if he could lapse "so far from the path of humility and sanity as to believe that the eternal destinies of the world" were committed to him? This difficulty, Machen argued, never seemed to trouble liberal Protestant devotion to Jesus as a model of religious experience. Liberal allegiance to Jesus, in Machen's view, avoided the reality of sin and the message of grace.[29]

Miracles presented further difficulties for the liberal image of Jesus as the "fairest flower of humanity." Machen did not mention miracles simply to argue for the truth of Christianity, as previous Princeton theologians had. Nor did he say that liberals who doubted the veracity of miracles denied the Bible's truthfulness. Instead, he tried to show that miracles constituted the heart of Christianity. For Machen, miracles were not evidence of the Bible's superiority but rather a manifestation of grace. Without a proper comprehension of the nature of sin, a person could not understand the occasion for a supernatural act of God. Once convinced of one's inability to merit salvation, however, the believer readily admitted that the only solution for sin lay in a miraculous act of God.[30]

Throughout *Christianity and Liberalism,* then, Machen stressed the supernatural character of Christianity in contrast to the naturalistic perspective of liberal Protestantism. This position was especially evident in the chapter on salvation, which was the longest and contained the core of his objections to liberalism. Machen maintained that Christianity and liberalism offered two entirely different views of salvation. Christians traditionally held, according to Machen, that Jesus was a savior, not because he inspired people to lead good lives but because he bore the guilt of human sin in his death on the cross. Machen thus launched a thirty-five-page defense of the doctrine of the vicarious atonement. To the objection that it was too exclusive, he countered that it was only narrow if the church ignored its responsibilities to preach to the lost. To the objection that one person could not bear the punishment of another, he answered that Christ was no mere person but the "Lord of Glory." To the further objection that the atonement embodied a degrading view of God's love, he responded that the doctrine actually enhanced an understanding of divine love because God had made the sacrifice. The very term *gospel,* Machen asserted, implied this conception of Christ's death. *Gospel* meant "'good news', tidings, information about something that has happened." Christianity, he argued, "must be abandoned altogether unless at a definite point in history Jesus died as a propitiation for the sins of men." Christianity and liberalism were two different religions, then, because of their divergent attitudes toward the death of Christ. For liberals it was a symbol of self-sacrifice and a model for the Christian life, but for conservatives it was the only remedy for human sinfulness.[31]

Certainly, such an impassioned defense of Presbyterian orthodoxy surprised audiences accustomed to reading fundamentalist discussions of premillennialism, evolution, and inerrancy. Indeed, the novel aspects of fundamentalism have obscured the traditional doctrines that the movement also tried to defend and preserve. If Machen identified with fundamentalists it was not because of similar views of history, common concerns about evolution, or even a shared understanding of biblical authority. Rather he sided with the movement because he believed it reiterated traditional Christian convictions about sin and grace against the humanitarian theology of Protestant liberalism.

The theological content of *Christianity and Liberalism,* however, should not obscure the book's cultural implications. Machen wrote at a time when a significant number of intellectuals and writers had become increasingly skeptical and critical of American ideals. This disillusionment was especially evident in the literary world. Writers such as

F. Scott Fitzgerald and Ernest Hemingway, who rejected the values associated with small Midwestern towns, lived as expatriates in France and Spain. Others who stayed at home, such as Sinclair Lewis and H. L. Mencken, launched sometimes vicious attacks upon the provincialism of middle-class life. Dissatisfaction with American culture led also to a variety of artistic innovations. In poetry, T. S. Eliot and Ezra Pound experimented with free forms of verse, not strictly for the sake of defying genteel standards but also to explore questions of integrity and precision in artistic expression. Innovations in poetry in turn stimulated new developments in literary criticism which made aesthetic criteria the basis for critical judgment and spurned older approaches as overly moralistic and sentimental. Likewise, fiction manifested disenchantment with American idealism, from Lewis's lampoon of the Babbitts of the business world to Hemingway's stark depiction of human nature. While rarely arriving at an aesthetic or cultural consensus, intellectual life in the postwar decade was unified by disrespect for tradition. The heritage of British-speaking Protestantism especially came under searching attack as intellectuals saw Puritanism behind every moral crusade from Prohibition to movie censorship.[32]

Although signs of intellectual discontent were evident before World War I, the experience of war gave criticisms of American life greater urgency. The rationale for entering the war in April 1917 was littered with reassertions of the country's innocence and providential role in human history. President Woodrow Wilson repeatedly told the nation that the war to make the world safe for democracy was the fulfillment of America's moral purpose. The experience of many intellectuals who served at the front, however, directly challenged such a reading of the war. For them, whether they were driving ambulances or engaging in combat, the war exposed the contradiction between the ideals for which the war was fought and the grim reality of combat and suffering. In the war's aftermath, moreover, as negotiations at Versailles degenerated into disputes over land and war reparations, American idealism appeared to be even more of a charade. The outcome offered proof of the absurdity of the righteous fervor that had fueled the war. Postwar cynicism was summarized well in Hemingway's *A Farewell to Arms* (1929) where he wrote, "I was always embarrassed by the words sacred, glorious, and sacrifice . . . Abstract words such as glory, honor, courage or hallow were obscene beside the concrete names of villages, the numbers of roads, the names of rivers, the numbers of regiments and the dates."[33]

Machen's rejection of liberal Protestantism echoed the postwar loss of faith. *Christianity and Liberalism* censured liberal optimism and idealism for reasons similar to those of other writers and intellectuals who thought America's moral outlook did not comprehend the darker side of human affairs. Throughout the book Machen charged liberal Protestantism with ignoring the depths and effects of human turpitude. Preaching in the churches was especially deplorable. The liberal preacher comes forward not with the authority of the Bible but with the appeal of goodwill. He says, "You people are very good . . . you respond to every appeal that looks toward the welfare of the community." And of course, Jesus is the model for such goodness, "something so good that we believe it is good enough even for you good people." Such an attitude was especially evident, Machen argued, in the liberal conception of God's love. Modern preachers had reduced the ruler of the universe to a loving father who would never "permanently inflict pain upon his children." Not only was this God uninteresting—"nothing is so insipid as indiscriminate good humor"—but the liberal deity was ultimately unappealing. Religion had to offer more than simply "looking on the bright side of God." In a statement that evoked the critical temper of the 1920s Machen declared that "a one-sided God is not a real God." Only a God enveloped in "impenetrable mystery" and "awful righteousness" could satisfy the soul.[34]

Just as the cruelty and destruction of World War I was partly responsible for disillusionment among America's younger intellectuals and writers, it also helps to explain Machen's indictment of Protestant idealism. To be sure, his Calvinistic convictions about human sinfulness predated his service at the front, but the horrors of the war confirmed those views while making liberal notions all the more objectionable. For instance, Machen would sometimes refer to the war as evidence that liberal optimism was naive. The war proved that the accomplishments of technology, science, business, and education could not cure "the disease of sin." Furthermore, liberal reforms merely palliated "the symptoms of sin" but only historic Christianity attacked the disease's roots. Machen also criticized mainstream Protestant reactions to the war. Rather than fostering humility and soul searching, the optimism following victory had yielded an inordinately high estimate of human goodness and made Germany a convenient scapegoat for evil. Many preachers, Machen complained, had tailored the gospel to fit postwar confidence. Such preaching was useless because it encouraged people to rest their hopes for salvation and world peace on the "merit of their own self-sacrifice."[35]

While the war was a catalyst for Machen's criticism of mainstream Protestantism, his perception of the war differed substantially from that of other fundamentalists. Machen had been initially critical of the

Allies' aims and viewed America's involvement with much skepticism, but for many conservatives the war elicited both sharp criticism of American society and unrestrained patriotism. On the one hand, fundamentalists believed that democratic governments, by indiscriminately allowing sinful people to rule, were signs of the end of the age, a time when anarchy would reign. On the other hand, fundamentalists were conventional American Protestants who believed that Christianity was crucial to the prosperity and well-being of the nation. As a result, when some liberal Protestants during the war condemned fundamentalists for being unpatriotic, they responded with pronounced expressions of loyalty to the United States and admonitions about the dangers of German theology and biblical criticism for American society. Indeed, at the same time that fundamentalists defended their patriotism, they countered that by importing German ideas liberal Protestants were undermining Christian civilization in America. The war transformed fundamentalism into a movement that, while cautious about the effects and benefits of social reform, identified the cause of Christianity with the United States in a way not entirely different from liberal Protestant notions about America's moral purpose.[36]

In the same way that Machen's estimate of the war diverged from that of other fundamentalists, the occasion for his opposition to liberalism was also significantly different. The war, the threat of German infidelity, and a concern for America's Christian identity politicized fundamentalism and led to the campaign against evolution in which a politician, William Jennings Bryan, became fundamentalism's chief spokesman. In contrast, the issue that provoked Machen's opposition to liberalism was church union. His concerns were not with the survival of Christian civilization but in fact questioned the very notion of using religion for social ends. For Machen, the Interchurch World Movement and the American Council on Organic Union, not higher criticism or radical theology, were poignant examples of what was wrong with American Protestantism. Both ecumenical endeavors built upon the moralistic ethos of the progressive era and seized the opportunities presented by the Allies' victory but failed to distinguish between the mission of the church and the aims of the nation. The purpose of the movement, according to its founders, was to unite the Protestant churches of North America in a unified program of Christian service, thereby making available the "values of spiritual power" and meeting the "unique opportunities of the new era." To this end, the organization prepared a "scientific" survey to assess the world's religious needs, and applied the principles of big business to put the religious resources of the country on an efficient and economical basis.

Beyond its stated purpose the Interchurch World Movement was also one further effort by Northern Protestant church leaders to preserve the Puritan-Evangelical moral tradition in the face of enormous social and cultural challenges. Signs of Protestant cultural aggressiveness permeated the movement. The official Interchurch World Movement hymn sheet contained "Soldiers of Christ Arise," "The Battle Hymn of the Republic," and "Onward Christian Soldiers." The organization also embraced Americanization as a form of evangelism. According to one article in a Presbyterian periodical that interpreted the results of survey data, preserving the United States as one nation with "common feeling, language, habits, customs and moral and spiritual attitude" required a process of assimilation that centered on the "largest racial group, the old white stock."[37]

The aims and sentiments of the Interchurch World Movement are important for understanding the nature of Machen's opposition to liberal Protestantism and how that opposition was linked to the war. Although the Interchurch World Movement eventually failed because of overly ambitious plans and meager financial support, the cooperative and reformist spirit that had inspired it continued, from Machen's perspective, to permeate mainstream Protestantism. On the final page of *Christianity and Liberalism* Machen described the standard postwar worship service, one that illustrated the errors of crusading Protestantism. Rather than looking beyond the turmoil of the world, churches were filled with news of and advice about society's problems. "The preacher comes forward" not with the hope of salvation but with "human opinions about the social problems of the hour" or easy solutions to the "vast" problems of human misery. Then, after the sermon, the service closes with "one of those hymns breathing out the angry passions of 1861." The church, Machen concluded, had ceased to offer refuge for the weary soul seeking peace only to become captive to "the warfare of the world."[38]

Thus Machen criticized Protestant liberalism for social as well as theological reasons. American churches, he charged, had abandoned considerations of heaven or the immortality of the soul and made society the focus of their attention. In the process, religion had become merely a means for maintaining an orderly and productive society. Even businessmen and politicians, he added, were convinced that religion was necessary for social improvement. So, for instance, religion was called upon to address the problems arising from immigration, a tactic that was commonly called "Christian Americanization." But according to Machen, who could barely hide his ridicule, the help government and churches provided to immigrants amounted to little more than offering "the blessings of liberty" with "a Bible in one hand and a club in the other." He also objected to those who advocated religion as a solution to the problems posed by industrialization, conflicts between nations, and the threat of communism. Using religion as a means for solving social ills, Machen asserted, was altogether different from Christ's·"stupendous words" which demanded utter loyalty from his followers, even to the point of hating father and mother. Ever since the Civil War, he complained in a letter to his mother, the United States had been transformed into a "centralized, and probably militarized country, with abandonment of all the old precious ideals of free speech and religious liberty and toleration." "When I turn for refuge to the church," he continued, "I find there exactly the same evils that are rampant in the world—centralized education programs, the subservience of the church to the state, contempt for the rights of minorities, standardization of everything, suppression of intellectual adventure." He confided that his only hope was the belief that the gospel offered "blessed relief" from "the sinful state of affairs commonly known as 'hundred-per-cent Americanism'."[39]

Machen's opposition to Protestant Americanism added a Southern flavor to his critique of religious modernism. His condemnation of church union and the functional view of religion it embodied evoked the Southern Presbyterian doctrine of the spirituality of the church, an idea that the church's mission of proclaiming the gospel was not to be confused with political or social matters. This perspective made Machen suspicious of Northern Protestant efforts to unite the largest denominations in a national crusade. In fact, his hostility to church union became all the more extreme when the Interchurch World Movement began to include a picture of Abraham Lincoln on promotional posters. To Machen, little separated the optimism and moralism of 1920s Protestantism from the cultural outlook of the antebellum Republican party.[40]

While Machen's criticism of religious modernism echoed postwar discontent, his attention to religious language also paralleled a growing concern for the meaning of words among American intellectuals. A complaint that Machen repeatedly made throughout the fundamentalist controversy was that liberal Protestant clergy were using traditional Christian phrases and words dishonestly. At several points in *Christianity and Liberalism*, for instance, Machen took issue with the hypothetical liberal minister who reassured parishioners of his soundness by affirming a specific doctrinal tenet, such as Christ's deity, the virgin birth, or the atonement. The trouble, Machen said, was that liberals attached to their theological affirmations a "different meaning from that which is attached to them by the simple-minded person to whom he is speaking." They were guilty of violating the principle of "truthfulness in language" because their words had a different meaning for "theologically trained persons" than for "old-fashioned Christians."[41]

An extreme example of Machen's concern for language came in the sermon that sent Henry Van Dyke looking for another church. Here Machen parodied the liberal notion that each generation had to interpret the Bible or the creed according to its own time and place. Did not the modernist preacher, Machen wondered, hold to a static view of language when it came to such questions as whether six times nine equaled fifty-four or whether the Declaration of Independence was signed in Philadelphia? Why, then, was the theological affirmation of Christ's resurrection any different? According to Machen, the standard liberal response was "Of course we accept the proposition that 'the third day he arose again from the dead'" but because each generation has a right to interpret the creed in its own way "we interpret that to mean 'the third day He did not rise again from the dead.'" Machen's own rejoinder was to fear for the future of human language. "If everything that I say can be 'interpreted' to mean its exact opposite, what is the use of saying anything at all?"[42]

Interestingly, Machen first voiced objections to liberal Protestant double-talk during his attack upon the plan for church union. He was particularly alarmed by the creedal basis for union. Machen observed that the plan set the confessions of the Lutheran, Episcopal, Congregational, and Presbyterian churches on an equal footing, even though some of the statements in those creeds were "sharply contradictory" to each other. He also noted that the creedal platform for union subordinated each denomination's confessional standards to a "common faith" that was "studiously vague and colorless." It merely affirmed the trinity, the church, the Bible, and eternal life, thus substituting "meaningless generalities" for statements of faith that were the "carefully formulated result of centuries of controversy." The creed was so vague that even Unitarians could subscribe to it. Machen rejected the suggestion that this was an effort to put into simple words what had traditionally been stated in technical theological language. Rather, it was further evidence of the church making Christian truths subservient to specific social ends. Protestant leaders appealed to a vague set of ideals, stripped of the specifics of Christian theology, so that the churches could respond more effectively to the nation's ills.[43]

Although Machen's concern for language was shared by fundamentalists who did not want the gospel obscured by subtlety or paradox, his ideas also reflected developments in the literary world. In poetry, figures such as Ezra Pound and T. S. Eliot spawned a conception of poetry that reacted sharply against the "cosmic utterance" of Victorian verse. They believed that an artist should communicate precisely and honestly, and argued for aesthetic principles that valued economy and exactness in expression. This endeavor to free poetry from didacticism and sentimentality prepared the way for the New Criticism of the late 1920s and 1930s, which paid careful attention to the formal characteristics of artistic expression in order to make aesthetic values independent of social, moral, or political considerations. The emphasis on simplicity of expression was also evident in the fiction of Hemingway and Gertrude Stein where the formal and stylistic qualities of prose conveyed the immediacy of experience in a realistic manner. These literary innovations rejected ideas for facts. As one critic has written, the 1920s displayed an "almost paranoid fear of the abstract phrase." Modernist writers pruned noble sentiments and abstractions from literature and replaced them with "the object, the thing, the experience in itself stated boldly and without rhetorical flourish."[44]

While Machen faulted Protestant liberalism for its perpetuation of sentimental rhetoric and hollow ideals, his concern for precise and honest religious discourse differed from modernist developments in one very significant respect. Rather than abandoning the certainties of the past for a world without meaning as many modernist intellectuals did, Machen rejected the idealism of liberal Protestantism in order to return to the truths of Presbyterian orthodoxy. Nevertheless, the verities of historic Christianity were for Machen markedly different from the abstractions of liberal Protestantism. The doctrines that he expounded and defended in *Christianity and Liberalism*, as he never tired of noting, were grounded in reality. "Christianity depends," he wrote, "not upon a complex of ideas but upon the narration of an event." Christian salvation was not an idea to be discovered but "something that happened." The liberal preacher offered exhortation and uplift but the conservative minister preached a historical event. Thus, Machen's affirmation of traditional Christianity manifested the preference for facts and events over ideas that modernist writers also exhibited during the 1920s. Indeed, what gave *Christianity and Liberalism* wider appeal, even to readers for whom Machen's beliefs were unrealistic and unbelievable, was that the book debunked American idealism on theological grounds, a feat that intellectuals unfamiliar with Protestant orthodoxy could not attempt and that fundamentalists devoted to a Christian America were loath to try.[45]

The reception of *Christianity and Liberalism* followed predictable patterns. For fundamentalists it was a welcome addition to their arsenal. The editor of *Sunday School Times* immediately saw the advantage of Machen's learned assistance. Liberals who charged the movement with "ignorance" and "obscurantism" would now have to revise their assessment in the light of Machen's "scholarship and keenness." When J. C. Massee, the pastor of Boston's Tremont Temple and leader of fundamentalism in the Northern Baptist Convention, read Machen's pamphlet on Christianity and liberalism he expressed gratitude as well as surprise because he did not "know there were any men in seminaries who would write such articles." Meanwhile, the reviewer for the *Presbyterian* said that among the younger Christian scholars, no one had "given a better account of himself than J. Gresham Machen."[46]

The book also received favorable comments from the wider reading public. The *New York Herald Tribune* advised liberals to read *Christianity and Liberalism* before undertaking any further reconstruction of Christianity. The *Toronto Globe* praised Machen as a writer "of ample erudition" and "compelling force." Although *The New Republic* and *The Nation* did not acknowledge Machen by name, both magazines printed editorials soon after the publication of *Christianity and Liberalism* that admitted the strength of fundamentalist arguments that resembled Machen's. According to *The Nation*, "Fundamentalism is undoubtedly in the main stream of the Christian tradition while modernism represents a religious revolution as far-reaching as the Protestant Reformation." *The New Republic* declared that the modernist's use of Christian terminology was dishonest. Its editors encouraged liberals to "meet fundamentalism on its chosen ground" and set forth a common understanding that Christians could substitute for "authoritatively interpreted dogma."[47]

It is no surprise that liberal Protestants did not react as favorably. Presbyterians responded first and labeled Machen's charges slanderous. William P. Merrill, the popular pastor at New York's Old Brick Presbyterian Church, asserted that if liberalism were as "deadly and pernicious" as Machen claimed most modernists would line up with conservatives. A reviewer for the *Presbyterian Advance* wrote that according to Machen's definition of liberalism the church contained no liberals. Meanwhile, Nolan R. Best, editor of *The Continent*, accused Machen of impeaching the "sincerity of the evangelical position" occupied by "admittedly progressive" Presbyterians. Had Machen been judicious in his description of liberalism, Best wrote, he might have gained respect. But the book was "so totally lacking in the fundamental element of fidelity to facts" that it was "simply an offense against the ninth commandment." Gerald Birney Smith, the reviewer for the *Journal of Religion*, spoke for many liberals when he compared Machen's tactics to those of the pope.[48]

Machen had feared this kind of reaction and in the book's introduction had tried to anticipate liberal hostility. His primary purpose, he wrote somewhat disingenuously, was the rather abstract one of evaluating ideas. By comparing the teachings of historic Christianity with those of modernism he believed he could show that the two systems were different. Of course, Machen's aim went well beyond mere analysis. He also hoped to make conservative opposition to liberalism within the churches more stalwart. Yet when Machen wrote that he was using the word "un-Christian" in a descriptive sense, not as a personal attack or "as a term of opprobrium," he was not far from the mark. Machen did have a broad range of contacts and participated in a variety of activities outside church circles. No matter how insincere liberals may have thought him to be, Machen's social and cultural activities accurately reflected his statement that "ties of blood, of citizenship, of ethical aims, of humanitarian endeavor" united him to liberals in a variety of ways that might still "serve some purpose in the propagation of the Christian faith."[49]

Nevertheless, Machen was sensitive to the charge that he had failed to name names and cite texts. In footnotes he did refer to Fosdick and Lyman Abbott but made a conscious effort to avoid personalities and to concentrate on ideas. Machen had in fact kept regular tabs on Fosdick by obtaining copies of the latter's sermons and from reports of conservative ministers in New York. Yet he made sure that this surveillance remained above board and counseled one of his sources that sending a stenographer to record Fosdick's sermons was improper. When Machen finally consented a year after the publication of *Christianity and Liberalism* to debate in print the soundness of Fosdick's views he did so reluctantly. His tactic of avoiding personalities looked all the more wise when Fosdick reacted to Machen's article in this debate as a "miserable representation of what I said, murdering the king's English in a way that I never was guilty of." "Never in all my ministry have I been treated like this before," Fosdick continued, "and there is no excuse whatever for such a thing's happening." Outbursts such as this confirmed Machen's fear that accusing individuals of liberalism would be construed as a personal attack. Still, he believed that courtesy was "quite consistent with a clear presentation of the issue" and became annoyed that liberals so frequently responded not by reflective refutation but rather with emotional denials.[50]

Despite negative reactions, Machen did force liberals to respond with definitions of their own movement. In 1924 William P. Merrill wrote *Liberal Christianity,* and Shailer Mathews, a Baptist minister and dean of the University of Chicago's Divinity School, published *The Faith of Modernism.* Both were written with Machen's book in mind. Neither author actually denied Machen's description of liberal beliefs and assumptions. Where Machen and his liberal respondents disagreed was whether liberalism could still be called Christian. From Machen's perspective, of course, liberalism was a counterfeit form of Christianity, while Merrill and Mathews considered liberal beliefs to be fully within the Christian fold. Although they would not concede Machen's point that two different religions were competing for the soul of American Protestantism, they did concur with Machen that liberals and conservatives held antagonistic conceptions of Christianity. Mathews even admitted that if Christianity were viewed simply as a theological system inherited from the past, the charge that modernism was un-Christian was "logically sound."[51]

The books by Merrill and Mathews also appeared to substantiate Machen's claim that liberal Protestantism was infused with sentimentality and idealism. Although both authors acknowledged the reality of human sinfulness, in the end they reverted to the platitudinous uplift that modernist intellectuals and conservative Protestants found hollow. According to Mathews, Protestant modernism called believers to "heroism and joy" because of confidence in the "cosmic God" who "loves and helps and saves." "The present is evil," Mathews added, but the underlying conviction of Christianity is that "the future may be better." He explained that a fundamental belief of the modernist was that "good will, though never fully realized, is of the nature of God, and is the law of progress." Goodwill was the only foundation upon which society could be safely built and the only motive that reproduced in human life the "spirit of God and example of Jesus." The beneficent and progressive nature of God meant that even the worst of situations, such as a natural catastrophe, was an "unexplained" operation of "cosmic Love" that constantly added "the better to the good" and taught that "men cannot live by bread or comfort alone but by the choice of that which is personal and loving."[52]

Merrill also denied that liberalism was nothing more than positive thinking in Christian garb, a defense that did not differ substantially from Mathews's. Christianity, according to Merrill, was "the religion of personality" or "personal friendship with the Father through Christ" and resulted in "pure, loving personal relationships." In a society that was becoming increasingly mechanistic and impersonal, the personal character of Christianity made it the only hope. What the world needed most, Merrill wrote, was a faith that could master the forces of modern life, that could keep the human spirit "strong, well-poised, dominant, masterful, amid the riot of new facts and forces that deafen and dazzle the soul." Christian humanitarianism had much to commend and God was at work in the forces of science, democracy, and social unity. Nevertheless, only Christ could deliver modern men and women from "bondage to a mechanistic view of life." Merrill did not seem to be troubled by the tension between God's presence in modern society and the mechanistic view of life that modern society was encouraging. For him the recognition that Christ was "living in our life today" would be a sufficient remedy for the world's ills.[53]

In sum, these liberal rejoinders to Machen evoked the very idealism that Machen had attacked. While claiming that modernist Christianity was more realistic than fundamentalism, Mathews did not appear to notice how ethereal his ideas about God were. "We want no God we pity," Mathews wrote, "but one who, like some hyperbola comes out from infinity into fellowship with men, only to reach out again to infinity." Neither was his meaning altogether clear when he declared that "to find God in natural law and evolution is an assurance that love is as final as any other cosmic expression of the divine will." For Mathews and Merrill the nature of religion made such imprecision and vagueness necessary. In fact, Merrill admitted that liberalism was not as exact in its language as conservative theology. This was inevitable, he thought, because the liberal knows that " 'nothing worth proving can be proved,' that no ultimate reality of the spiritual life can ever be adequately expressed in a definition or formula." Mathews concurred that the God of the modernist was not a "fully understood God." Rationalism could never satisfy the human heart. Such a riposte was standard in the liberal repertoire but did not prevent the likes of Walter Lippmann from charging that the liberal God was one to which the average person would not readily respond.[54]

Machen's *Christianity and Liberalism*, thus, registered a telling criticism of liberal Protestantism at a time when many in the intellectual world were also questioning and abandoning the teachings of the established churches. In Machen's estimate, liberal Protestantism was as antithetical to the teachings of historic Christianity as it was far removed from the truths that World War I had revealed about human nature and social progress. Yet for all of their optimism and idealism, liberal Protestants contended tenaciously that their religion was the only form of Christianity compatible with modern science and that could win those same intellectuals who were leaving the church. As the conflict over evolution drove the fundamentalist controversy out of the churches and into state legislatures, the argument that liberalism was the only form of Protestantism conversant with science took on even greater plausibility. Responding to it would require Machen to switch from the pejorative claim that liberalism was un-Christian to the equally provocative assertion that liberalism was at best unscientific and at worst anti-intellectual.

# CHAPTER FOUR

# Science and Salvation

> The purpose of science is to develop without prejudice
> or preconception . . . the facts, the laws, and the processes of
> nature. The even more important task of religion, on the
> other hand, is to develop the consciences, the ideals, and the
> aspirations of mankind.  *Robert Andrews Millikan (1924)*

Although denominational infighting among Presbyterians and Baptists generated its share of publicity, the most visible and best remembered episode of the fundamentalist controversy was the Scopes trial. For some, the petulant and sarcastic exchanges between Clarence Darrow and William Jennings Bryan were part of a larger contest between popular religion and scientific expertise, while for others they signified a struggle between rural backwardness and urban sophistication. The contestants themselves were hardly ambivalent about the significance of teaching evolution in public schools. Darrow's purpose was to prevent "bigots and ignoramuses" from controlling American education. Bryan, in contrast, said he was only trying to defend the Bible against the "greatest atheist or agnostic" in the United States. Darrow's and Bryan's vitriolic rhetoric obscured such weighty matters as parental control of public education and the tension between public opinion and scientific expertise. Whatever the larger meaning of the Scopes trial, it did spawn a new round of literature on the vexing questions surrounding science and religion.[1]

Machen, whose own arguments often contrasted the genuine faith of the average Christian with the artificial theorizing of theologians and critics, had an opportunity to participate at Dayton. Several weeks before the trial, he received a letter from William Jennings Bryan asking him to testify as an expert witness. The letter was postmarked Coconut Grove, Florida, and Machen received it at his family's summer residence at Mount Desert Island, off the coast of Maine. The difference between those two addresses said a good deal about the dilemmas facing Machen as the ecclesiastical debates of the fundamentalist controversy boiled over onto questions about science and religion. Coconut Grove was the stage for Bryan's famous Bible classes that through newspaper syndication reached millions of Protestants who shared the statesman's common-sense, intuitive, and populist approach to Christianity. Seal Harbor, Maine, in contrast, was the summer home for many cultural and religious elites, and represented the social world of mainstream Protestantism and the academic establishment. In fact, the local church where Machen worshiped (and preached on more than one occasion) was an ecumenical project of the town's wealthiest summer resident, John D. Rockefeller, Jr.[2]

The evolution controversy revealed the increasing chasm between the worlds of popular evangelicalism and mainstream Protestantism. By pitting the faith of the people against the religion of the academy, or the fundamentals of the faith against scholarly inquiry, the 1920s debates about science raised a conundrum for Machen. Religious liberals and conservatives were, in the words of Paul Carter, "more inclined to insist that one climb out upon the stream's right or left bank." Evolution presented Machen not merely with the age-old intellectual dilemma of reconciling reason and revelation but, more important, also forced a choice between two religious cultures, one dominated by genteel Protestantism where learning and scholarship enjoyed great prestige, and one devoted to evangelism and missions where fidelity to the Bible mattered more than academic credentials. His decision not to testify at Dayton indicated that despite his commitment to historic Christianity he was still attached to the world of the university. Nevertheless, throughout the controversy over evolution Machen would labor to construct a mediating position between modernists and fundamentalists that reconciled the seemingly backward ideas of traditional Protestantism with the findings of modern science.[3]

The conflict over evolution, undoubtedly, took many clergymen and scientists by surprise. Some may have been old enough to remember the so-called war between science and religion of the post–Civil War era. But the truce worked out in the late nineteenth century calling for a separation between the claims of science and religion seemed sufficiently durable to satisfy all but a few skeptics and now the fundamentalists. What made the new controversy all the more perplexing was that developments within physics were yielding a picture of the universe that was just as problematic for traditional Christian convictions as Darwin's principle of natural selection. Still, the old remedy still seemed workable. Religion, many continued to say, concerned piety and morality while science explored what was observable, rational, and physical. Conflict was unlikely as long as scientists and churchmen knew their place.[4]

This strategy for harmonizing religion and science was often invoked during the 1920s. One writer attributed the controversy to the failure of fundamentalists to recognize the different purposes of science and religion. Facts were the "business of science," he argued, while religion aimed at making "war against evil" and establishing "righteousness, . . . peace and good will." Kirtley F. Mather, a professing Baptist who taught geology at Harvard, believed that opposition to evolution stemmed from materialistic conceptions that contradicted Christ's teaching of "fellowship and self-sacrifice." Mather's solution was to infuse evolution with "moral values of the finest Christian type" that delineated the "role of service . . . during geologic history." Interestingly, this solution made biblical scholars important allies of scientists who were looking for cover. Many of the latter believed that the newer findings in New Testament studies had identified Jesus' ethical teachings and moral example as the essence of Christianity. Scientific research on human origins had no bearing on Christ's life and example and, therefore, little to do with the message and mission of the modern church. Some ministers and scientists even pointed out the striking similarities between the evolution from lower to higher forms in the natural world and the parallel progression of moral teaching in the Bible from the coarse laws of Israel to the refined sensibilities of Jesus.[5]

Another common feature in the truce between religion and science was the distinction between religion and theology. Many attributed the conflict between evolution and Christianity to a basic misunderstanding. Fundamentalists had mistaken their own doctrines—biblical inerrancy, the virgin birth, the resurrection, and the atonement, for example—for the essence of Christianity. But controversy would disappear once Christianity was understood apart from formal theology. Devotion to Jesus again prompted many social reformers, scientists, and clergy to isolate his teachings from the church's historic confessions. The Bible, accordingly, was not a book of doctrinal teaching, as fundamentalists maintained, but a collection of inspirational writings. Furthermore, genuine Christian faith did not depend upon intellectual assent to theological propositions. Instead, it was the record of vital religious experience. Nurtured by the anticonfessional character of American Protestantism and the influence of philosophical idealism in the late nineteenth century, this distinction between theology and religion was best summarized by Shailer Mathews, dean of the divinity school at the University of Chicago, when he wrote, "Christianity is not a hard and fast system of philosophy or orthodoxy" but rather "the attempt of men to rely upon Christian principles in meeting the needs of their actual life-situations."[6]

Ironically, by drawing the lines so sharply between religious experience and theological expression, liberal Protestants appeared to be relinquishing concern for the intellectual implications of Christianity to fundamentalists. To be sure, liberals were far more involved and established in academic circles than fundamentalists and could make a good case that their recasting of Christianity was accomplished with the assistance of modern learning. Yet fundamentalist attention to the theological ramifications of science was no less intellectually serious than liberal efforts to adapt Christianity to modern thought. Throughout the debates over science fundamentalists exhibited a strong commitment to intellectual consistency and scored liberals for abandoning the enterprise.[7]

One way of achieving cognitive coherence was to insist that modern science conform to the Bible. Of course many fundamentalists defended the veracity of Genesis against Darwinism, but the most notable and influential were the creation scientists, George McCready Price and Harry Rimmer. Price taught geology at several Seventh-day Adventist schools, wrote many books on science, and was the only living scientist Bryan could claim for support during the Scopes trial. Price was ever alert to discrepancies in the fossil record. All over the world, he argued in *Back to the Bible*, rocks could be found that were out of order and that contradicted the "invariable order of the fossils" scientists had imposed upon the data. Rimmer, whose only scientific training came during a year's residence at a homeopathic institution that required no more than a high school diploma for admission, was a Presbyterian minister and evangelist well skilled in public delivery. He gave thousands of lectures and thrived on pointing out that evolutionary theory contradicted such basic facts of elementary science as the variety of cells, a reality that ran counter to the uniformity of cells assumed by the scientific establishment. Together, Rimmer and Price popularized among fundamentalists a formidable and common-sense alternative to mainstream scientific views.[8]

The details of the creationists' arguments, however, are not as important as their larger claims about the relationship between science and religion. Although their methods and arguments were often spurious, fundamentalists used science to defend their understanding of the Bible. Rather than reading scripture as a source of moral and spiritual uplift, they developed a science that began with the historical and scientific facts of the Bible. Fundamentalists insisted that all truth was ultimately from God and therefore harmonious. God was the author of both creation and Scripture, Rimmer wrote. "It follows as an elemental fact, *that the Word of God and the works of God must agree."* Price shared Rimmer's sentiments. "To me religion and objective facts are only different aspects of one great unity." Some might content themselves with a religion that avoided confrontation with the atheism of modern science but not the faithful remnant who still believed the Bible to be the very word of God.[9]

Machen, whose views on evolution will be discussed later, followed a similar strategy for reconciling science and scripture but turned to the New Testament rather than the first chapters of Genesis. In his scholarship of the 1920s Machen repeated the theme that was prominent in his work on the apostle Paul. From its inception Christianity was a religion that depended on history. At the very minimum, Christianity hinged upon a man who lived and died in first-century Palestine. This meant that it was impossible to reduce Christianity to a complex of ideals that stood above critical scrutiny. The events surrounding Jesus' life and the emergence of the Christian movement were not only pivotal for understanding the nature of Christianity but also phenomena that could be subjected to scholarly inquiry. So the crucial issue in debates about science and Christianity, Machen believed, was the historical figure of Jesus, not the creation of human life. Any satisfactory harmonization of Christianity and science could not equivocate on the details of Jesus' life and death.[10]

This line of reasoning gave special force to Machen's final scholarly monograph, *The Virgin Birth of Christ,* which stemmed from the Thomas Smyth Lectures delivered at Columbia Theological Seminary in Columbia, South Carolina, in 1927 and published by Harper and Brothers in 1930. Coming as it did on the heels of the modernist-fundamentalist controversy, the book, no matter how learned, reinforced Machen's identity as a fundamentalist. For conservatives the virgin birth was a real historical event that proved Christ's divinity and sinlessness, while for modernists it was a symbolic expression of Jesus' incomparable superiority. Machen's volume, however, stood midway between these positions. While affirming the historical reliability of the biblical narratives, he resisted the fundamentalist tendency to look at the virgin birth strictly from the perspective of scripture's inerrancy.

With liberals he shared a willingness to explore the historical origins of the doctrine but refused to rule out the possibility of miracles. *Virgin Birth* was, therefore, one of the last efforts to combine faith and learning by an older generation of conservative biblical scholars who taught at respected institutions, looked skeptically upon popular interpretations of the Bible, and valued advanced learning.[11]

Machen's decision to publish with Harper and Brothers came as something of a surprise. His previous books had been published by Macmillan, as would later collections of sermons. Machen explained, somewhat weakly, to his editor at Macmillan that he switched to Harper because Macmillan had had trouble selling his books. He added that he was unaware of Macmillan's continuing interest in his work. The truth was that Machen was not pleased with the way Macmillan had marketed his books. With *The Origin of Paul's Religion*, Machen had to buy 500 copies at $750 before Macmillan would agree to publish it. Machen also thought Macmillan had priced *Christianity and Liberalism* too high. Finally, he thought that Macmillan had been too cavalier about the editorial details of his *Greek Grammar*.[12]

Ironically, for all Machen's misgivings about Macmillan, Harper decided to market *Virgin Birth* to fundamentalists rather than to the academic audience that Machen desired. He had asked his editor not to promote the volume as a "controversial book on the conservative side." As it turned out, *Virgin Birth* failed to make an impact upon popular audiences. It primarily attracted the attention of academics, partly because professional biblical scholarship had become too specialized for the person of average intelligence, no matter what his or her religious predisposition. Equally important to the book's lukewarm reception among mainstream fundamentalist circles was the increasing popularity of dispensationalism, an anti-elitist method of interpretation designed to preserve the Bible's authority and to offer an alternative to modern critical theories. Conservatives who did read the book were daunted by the sheer enormity of *Virgin Birth*'s scope. Machen, who was usually reserved about his own abilities and at one point in the process of revision complained that he was merely "rehashing" material he had written as a young man, pitched to his editor that the book was "the most comprehensive presentation of the subject" ever made. He believed "its collection of historical materials and wealth of bibliographical information" alone were indispensable to serious students of the New Testament. Reviewers agreed. The writer for the *Times Literary Supplement* called the book "elaborate, learned, and full." The review in the *Herald Tribune* praised Machen for his "extensive and profound scholarship" and called the book a credit "to the reputation of American theological learning." Meanwhile, Henry J. Cadbury wrote in the *Christian Century* that Machen's monograph was indispensable for making so much German scholarship available to English-speaking audiences.[13]

Yet for all of the book's sophistication, the main argument was quite simple. A well-formulated belief in the virgin birth was not a late addition to the Christian creed but extended back to the church of the early second century. Such early evidence suggested that the best historical explanation for the belief was its correspondence to historical reality. Despite this straightforward conclusion, the book again demonstrated Machen's considerable abilities and prompted one reviewer to write that "modernists [did] not have all the scholarship on their side." This remark must have pleased Machen, whose purpose in part had been to provide evidence that "the scholarly tradition of the Protestant Church [was] not altogether dead."[14]

More important, *Virgin Birth* furthered the fundamentalist attack upon the separation of Christianity and science that dominated American Protestantism. Throughout the New Testament, Machen argued, the apostles depicted their religion as one tied to history. Being a Christian involved not just following certain ethical principles but also holding to definite propositions about Christ's life, death, and resurrection. "There can scarcely be a greater error" than to regard religious truth "as in some way distinct" from scientific truth. The virgin birth could not be considered true in the realm of religion and false in the realm of science. By treating the Bible as a book of inspiration rather than as a book of "external history," liberals had embraced a halfway position that was "utterly inconsistent and absurd." The modernist idea of biblical authority implied that Christianity was independent of whether such a person as Jesus had ever lived upon the earth. But by appealing to Jesus' authority and example liberals still made their faith dependent on history. Machen saw signs that some theologians had begun to construct a "Christless Christianity" that even made Jesus' actual existence unnecessary. Still, most popular exponents of liberalism, Machen lamented, with complete disregard for logic or history went on "cheerfully" asserting that the Bible's authority lay strictly in the sphere of religion, all the while assuming that the Bible was truthful in "its attestation of the existence of Jesus."[15]

This kind of argument—that liberals were insensitive to the intellectual ramifications of biblical history—laid the basis for Machen's larger claim that Protestant modernism, not fundamentalism, was unscientific. It also explains his stress upon the historical reliability of the Bible. Unlike most fundamentalists, who focused on the dangers of evolution and tried to find scientific justification for their understanding of Genesis, Machen concentrated upon the historical problems surrounding the New Testament. The Bible, he said, made assertions about events in first-century Palestine upon which both liberal and conservative Protestant conceptions of Christianity depended. Although scripture did not deal with many departments of science, Machen thought the events surrounding Christ and the early church were as much the proper subject for scholarly inquiry as events in Greece or Rome. For this reason Machen concluded that separating Christianity and science was impossible. Furthermore, he continued the criticism he made in the 1910s that the liberal understanding of Jesus as a great moral teacher and example could not bear the weight of modern critical scholarship. An increasing number of New Testament scholars, Machen observed, recognized the impossibility of separating the Jesus of history from the Christ of faith, thus making the claim that modern criticism supported liberal Protestantism all the more dubious. By confining himself to the implications of his own academic discipline for popular belief, Machen avoided the fundamentalist habit of appealing to amateur scientists and disrespected theories of biblical interpretation that most scholars and learned lay people scorned.[16]

In *What Is Faith?*, another semipopular book published in 1925 by Macmillan, Machen appeared to be moving beyond his own area of competence. The book was his most sustained complaint against the separation of religion from science, and of religious experience from theology. In it Machen made statements that sounded more like those of an antebellum Protestant divine than a twentieth-century academic. For instance, Machen wrote that theology was "just as much a science as chemistry." Both disciplines, he explained, aimed at objective truth and were concerned with the acquisition and orderly arrangement of truth. Or again, like earlier theologians, Machen regarded the Bible as the theologians' storehouse of evidence. It contained the facts that theologians used for their scientific discoveries and explanations. Such a perspective, in the judgment of many, revealed an epistemology that contradicted Machen's own Calvinistic beliefs about the fallenness of human reason, overestimated the powers of science, and departed from historicist conceptions of knowledge that said truth was relative to particular times and places.[17]

Despite the problems raised by Machen's conception of religious knowledge, the larger point of *What Is Faith?* did not lack merit. Indeed, his purpose was to defend the primacy of the intellect in religion and to break down the "false and disastrous" distinction between knowledge and faith. In short, Machen wanted to show that Christian faith depended upon knowledge and that because Christianity consisted of certain assertions about historical and metaphysical reality it could not be sheltered from scholarly investigation.[18]

At the most basic level, Machen held that faith was an act of trust that required knowledge about the object of faith. For example, the early church made knowledge about Jesus central to its message and identity. It did not try to imitate the faith of Jesus as religious liberals were suggesting but made Jesus an object of faith. The knowledge of Jesus that was implicit in the early church's confession did not consist merely of certain historical occurrences, as important as those were; it also involved an explanation of those events. In other words, the Christian religion entailed doctrine. Theology was thus integral to Christianity. And following the example of the early church Machen recommended that modern church membership be restricted to those believers with an adequate understanding of their denomination's doctrinal standards. Although theological knowledge did not make one a Christian, it redressed the modern tendency to divorce faith from knowledge.[19]

By emphasizing the intellectual aspects of Christian faith Machen did not espouse the naive confidence in human reason of which he and other fundamentalists were sometimes accused. He admitted that philosophical developments since Kant's critique of reason had raised many "interesting problems" and "puzzling antimonies" for a common-sense view of truth. But while these difficulties revealed the limitations of the human intellect they did not imply that the mind was entirely unreliable. Machen was unwilling to relinquish the belief that truth could be attained. To do so would be a "sin against the light of reason itself; and if the light that in us be darkness, how great is that darkness."[20]

Machen's more pressing concern was not just to defend the powers of the intellect but also the possibility of knowing God. Religious knowledge, according to Machen's theological convictions, was not something that humankind derived from its own speculations. Rather, a genuine knowledge of God came only through revelation. Knowledge, in this sense, was not meant to convey the idea of certitude based upon scientific proof. Machen was especially critical of the influence of empirical science which had restricted knowledge to observation irrespective of information received from other sources such as revelation or tradition. He held that God had constituted the human mind in such a way that it was capable of receiving revelation and that God had in fact revealed himself to and through the biblical writings. The central convictions of the Christian religion were based not upon human powers of observation but upon the testimony of the biblical authors. To be sure, the testimony of scripture could turn out to be false, but to judge it so without a proper evaluation was a "serious intellectual fault."[21]

Furthermore, religious knowledge rooted in the biblical narrative was not exhaustive. Human knowledge of God, Machen conceded, was infinitesimal compared with what could not be known. But partial knowledge was not necessarily false knowledge and did not mean that the project of theology should be abandoned. The limitations of the theological enterprise actually resulted in another favorable comparison with science. Machen was well aware that the theology he defended, seventeenth-century British Calvinism, seemed to undermine the kind of progress upon which scientific development hinged. Twentieth-century theology, accordingly, should advance beyond seventeenth-century formulas in the same way that modern science had advanced beyond older conceptions of the universe. Nevertheless, this analogy broke down in Machen's view because theological differences between liberals and conservatives were the result of different conceptions of truth. The liberal theologian, unlike the scientist, did not intend his formulations to be true, even if only for one generation, but believed that theology was merely the symbolic expression of religious experience. In contrast, conservative theology followed scientific practice by striving to explain and systematize the data of revelation. It did not yield static and comprehensive explanations because human understanding of scripture was always limited and new insights required theological revision just as new learning was always uncovering new evidence. Yet conservatives, like scientists, were aiming at "increasingly close approximations to an objectively and externally existent body of facts" while liberals advocated change merely because it suited a "particular generation or a particular group of persons."[22]

Nevertheless, Machen acknowledged that theology and science were different in methods and subject matter. By science Machen most often meant systematic inquiry and organized learning. These goals, he believed, united all academic disciplines, from the physical sciences to humanistic and theological disciplines. But while all scholars probed various aspects of creation, the theologian studied the natural world, the human conscience, and above all the revelation of scripture. Because of the relatedness of human knowledge, apologetics, a branch of theology defending the truth of Christianity, was an essential component of theology. With Machen's stress upon the intellectual aspects of faith his advocacy of "external proofs" for Christianity came as little surprise. He defended natural theology's arguments for the existence of God as good ones despite Kant's criticisms and called for a "truly comprehensive apologetic" that included theistic proofs, historical evidence of the New Testament, and metaphysical considerations. Such reasoning was not sufficient to produce faith but still was necessary because without an objective and external reality that individuals could trust, salvation was impossible. The facts of Christianity were true "for angels and for demons," "whether we cherish them or not."[23]

But, Machen conceded, theology was different from other kinds of inquiry. A conviction of Christianity's truth could not come through intellectual argument alone. Conviction of sin was necessary. Machen insisted that all the evidence for Christianity was completely unconvincing without a sense of sin's dire consequences. Without this, the stupendous and miraculous events surrounding Jesus' life were unbelievable because they were so unusual. Individuals under the conviction of sin, however, could accept the biblical accounts because they knew that the only chance for salvation lay in a supernatural and gracious act of God. This sense of sin was no mystical experience that transcended reason but rather it transformed the intellect into a "trustworthy instrument for apprehending truth." The qualifications for good theology, then, were the same as that for ordinary belief: conviction of sin and knowledge of God's redemptive acts revealed in the Bible. By stressing the intellectual aspects even in the subjective dynamics of religious experience Machen, in effect, made theologians out of all believers. Only in the act of regeneration, he explained, once the "blinding" effects of sin had been removed, could the truth of Christianity be understood properly.[24]

Machen contrasted this idea of faith with what he called the anti-intellectual approach prevalent in Protestant liberalism which regarded faith as a particularly intense form of religious experience. In fact, liberalism was for Machen just one more example of a lamentable intellectual decline in American society. Ignorance of the Bible among seminary students as well as theological naiveté on the part of many clergy were just two examples of the modern church's woeful ignorance. Machen attributed this problem in part to the decline of doctrinal teaching and preaching within the churches and to the demise of the home as an educational institution. But the ultimate source of religious ignorance was the edifice of liberal Protestant theology constructed upon the thought of Immanuel Kant, Friedrich Schleiermacher, and Albrecht Ritschl. People no longer cared about theology or the details of their Bibles because ministers were telling them that theology and the Bible were simply symbolic expressions of an ineffable religious experience. To be sure, liberalism possessed an "elaborate philosophical grounding" and so was not inherently anti-intellectual. But by depreciating the intellect and exalting the feelings in its place religious liberalism had fostered intellectual decline in the mainline churches.[25]

Surprisingly, Machen's conception of religious knowledge also put him at odds with conservative evangelicals. Central to the revivalist tradition in America was the conversion experience. By stressing a personal experience of grace, promoters of revivals from the colonial awakenings of Jonathan Edwards to the urban crusades of Dwight L. Moody and Billy Sunday encouraged the idea that everything of value in the Christian faith had to originate with the individual's subjective encounter with God, revelation, or the church. Furthermore, the demand for the individual to decide for Christ undermined respect for the past, especially traditions of learning. Revivalists encouraged all people, whether educated or illiterate, to judge the merits of Christianity irrespective of previous generations of believers. To be sure, evangelicalism throughout the nineteenth century had fostered conservative views about the authority and truthfulness of the Bible. But the centrality of the conversion experience in the evangelical understanding of Christianity meant that theology was sacrificed for evangelistic outreach and popular or democratic conceptions of Christian faith and practice.[26]

Machen used a review of E. Y. Mullins's *Christianity at the Crossroads* (1924) to challenge the experientialism of the evangelical tradition. Mullins was president of Southern Baptist Theological Seminary in Louisville and worked out of a theological tradition that pointed to the transforming power of religious experience as evidence of Christianity's truth. Machen was critical of Mullins's apologetic precisely on the issue of the relationship between religion and science. Mullins argued that religious experience was impervious to changes within philosophy and science. Religion, he wrote, "has its own methods, its own criteria of truth, its own approach to the great Reality, and its own conditions for attaining certainty." In other words, the individual's conversion, not the findings of science or conclusions of philosophy, determined the truth of Christianity. Even though Machen also argued that regeneration was necessary for a proper understanding of Christianity's truth, he faulted Mullins for making the same error that liberal Protestants made. By deducing from the necessity of conversion that religion and science approached knowledge differently, Mullins's position, Machen argued, ultimately led to skepticism because it exempted religion from the norms of rational discourse. Machen agreed with Mullins that many of the so-called conflicts between religion and science were imaginary. Yet, while the Bible was not a scientific textbook, it did make claims about history and the nature of human existence that could not be separated from the larger question of whether those claims in fact corresponded to reality.[27]

The primary issue that the debates about religion and science raised for Machen, then, was the proper way to reconcile the claims of faith and reason. While Machen strove to persuade unbelievers of the truth of his religion, his principal aim was to show believers that, while attractive, the tactic of segregating faith from critical scrutiny was a poor strategy. It was attractive because it seemed to be an easy way out of conflict with science to say that religion had its own criteria for adjudicating truth claims. But it was a poor solution because scientific examination would ultimately subject even religious experience and moral idealism to critical investigation. "Mere concessiveness" would never succeed in avoiding intellectual conflict. To have any intellectual credibility Protestants on both sides would have to defend the claims of their faith, whether the philosophical idealism of liberals or the biblical narratives of conservatives.[28]

One of the reasons Bryan asked Machen to testify at Dayton may have been an article that the Princeton professor wrote for the *New York Times* only one month before the Scopes trial. The editor had requested from Machen a description of the reasons why fundamentalists opposed evolution. Machen, who had given little attention to evolution, suggested a defense of historic Christianity instead. His piece, "What Fundamentalism Stands for Now," ran on the front page of the Special Features section opposite an article by Vernon Kellogg, a zoologist and secretary of the National Research Council, entitled "What Evolution Stands for Now." Machen rehashed arguments from *Christianity and Liberalism* and *What Is Faith?* He claimed that conservative Protestants did not oppose science but actually had the facts on their side. The facts to which he appealed were doctrines concerning God and man and the historical events recorded in the New Testament. Conservatives could not abandon to natural scientists the "entire realm of fact" in order to reserve for religion "merely a realm of ideals." If Christianity was true, it was true for scientists as well as theologians, for unbelievers as well as believers.[29]

By avoiding the subject of evolution Machen displayed some political savvy. He did not think that the creation accounts in Genesis were crucial to the differences between conservatives and liberals. As he explained to Bryan his reasons for not testifying at Dayton, evolution was beyond his own expertise. Machen did not make his views on evolution known publicly throughout the controversy although he did express them in personal correspondence. The closest he came to taking a public stand on evolution during the 1920s was when he reprimanded Phi Beta Kappa for adopting policies that he thought made teaching evolution a criterion for membership. But here Machen's reasons had more to do with the nature of academic freedom than with biology. His public reticence on this controversial issue in all probability stemmed more from ambivalence than from hesitation about entering the public debate surrounding evolution. Throughout the fundamentalist controversy he seemed to thrive on agitation. What was one more dispute?[30]

There is also evidence to suggest that Machen avoided the subject of evolution because he was not troubled by alternative views of creation. He grew up in a Christian home where his parents had in all likelihood come to terms with Darwinism. His niece Mary Gresham Machen said that when the General Assembly of the Southern Presbyterian Church (PCUS) met in Baltimore in 1881 the Machen residence was the meeting place for those in sympathy with James Woodrow. The uncle of Woodrow Wilson, Woodrow taught at Columbia Theological Seminary and, despite the efforts of his supporters who met in the Machen home, was dismissed by the General Assembly for his efforts to reconcile Genesis and evolution.[31]

Undoubtedly, another influence upon Machen's thinking about evolution was the Princeton theologian Benjamin Breckinridge Warfield. While defending the Bible's inerrancy, Warfield also argued that the Genesis narratives were compatible with the idea that God had providentially superintended evolutionary developments in the origin of the human form and had supernaturally intervened to create the human soul. The only place in the creation of humanity where Warfield thought it necessary to insist upon supernatural and direct divine activity in the evolutionary process, therefore, was in the creation of the human soul, the place that he believed bore the divine image. With that one qualification made, Warfield could assert in 1915 that the Calvinist understanding of creation not only allowed for evolutionism but for "pure evolutionism." Machen appeared to accept Warfield's views. When he responded to queries about evolution he usually directed inquirers to Warfield's writings. Machen did not believe that evolution alone could explain the origin of human life nor did he believe that evolution was incompatible with divine creation. He thought it possible to accept evolution in providential terms, "as God's way of working in certain spheres . . . through nature." And like his mentor, he was careful to distinguish between God's creative power to bring life into existence out of nothing (*ex nihilo*) and divine providence, which involved God's superintendence of existing natural forces and laws. "The uniqueness of redemption in Christianity," he wrote, depended upon a distinction between supernatural (creative power) and natural causes (providence).[32]

Yet when Machen spelled out his understanding of creation for publication he garbled some of Warfield's subtleties. The occasion was a series of radio addresses on Christian theology delivered in 1936. In his homily "Did God Create Man?" Machen made the point that God did create humankind in a supernatural sense. Like Warfield, Machen held that the origin of human life depended on both natural developments and divine intervention. And following Warfield, he also thought that the supernatural creation of human life, as distinguished from the providential course of natural development, referred specifically to the creation of the soul, not the human form. Creation in the image of God, he explained, could not refer to the human body because God was spirit.[33]

Unlike Warfield, however, Machen drew back from the idea that the human species had evolved from lower forms of life. His hesitations showed sympathy with fundamentalist hostility to evolution. Machen believed that there were significant gaps in the biological and geological evidence for evolution and that naturalistic presuppositions had led scientists to overlook these problems. Nevertheless, he resisted the tendency of creationists to attack the scientific establishment and to set up a rival science of their own. Machen acknowledged his own incompetence to judge the scientific data even though he did not want the issue to become strictly a matter for scientific experts. For evolution, he believed, ultimately concerned one's understanding of the nature and meaning of the universe.[34]

So Machen looked to Christ's birth to reveal the problems of an evolutionary account of human life. Similarities in bodily structure between Jesus and other men had not prevented conservative theologians from accepting the virgin birth. In fact, historic Christianity had always asserted that miracles were interwoven with natural events. In the case of Christ's birth, this meant that Jesus' body was produced not merely by the ordinary course of nature but also by a supernatural act of God. Despite great differences, Machen said, this same principle applied to the creation of human life. Physical similarities between human species and lower animals did not disprove God's supernatural creation of human life. The crucial issue was not the nature and scope of the scientific data but the theological implications of evolutionary theory. If evolution entailed a denial of God's creative and miraculous power, then it was incompatible with Christian theism, a proposition in keeping with Warfield's perspective. But Machen wavered over the converse idea—one that Warfield would have affirmed—that evolutionary theory was acceptable as long as it made room for divine intervention.[35]

Despite questions about evolution, Machen made points about science more generally in his essay for the *New York Times* which were closer to those of his newspaper rival, the zoologist Kellogg, than to the views of fundamentalists. Machen did not attack evolution itself but rather the way in which liberal Protestants had selectively accommodated new learning in all spheres of academic inquiry. While professing to offer to the modern world a version of Christianity compatible with advances in science, religious modernists overlooked what was going on in the world of biblical scholarship. To be truly scientific, Machen argued, modern Christians would have to heed the problematic findings of biblical scholars who had concluded that the Christ of the scriptures was altogether different from the Jesus of the modern church. They could not assume that science confirmed middle-class morality and American ideals. Kellogg made a similar point about the natural sciences, complaining that average Americans welcomed the technological advances of science but objected when scientists used the same methods to support evolution. Kellogg thought that evolution was just as much a fact as the automobile. Kellogg and Machen were united in maintaining that the public could not have it both ways; if it chose to accept science, whether biology or higher criticism, then it would also have to accept science's disquieting realities along with its comforting achievements.[36]

The affinity between the form of Machen's and Kellogg's arguments is important for what it shows about the place of science in the fundamentalist controversy. The differences between liberals and conservatives have often been attributed to divergent attitudes toward science, an interpretation that parallels mainstream Protestant explanations from the period. Modernists, accordingly, showed the influence of twentieth-century philosophical developments that viewed science in organic and evolutionary categories and recognized the effects of individual and cultural influences on observation. Fundamentalists, in contrast, adhered to early modern models and held that scientific truth was fixed, static, absolute, and objective.[37]

This way of viewing the differences between modernists and fun-

damentalists has significant liabilities. First of all, it neglects the persistence of mechanistic and static conceptions of science and religion
that were common in the scientific community as well as in mainstream religious circles. When scientists and liberal clergymen defended their own religious views, they might have argued that truth
was embedded in the development of culture, relative to time and
place. But when they turned to scientific matters they invariably appealed to the facts and insisted that fundamentalists did not have the
slightest clue as to what the facts were. According to Harry Emerson
Fosdick, even though science expanded and grew, its truths were discovered "once and for all." The findings of Copernicus were "final";
"this earth does move; it is not stationary; and the universe is not geo-
centric." Moreover, proponents of liberal Protestantism were no less
adamant in asserting that certain aspects of Christianity escaped the
process of history and were therefore absolute. For some, the teachings
of Jesus remained universally true, while for others religious experience transcended time and place.[38]

Second, attributing the differences between modernists and fundamentalists to different conceptions of science misses an important
theme in the controversy over evolution. Liberals and conservatives
debated the merits of modern science more often in terms of social
consequences than in the language of epistemology. Many fundamentalists, for instance, not only blamed Darwinism for the 1914 war but
also for the rise and spread of communism around the world and for
the moral decline of American society. In contrast, defenders of evolution, from Robert Andrews Millikan to Harry Emerson Fosdick,
pointed to the theory's social benefits. As the American Association
for the Advancement of Science resolved in 1925, evolution "is one of
the most potent forces for good" having promoted "the progress of
knowledge," "unprejudiced inquiry," and "humanity's search for
truth in many fields." Machen himself deplored this type of argument,
whether from the left or right. In his correspondence with Bryan he
corrected the statesman's utilitarian indictment of evolution. Bryan
had claimed that teaching evolution diverted attention from the great
practical problems of life to "useless speculation as to the distant past
and the distant future." Machen observed that this reasoning was hostile to pure science and would limit education to merely practical matters. Likewise, he criticized pragmatic defenses of Christianity. "It is
no proof of the absolute truth of Christianity," he wrote, "that it has
made the world better: for that achievement it shares perhaps with
other religions, though no doubt they have it in far less degree."[39]

Rather than revealing antagonistic conceptions of science and truth,

Protestant debates over evolution manifested significant differences over the nature and purpose of Christianity. Liberal Protestantism reflected the widening influence of the social sciences and of a functional approach to religious ideas. This development was tied to efforts to construct a scientific rationale for many of the values that Protestants held dear and to implement those ideals in society. Religious or philosophical truth did not conform to a fixed and abstract reality but developed out of practical and daily experience. John Dewey's understanding of religion in *A Common Faith* (1934) expressed in less Christian terms the impulse that lay behind religious modernism. Like liberal Protestantism, Dewey wanted to emancipate religion from dogma and to infuse human affairs traditionally regarded as secular with religious qualities. To be sure, Dewey was critical of Protestantism and was uncomfortable with theology and the church as outlets for religious experience. Still, Dewey agreed with the "crucial contention" of religious modernism that the traditional disjunction between the sacred and the secular or between church and society was invalid.[40]

Shailer Mathews, Machen's theological opponent, made clear why the traditional Christian distinction between the sacred and the secular was no longer workable in modern society. Christianity's purpose, according to the University of Chicago professor, was to improve humankind's social condition but fundamentalists, with their theological fastidiousness, were obstructing such progress. The world needed new control over nature and society but was told that the Bible was inerrant. Society needed a means for redressing class strife but heard only the doctrine of the atonement. People needed to find a spirit of love and justice but fundamentalists declared that love without orthodoxy would not save one from hell. The world wanted to find God in the development of nature but was informed that evolution excluded belief in God. Modern knowledge required "faith in the divine presence in human affairs" but conservatives responded with the doctrine of the virgin birth. Society's hopes "for a better world order" foundered on the fundamentalist advice "to await the speedy return of Jesus Christ." Mathews concluded that orthodoxy had lost its appeal because it had "no message for the world's new needs."[41]

Throughout *What Is Faith?* Machen objected to arguments like Mathews's, insisting that liberal Protestantism was founded upon a "pragmatist" view of truth. The modernist theologian, Machen wrote, regarded his own formulations as merely symbolic expressions of religious experience. The sole criteria for truth, then, was whether a particular theology improved the quality of life for individuals and society. Machen opposed this understanding of Christianity because it rejected theological and metaphysical considerations and reduced Christianity to humanitarianism. Modernist preachers, Machen charged, were guilty of focusing strictly on the problems of this world without considering the "great beyond of mystery." Questions about humanity's place in the universe, the meaning of suffering and evil, and the "unfathomed mystery" of eternity could not be dismissed as idle speculation. Although they were the battleground of theologians, these considerations were also the "very breath of our Christian lives." In a sense, Machen was no less concerned than liberal Protestants with the practical consequences of theology. But he differed from liberals by judging religion's effectiveness from the perspective of life in the next world, not this one. Machen believed that liberal Protestantism might improve the conditions of society but solving social problems was not the end of Christianity. Instead, to be truly meaningful any religion had to conform to the realities of the spiritual world and satisfy the needs of the human soul; it had to overcome the enormous gulf that separated sinful people from a holy and transcendent deity. Machen thus affirmed a metaphysical reality that modernists seemed to deny. For him, beliefs had to conform to this higher reality. If they did not, they were neither true nor useful.[42]

It should be noted that Machen and other fundamentalists were not alone in conceiving of religion as chiefly concerning eternal and spiritual realities. Conservative intellectuals such as the New Humanists and Southern Agrarians also criticized the antiformalism of American social thought for disregarding metaphysics, took issue with the functional approach to ideas that dominated the social sciences, and attacked the mainline churches for succumbing to such thinking. These writers and literary critics believed that liberal Protestantism's appropriation of science was responsible for reducing Christianity to altruism. In turn, they called for a defense of Christianity that would recover a sense of otherworldliness, even if that meant rejecting science. The New Humanist Paul Elmer More, a classicist at Princeton University, criticized liberalism for abandoning Christian supernaturalism and called for a renewed commitment to the doctrine of the incarnation. Likewise, John Crowe Ransom, a principle figure among the Southern Agrarians, urged Christians to rediscover the "God of thunder" and abandon the "soft modern" Christ of mainstream Protestantism. Religion for these humanists was not a reflection of social or material factors but a manifestation of humanity's spiritual capacity and the primary reality of human existence. Religion's purpose, according to More, was "first of all and last of all to offer to a soul despairing of this world's peace the promise of eternal life."[43]

Nevertheless, Machen's defense of old-time religion diverged from these criticisms of other conservative intellectuals in two significant ways. First, supernaturalism was central to Machen's understanding of Christianity. He accepted the miracles narrated in scripture as historically reliable. Moreover, the historical character of Christianity made it impossible to separate religion from scientific exploration. Religiously minded humanists, in contrast, were more inclined to regard miracles as myths that figuratively taught metaphysical truths. Second, rather than rejecting science and appealing to tradition or revelation as other humanists did, Machen continued to appeal to science to justify his beliefs. In contrast, conservative intellectuals with humanistic training regarded the explanatory powers of science with suspicion and argued that the humanities yielded a higher and more permanent truth. Part of the reason for this difference was Machen's own scholarly instinct, which valued specialized research more than the cultivated generalism of many older humanists. Still another difference was Machen's identification with intellectual habits stemming from the American Protestant accommodation of the Enlightenment, a tradition that bound Christian expression closely to the assumptions and procedures of detached, rational, scientific inquiry. Thus, while Machen and other conservative intellectuals agreed that Christianity involved a series of doctrines concerning the nature of life and the universe that could not be separated from metaphysics or dogma, he could not be diverted from the lure of science.[44]

In the end, the controversy over evolution revealed a polarization within American Protestantism about the nature and scope of divine activity in nature and human history that had far-reaching consequences for popular and learned understandings of Christianity. Previous generations of theologians had affirmed that God was both active in and transcended creation. The triumph of science allowed little room for affirming such a paradox. Consequently, liberal Protestants accommodated science and affirmed divine immanence while fundamentalists, for reasons having to do with evangelism and missions, tilted toward divine transcendence.[45]

Liberals endeavored to uphold traditional Christian mores while applying those truths to all areas of life, to the culture as well as the church. The hallmark of liberalism was a conscious adaptation of religious ideas to modern culture and the affirmation that God was immanent in human history and was establishing a righteous kingdom through social progress. By affirming God's presence in all aspects of culture and by overturning the distinction between the sacred and the secular, liberals, in effect, were saying that special and miraculous instances of divine intervention were unnecessary to Christianity. In fact, liberals believed that evolution offered the best evidence of God's existence and presence in history. Yet the liberal Protestant appropriation of evolution also displayed the positivistic tendency to limit legitimate explanations strictly to physical and natural causes. While affirming God's presence in natural causes, liberals viewed miracles as a prescientific way of explaining natural phenomena. From this perspective, fundamentalists' stress upon miracles was not only oblivious to God's immanence in daily existence but was also at odds with modern science.[46]

Shailer Mathews, speaking for many liberals, admitted that a rejection of miracles seemed to banish God from the world, deny divine freedom, and destroy the heart of religion. Yet God's existence did not depend upon the supernatural. Miracles were "unthinkable" to people living in a scientific age and were no longer necessary for explaining God. Rather than limiting God, science actually led to an better understanding of God's presence in the world. "The unity of cosmic order, discoverable law, and evolution" made it apparent that God no longer appeared occasionally in "some inexplicable violation of accustomed experience." For Mathews, Christianity was a way of "tapping" God's presence and applying the "force of love to whatever one has to do."[47]

Such a view severely weakened Christian doctrines of sin and grace. If God was active in all areas of life, or even to some degree in all religious experience, what was the point of or need for the church and Christianity? Fundamentalists opposed evolution precisely because of its naturalistic and relativistic implications and attacked it primarily on religious rather than scientific grounds. For them, creation had to be miraculous in order to preserve the idea of God's supernatural and gracious intervention into human history. But the fundamentalist emphasis upon the supernatural also encouraged suspicions of science. By so zealously defending miracles as signs of God's activity, fundamentalists tended to deny the Christian doctrine of providence that taught that God was actively involved in human history and nature. For fundamentalists, the idea that God could be known through scientific inquiry smacked of naturalism and so they became increasingly hostile to the academic enterprise.[48]

Machen tried to construct a mediating position that subordinated the naturalism of liberal Protestantism to the supernaturalism of fundamentalism but still kept the two ideas together. With conservatives he believed that Christianity depended upon the miraculous intervention of God into human history. Human depravity had made the supernatural the very "ground and substance" of the Christian faith. But

Machen also believed that fundamentalists were in error by failing to distinguish between providence and grace—between God's natural and supernatural activity—and, as a result, had an impoverished understanding of divine activity in creation and the merits of scholarly explanations. In turn, he agreed with modernists that God was actively present in nature and history and that science yielded true even if partial knowledge of God. For him, the crucial difference between historic Christianity and liberalism had more to do with antagonistic ideas about Christ and the nature of salvation than with divergent accounts of creation. As Machen explained in his article in the *New York Times*, Christianity depended upon what Christ did at a definite point in history. By trying to shift debate from evolution to the historical Jesus, Machen hoped to make plainer to both conservatives and liberals what was at stake in the controversy over science.[49]

Despite Machen's effort to reconcile modern science and historic Christianity, he could not avoid the fundamentalist label. In June of 1927 the trustees of Bryan Memorial University at Dayton asked Machen to preside over their newly founded institution. According to the president of the trustees, F. E. Robinson, Machen was "one of the most scholarly and conservative theologians in America." Invitations like this one were not uncommon. The trustees of Ohio's Cedarville College also asked Machen to become president of their institution. Machen's preference for seminary education also led some conservatives to talk of founding a new fundamentalist seminary. W. E. Biederwolf's Winona Summer School of Theology in Indiana was one possible site for such a venture. Yet Machen was not inclined to join the ranks of fundamentalist educators whose interdenominational policies, he believed, undermined the importance of confessions and the institutional church, and whose educational goals departed from traditional aims and purposes. For this reason, Machen looked more favorably on invitations from Columbia Theological Seminary, a Southern Presbyterian institution in South Carolina, to teach New Testament, and Knox College, a Canadian Presbyterian school, to be its principal. Nevertheless, he turned down all invitations in order to remain at Princeton. He not only identified with his alma mater's theology and mission, but hated the thought of leaving behind its superior library.[50]

Machen was an obvious choice for conservative Protestants who wanted to establish alternative institutions but his views on education, like his ideas on science, ran counter to those of most fundamentalists. The typical fundamentalist institution was the Bible college or institute, designed to give young adults with meager educational backgrounds the basic skills for work in evangelism and missions. Machen, in contrast, believed that the work of the church was best conducted by educated clergy, that seminary training was necessary for ministers, and that a liberal education was a proper prerequisite for theological study. So while he graciously declined the offer of Bryan University, Machen knew that he would have been out of place at a fundamentalist school. As the brief exchange between Bryan and Machen prior to the Scopes trial made clear, the fundamentalist focus upon practical consequences of ideas and hostility to theoretical considerations did not sit well with Machen, who thought such attitudes were hostile to genuine learning. The limitation of education to merely practical matters was, according to Machen, "one of the greatest evils of the day."[51]

Educational as well as theological conservatism informed Machen's attitudes toward all levels of learning. In the same way that he deplored a view of faith that stressed religious experience over doctrinal knowledge, Machen criticized contemporary educational reforms that emphasized students' personal development at the expense of instructional content. Moreover, as a biblical scholar with a classicist's training, he favored older educational methods and curricula that stressed learning the basics. He especially faulted the functional obsession of modern education. Its aim, he said, was to assist people "in the art of living" but it never asked what made life worth living. These "absurd" pedagogic theories, furthermore, depreciated the hard and routine work of learning facts. Rather than creating an environment where students could meaningfully integrate their world and express themselves, Machen believed the teacher's sole duty was to lecture and that the student's responsibility was to listen, take notes, and memorize. Machen admitted that older educational methods may have overemphasized memorization at the expense of critical thinking. The student who only repeated what the teacher said was unsatisfactory, but no worse than the modern student who tried to analyze and criticize something he or she did not adequately understand. "It is impossible to think with an empty mind," Machen wrote, and thinking without sufficient knowledge was precisely the danger that he saw in modern methods of education.[52]

Machen's general remarks about education took specific form when he spelled out the nature of seminary education. The principle component of theological education should be biblical study. Consequently, he criticized the curricular reforms of many Protestant seminaries which were designed to make ministers more accessible to regular people and more responsive to everyday concerns. The model seminary for Machen was more a graduate school of theology than a professional institution that equipped ministers with specialized vocational skills. Other kinds of institutions or programs, he argued, could provide knowledge about other areas of life, whether matters of church administration or questions related to secular careers. Nevertheless, the minister, in Machen's view, was a "specialist in the Christian religion" not a "Jack-of-all-trades." No doubt, the Bible had to be applied to practical realities. But this was a long and arduous process, one learned best by experience, not in the classroom. The task of the seminary, then, was to provide students with those things that were best learned in school, not to acquaint them with every aspect of life or the ministry. This understanding of theological education put Machen at odds not only with some Protestant administrators who advocated that seminaries include more courses in the social sciences but also with fundamentalists who often stressed the techniques of evangelism and spiritual formation over formal biblical and theological instruction.[53]

Machen's decision to remain at Princeton during the fundamentalist controversy, then, was indicative of his views about scientific questions as well as educational matters. When forced to choose between the academic worlds of fundamentalism and mainstream Protestantism Machen was still more comfortable with the scholarly traditions of the religious establishment. Even though he thought old-line Protestant institutions were becoming hostile to conservative theology and were abandoning the traditional curriculum in order to make Christianity more relevant, liberal Protestantism, unlike fundamentalism, still had the resources and respect for learning that Machen believed necessary for the survival of historic Christianity. Only when the fundamentalist controversy disrupted his life at Princeton would he consider leaving that world to teach at another institution.

# CHAPTER FIVE

# A Question of Character

It will make all the difference to your success in life whether
you have a pleasing personality or the opposite, a personality which
arouses antagonism and dislike in those with whom you deal . . .
An agreeable personality often has an influence out of all proportion
to a man's ability or his position.   *Orisen Swett Marden (1921)*

A man who is lacking in depth of conviction, or one who is bitter
toward his fellow-believers, shows that he is out of fellowship with
our Lord and is not controlled by his Spirit.   *Charles Erdman (1926)*

Pressures confronting American denominations in the 1920s made it
easy to avoid the merit of Machen's arguments against mainstream
Protestantism generally and religious modernism more specifically.
Throughout the late nineteenth and early twentieth centuries, churches
experienced the same sort of bureaucratic transformation that was re-
shaping American business and government. As denominational leaders
faced problems stemming from numerical, financial, and programmatic
expansion, they often turned to scientific management and organizational efficiency for solutions. Thus, while liberals and conservatives disagreed profoundly on various points of theology, organizational realities dictated the resolution of the modernist-fundamentalist
controversy.[1]

The rise of a highly organized society undergirded by corporate
capitalism at the beginning of the twentieth century, cultural historians have argued, brought with it a new conception of the self. Self-
improvement manuals and guides published at the turn of the century

abandoned the older advice, which esteemed thrift, integrity, and industry. While these virtues had been effective in a producer economy, life in the corporate world demanded a different ethic. A winning personality, charm, and being well liked were far more effective than older values for making one's way in large, impersonal, and highly regulated organizations. What was true for business also became increasingly true for churches. As denominations grew and required greater managerial oversight church officials became especially sensitive to criticism and dissent. Discord not only threatened organizational unity but trangressed against the ideals of Christian harmony and brotherhood.[2]

True to this pattern, Presbyterian leaders, rather than answering Machen's arguments, dismissed him as temperamentally deficient. An early indication of this reaction surfaced in an unlikely source, a series of articles on *What Is Faith?* that appeared during the spring of 1926 in the *British Weekly.* The eight British theologians who discussed Machen's work were generally positive and respectful. Some complimented him for his forceful statement of conservative convictions while others took issue with his views about the Bible. Reactions to these articles in America, however, were not so cordial. In June, a Presbyterian pastor, Phillip Ellicott, wrote to the editor and objected to the polite tone of the series. Fundamentalists, he complained, were using the reviews to their advantage. The book that the magazine's contributors had "so complacently" reviewed was in fact the "battle cry" for conservatives who wanted to exclude from the Presbyterian Church all theological development since Calvin. When Machen thanked the *British Weekly*'s editor for the "courteous and dignified" discussion of his book he had good reason. For at the same time that this series was appearing, rumors similar to Ellicott's were spreading through the Presbyterian Church that Machen's criticism of the mainline churches had made him unfit to teach at Princeton.[3]

The disparity between American and British reactions to Machen foreshadowed the struggle that he would face throughout the rest of his career. While his scholarship and arguments were sufficiently cogent to win the respect of many intellectuals, whether secular or religious, within institutional Protestantism Machen's personality became suspect. These suspicions were partly the product of his audacity. Although he explained repeatedly that he was not questioning the sincerity of individuals, by labeling liberal Protestantism "un-Christian" Machen used inflammatory rhetoric that many easily concluded was pejorative. Who could blame respected liberal ministers for becoming upset with someone who challenged their honesty or conservatives for sympathizing with the accused?

Nevertheless, the shift from theological issues to Machen's character was as much the reflection of institutional realities as a plot by scheming denominational leaders. As Presbyterians debated his personality and as the majority of officials and church members rallied to the warm sentiments of Christian fellowship, the denomination may have failed to answer the substance of Machen's charges. But it did succeed in maintaining organizational solidarity and a wider sphere of influence. Thus, the controversy surrounding Machen and its resolution illustrate a larger point about twentieth-century church life: public relations and image control have often been more effective than confessional standards and church order for settling rifts within America's largest Protestant denominations. The underside of this maxim, one often overlooked in institutional histories, is the toll that preserving the size and influence of large Protestant denominations exacted from dissenting individuals. In Machen's case, his outspoken opposition to Presbyterian practices cost him dearly. After 1926 many Presbyterians would know him more for his spitefulness than his scholarship.

After the publication of *Christianity and Liberalism* and *What Is Faith?* Machen had little time for writing. His last significant work was *The Virgin Birth of Christ*, published in 1930. Two more books would appear, *The Christian Faith in the Modern World* in 1936 and *The Christian View of Man*, published posthumously in 1937, but these summaries of Calvinistic theology were originally produced for a local radio show that publicized Machen's new seminary, Westminster. He wrote nothing of a strictly academic nature for the last ten years of his life. Instead, he directed most of his energies to Presbyterian affairs.[4]

Machen's thoughts about the church directly challenged the dominant outlook of Presbyterian officials. While they strove for greater cooperation with other denominations he defended Presbyterian particularism. During a time when many denominations opted for greater administrative centralization, Machen opposed bureaucratic streamlining and advocated the authority of local churches and regional bodies. Furthermore, while many Protestant leaders thought denominations should tolerate and seek to reconcile diverse outlooks, Machen insisted that the theology of the Westminster Confession was normative for Presbyterians.[5]

Ironically, when discussing the church both liberals and conservatives seemed to contradict themselves. For instance, conservatives considered the Bible to be the word of God and took exception to the modernist portrayal of scripture as merely the work of human writers. Yet in denominational skirmishes, they were the ones who usually spoke of the church not as a divine institution but as a voluntary association in which majority rule should prevail. In contrast, liberal and moderate church leaders often attributed to the church the same timelessness and transcendence that fundamentalists found in the Bible. Although modernists thought much conservative theology could be explained away as the product of cultural conditioning, the same logic rarely applied to the church. In fact, liberals, who said the church was the body of Christ, scored fundamentalists for an excessively low view of the church and for introducing secular notions into ecclesiastical affairs.[6]

Machen was a prime target for this criticism. He often compared the church to a political party, saying it consisted of individuals joined in voluntary association to advance a particular set of ideas. Such an organization, he argued, had every right to exclude those who differed. While denominational leaders defended organizational reform in spiritual terms, Machen challenged such arguments by reminding the church of its legal obligations. His approach to ecclesiastical disputes may have been unconventional but was hardly surprising. Machen demonstrated a penchant for legal argumentation that would have made his father and older brother proud. In fact, he regularly sought advice from his brother Arthur on the constitutional aspects of denominational matters.

The crux of Machen's legal case for excluding liberalism from the Presbyterian Church was evident as early as 1923 with the publication of *Christianity and Liberalism*. In that book, however, his reasoning about the Presbyterian Church as an institution was overshadowed by the weightier objection that liberalism was a different religion from Christianity. Obviously, if liberalism was as bad as Machen said, it had no rightful place in the church. Still, his quarrel with liberalism involved more than theological infidelity. Religious modernism contained a flawed understanding of the church and violated the constitutions of old-line Protestant denominations. Thus, what began in *Christianity and Liberalism* as a theological critique shifted to questions of Presbyterian polity.[7]

Machen's conception of the church followed directly from his understanding of faith. If faith was primarily the intellectual comprehension of a message about Christ, the church's task was to make that message clear. Machen cited Christ's instructions to his followers—"Ye shall be my witnesses"—as a correct summary of the church's purpose. Christianity did not consist of religious experience that transcended doctrine nor was it an inward feeling of which doctrine was a manifestation. Rather, Christianity was fundamentally theological. The confession and catechisms of the Presbyterian Church underscored in Machen's mind the propositional nature of Christianity. He made much of the ordination vows required of Presbyterian ministers. To preach in a Presbyterian pulpit, clergy had to answer a series of questions. The first concerned belief in the Bible as "the only infallible rule of faith and practice," and the second stipulated acceptance of the Westminster Confession of Faith as "containing the system of doctrine taught in Scripture." These vows, Machen thought, limited the content of Presbyterian preaching and restricted the use of the denomination's financial resources. Presbyterian funds were held under a trust that bound the church to propagate the gospel as taught in the Bible and the Westminster Confession. To use those funds for any other purpose was a violation of that trust.[8]

While Machen advocated ecclesiastical intolerance, he also defended civil liberties and saw no contradiction between the two. In fact, he often portrayed conservatives as true defenders of religious liberty and charged liberals with failing to distinguish between private and public concerns. Fundamental to religious liberty in the United States, Machen held, was the distinction between voluntary and involuntary organizations. The state was an involuntary organization that admitted all born in its jurisdiction. In contrast, the church was an association that individuals joined voluntarily. The U.S. Constitution guaranteed religious freedom and the right of voluntary association and denied the state the power to abridge those freedoms. Thus, the norm for the state was tolerance of different religions, but private associations such as the church could limit membership upon whatever criteria they chose. Excluding liberal ministers from the church, then, was connected to religious liberty "in the closest possible way" because the right of private association was an essential element of civil liberty. "A creedal church seems foolish to the Modernist preachers," Machen wrote, "but if they are really tolerant they will recognize its right in a free country to exist and to maintain its existence by insisting that its accredited representatives shall not combat its fundamental purpose from within."[9]

Machen did not hesitate to apply the lessons of voluntary association to his own denomination. The Presbyterian Church was composed of a number of persons who agreed upon a certain message about Christ and desired to unite in the propagation of that message. No one was forced to join it; if others wanted to form another church for other purposes, such as promoting the kind of life exemplified by Jesus, they were free to do so. But for an organization with a definite creedal basis "to commit its resources and name" to a hostile or different message was "not tolerance but simple dishonesty." For Presbyterian ministers and elders to decry the confession's theology as outdated or teach that the Bible was a collection of inspirational writings was entirely unacceptable. Even if the liberal understanding of Christianity were correct, the Presbyterian Church was still incorporated as a body loyal to the Westminster Confession and so was obligated to propagate Calvinistic theology.[10]

While Machen believed that liberal Presbyterians should withdraw from the church, he made two qualifications. First, he stressed that he was not making a personal judgment about whether liberal ministers possessed true faith. Only God knew such matters. But the church in its corporate deliberations was fully competent to decide whether a minister's words and conduct departed from denominational standards. Second, Machen said he was only calling for greater regularity among the clergy and church officials. He believed the church should make room for believers stricken with doubts. "It would be a crime," Machen wrote, to cast out such "troubled souls." Liberal clergy who questioned Presbyterian convictions might continue as church members, but to make them leaders was sheer folly.[11]

Machen knew that his views smacked of intolerance but argued that this was precisely the point. From its inception, he wrote, the church had excluded deviant theological views. In contrast, the Presbyterian Church had become tolerant of doctrinal diversity but intolerant in organizational matters. Religious liberals, despite pleas for freedom and tolerance, according to Machen, undermined liberty in the "most serious" way. By forcing the church to tolerate opposing views, liberals threatened the principle of voluntary association. Voluntary organizations were by nature intolerant or else they would "cease to exist." The church, in this regard, was not entirely different from a political party. If people dedicated to Republican principles joined a Democratic club and began to use that club's name and resources for anti-Democratic purposes, most people would agree that the Republicans had acted dishonestly. To be sure, the church was more than a political organization. But the church, Machen believed, should be at least as honest as a political organization.[12]

Machen also pointed out that liberal pleas for broadness were actually quite narrow. Narrowmindedness, he explained, did not consist in an individual's devotion to or rejection of certain ideas. Instead, a narrow person rejected another's convictions "without first endeavoring to understand them." This was exactly what liberals had done, according to Machen. They blithely called for peace and harmony without ever considering the significant differences that divided liberals and conservatives. Liberals thought doctrine unimportant and so could coexist with conservatives in the denomination. Conservatives, in contrast, believed doctrine was of utmost importance and so could not come to terms with liberals. The two parties could not be more different. Liberals were not necessarily narrow for rejecting traditional dogma, but it was "very narrow and very absurd" to suppose that conservatives and liberals were essentially united in their aims. Such a position was akin to Protestants telling Catholics that both groups could unite for common religious purposes because the mass and church membership "are of course matters of secondary importance." Liberal Protestant proposals for unity did not involve compromise but rather a "complete relinquishment" of everything that conservatives held dear. Machen received support on this point from Walter Lippmann, who said that the liberal plea for tolerance and goodwill was tantamount to telling conservatives to "smile and commit suicide."[13]

The solution that Machen advocated followed directly from his understanding of the church. A separation of the two parties was the "crying need of the hour." Nothing engendered strife so much as a "forced unity within the same organization" of those who disagreed fundamentally in aim. The denomination had to reaffirm the "absolute exclusiveness of the Christian religion." Then it would no longer be attractive to prospective ministers and established clergy of liberal convictions. But Machen also warned that if liberals gained control of the church, conservatives would be forced to withdraw. By the end of the 1920s, however, a conservative withdrawal looked far more likely than a liberal exodus.[14]

The more Machen and other Presbyterian conservatives relied upon procedural arguments the more they ran up against sentimental notions of church unity or pragmatic ideas about organizational efficiency. Thus, while Machen pointed to denominational standards, his opponents countered with pleas for Christian unity. These appeals stemmed in part from the heritage of American evangelicalism. Systematic reflection and sustained analysis were not characteristic of Protestant traditions influenced by revivalism and pietism. Evangelicalism relied more upon intuition and charisma to understand and promote the gospel. Even though mainstream Protestants by the early twentieth century had lost some of their evangelistic fervor, they still favored sentiment over principled deliberation. The demands of organizational life in large-scale bureaucracies furthered this tendency. As denominations became more centralized, sincerity, likability, and being a team player became desirable traits in church leaders. Evangelical habits and organizational demands, then, made goodwill, not critical scrutiny, the best way to resolve church controversy.[15]

This development explains why conservatives faced such difficult odds in removing liberals from the church. Throughout the general assemblies of the 1920s, conservatives were able to block some liberal advances but could never gain control of the church's administrative apparatus. As the fundamentalist controversy dragged on, many Presbyterians believed that while conservative ideas may have been theologically preferable to liberal ones, conservative tactics were breeding a spirit of suspicion and bitterness in the church. Conservatives were thus put on the defensive. The more they pressed their case, the more disruptive they seemed. Furthermore, denominational officials, whose task was to avoid schism and promote the church's positive mission, had little trouble garnering support for restoring peace, even if it meant censuring conservatives.

Events at the 1925 General Assembly offer a good example of the obstacles conservatives such as Machen faced. Machen was not present at this gathering. Despite the popularity of his book, *Christianity and Liberalism*, the most visible conservative leaders in denominational politics were still William Jennings Bryan and Clarence Macartney, a popular pastor in Philadelphia (later in Pittsburgh) and a member of the board of directors at Princeton Seminary. Only after 1929 with the founding of a new Presbyterian seminary would Machen attempt to lead the conservative party. Until then, conservative Presbyterianism was anything but a unified party or coherent set of views. It ranged from the anti-evolutionism of Bryan to the confessionalism of Macartney. While this diversity prevented conservatives from electing their own candidate for moderator at the 1925 assembly, they did manage to block the licensure of two ministerial candidates from New York who would not affirm the virgin birth. The majority of Presbyterians were still sufficiently conservative to decide that this doctrine was, in the words of the assembly, an "official teaching" and the "established law" of the church. This ruling was also the closest conservatives came to excluding liberals from the church.[16]

But a conservative victory was short-lived. The presbytery of New York, traditionally more hospitable to liberal views and the stronghold of Presbyterian liberalism during the 1920s, would not abide by this decision. Henry Sloane Coffin, pastor of New York's Madison Avenue Presbyterian Church, read a statement to the assembly's delegates that threatened a liberal exodus if the ruling was upheld. Other ministers from New York also voiced their displeasure and willingness to leave the denomination. The threat of losing New York's considerable resources and the risk of depleting Presbyterian influence in the region forced leaders to reconsider their decision. To mollify Coffin and his colleagues the newly elected moderator, Charles Erdman, a colleague of Machen's at Princeton, proposed that a special commission be appointed to study the issues dividing the church and make recommendations that would restore "purity, peace, unity and progress." Erdman's proposal easily won the assembly's approval.[17]

An important factor in this turnabout was the emergence of a well-organized liberal lobby. The first signs of a liberal party surfaced in 1924 with the publication of the *Auburn Affirmation*, bearing the signatures of 150 Presbyterian ministers, many of whom were well-known modernists. Just before the start of the 1924 assembly, it was republished over the signatures of 1,274 ministers, roughly 13 percent of the denomination's clergy. The *Affirmation* appealed to the denomination's history of tolerating different interpretations of the Westminster Confession. It also stated that specific doctrines affirmed in 1923—biblical inerrancy, the virgin birth, the vicarious atonement, and the resurrection, for example—were "only theories." For some these doctrines were "satisfactory explanations" of the biblical data, but they were not the only theories allowed by the Bible or Presbyterian standards. Finally, the *Affirmation* called for greater toleration and argued that Presbyterians who affirmed these doctrines, no matter what their interpretation, were "worthy of all confidence and fellowship."[18]

The distinction between fact and theory was an argument that Machen opposed vehemently. From his perspective, the *Affirmation* revealed the telltale flaw of liberalism, that of making theology independent of and secondary to religious experience. The redemptive events mentioned in the document were not theories, he believed, but facts whose meaning the Bible supplied. By asking for tolerance in interpreting these doctrines, Machen thought the *Affirmation* reversed the "plain meaning" of both scripture and the confession and, in effect, left the church without a theological foundation.[19]

Liberals were also quite effective in thwarting conservative advances through denominational red tape. John Foster Dulles, who provided legal council for New York liberals and himself a Presbyterian elder, was quite successful in seeing that conservative pleas for discipline of liberal ministers were referred to standing committees of the denomination rather than to the General Assembly. Many of these committees were oriented more toward Presbyterian headquarters in New York than to the General Assembly which was made up of ministers and elders from all regions in the United States. Dulles admitted that in some of these cases the denominational committees did not have the proper jurisdiction to make such rulings. But in one instance where a review of committee work would have meant prolonging the General Assembly for several days, the delegates gladly acceded to the committee's decision.[20]

The election of Erdman as moderator in 1925 also stemmed from liberal endeavors to build closer relationships with evangelicals in denominational politics. Erdman had solid evangelical credentials. He had served as editor of *The Fundamentals*, a series of pamphlets published in the 1910s that opposed liberal biblical scholarship. He also had taught at Princeton Seminary since 1906, and had written many popular biblical commentaries. While conservative in theological matters, Erdman strongly desired to maintain the unity of the church. Liberals knew this and supported his candidacy for moderator with the hope that his platform of unity would hinder conservative efforts. Erdman, for his part, did not court liberals, but neither did he refuse their support. His program of "purity and peace and progress" was one that gave the upper hand to liberals who did not want to exclude conservatives but believed that both sides could render important service to the church. Conservatives could reach people with more conventional views, the argument ran, while liberals could win those wrestling with the dilemmas of modern life. Conservatives such as Machen, in contrast, believed that liberal and conservative views were irreconcilable. When he complained publicly that Erdman was merely a puppet for liberals and asked conservatives not to vote for his colleague, Erdman took offense. Thus, Erdman's candidacy and election split conservatives further and put Machen in the awkward position of playing the schoolyard bully to Erdman's sacrificial lamb.[21]

The report issued by the special commission that Erdman had appointed to quiet Presbyterian strife disclosed the growing perception that conservatives were to blame for acrimony in the church. This committee had met four times over the course of a year and divided into various subcommittees that studied the meaning of ordination vows, the doctrine of the virgin birth, the power of the General Assembly, and previous Presbyterian controversies. The commission also heard testimony from leaders on both sides, ranging from conservatives such as Macartney and Machen to liberals such as Coffin and William Adams Brown, professor of theology at Union Seminary (New York). Although it did not mention Machen by name, the commission's report directly repudiated his views. It found that the church's theology was not nearly as unequivocal as conservatives thought. Presbyterian history showed continuous rivalry between liberal and conservative views, a fact that gave precedent for diversity. Even the doctrine of the

virgin birth was unclear because men of "piety, conviction, and scholarship" took opposing positions. In turn, the commission celebrated
the denomination's pluralism. Despite geographical, racial, national,
and cultural differences, the denomination stood "with one heart beat-
ing at the center of its corporate life," bound together by the "shining
record" of its past, a faith engaged in the "rich loyalties" of the present
and inspired by the "holy promise of a fairer future." Still, diversity
did not mean theological indifference. The church continued to affirm
that God was the "vital and unifying and governing Personality"
who imparted "order, stability, and moral purpose" to the world. The
church also held that Christ was the "only Saviour" and that regeneration by the Holy Spirit was necessary for true faith. The commission even pointed to its own existence as evidence of the church's
soundness.[22]

Judged by Machen's concern for doctrinal precision, these affirmations were vague statements of Christian conviction designed to keep
the church from splintering. This became especially clear in the report's declaration of Presbyterian convictions. Presbyterianism, the
report declared, was more than just theology. It was also a tradition
and "controlling sentiment." Ties of the heart made it impossible for
ministers with liberal convictions to be at home in any other communion. Consequently, the commission recommended a policy of "constitutional toleration" that would "conserve such assets" without
endangering the fundamental beliefs of the church.[23]

Finally, the commission found that liberalism was not present in the
denomination. Members of the commission here showed some sympathy with Machen's concerns. Religious modernism, they believed,
should be excluded from the church. Their conception of liberalism
even sounded like Machen's: the belief that the Bible was only "traditional literature," that Christ was nothing more than a man filled
with the Holy Spirit, that his life and death were merely examples of
self-sacrifice, that he "never rose from the dead," and that he would
"never return to the earth." Yet they could find no one in the church
who held these views. Consequently, the commission gave the church
a clean bill of theological health.[24]

With liberalism ruled out as the source of controversy the report
blamed the "misjudgments and unfair and untrue statements" made
by conservatives. In a charge that would have significant repercussions
for Machen, the commission declared that conservative indictments of
modernism bordered on "libel and slander." Of course, a careful reading of Machen showed that he had not accused liberals of denying car-
dinal doctrines in as blatant a manner as the commission's definition

of liberalism. Rather, he held that modernists were using orthodox Christian terminology in equivocal ways. In his testimony before the commission, Machen pointed to the 1920 plan for church union, Harry Emerson Fosdick's preaching and the church's handling of that affair, the *Auburn Affirmation*, the licensure of candidates in New York presbytery who would not affirm the virgin birth, and the hostility of the denomination's boards to conservatives as evidence of liberalism within the church. Nevertheless, the commission interpreted Machen's criticism as an assault upon the loyalty of worthy Presbyterians and urged the General Assembly to silence those who continued to spread distrust and suspicion.[25]

From Machen's perspective the commission's report lacked both theological clarity and resolve. Undoubtedly, its stress upon the plasticity of Presbyterian theology can be explained by political necessity. The report was, in effect, a call for pragmatic tolerance and followed Henry Sloane Coffin's suggestion that "we ought to work harmoniously together and emphasize those things in which we agree." But for Machen's purposes this kind of resolution gave modernists the upper hand because it failed to recognize the significant doctrinal disagreements that existed between liberals and conservatives. Moreover, by making goodwill and sincerity the basis for toleration, the commission elevated sentiment over theology as the salient feature of Christian conviction. In effect, the commission made "moderate theological liberalism" legitimate. It also put Machen and other conservatives on a collision course with the Presbyterian hierarchy. The more conservatives insisted that liberals were at odds with the Westminster Confession, the more they appeared to manifest an un-Christian spirit.[26]

The special commission's report met little opposition at the 1926 General Assembly. Conservative acquiescence remains a mystery but again suggests divisions within conservative ranks. Machen, who was lecturing in Britain, wired Macartney that if conservatives voted for this report "all the sacrifices of the past few years will go for nothing." He also believed that the report "[did] away with the foundations of Presbyterian doctrine and law" because it put loyalty to the church above faithfulness to the Bible and the confession. Macartney tried to amend a section of the report concerning the assembly's power but his brother Albert, who had liberal sympathies, upstaged him when he declared that liberals and conservatives were virtually identical. "We were brought up together," Albert told the assembly, "and our mother sang the same hymns to us . . . We didn't know what those words meant then, but it was the same Christianity we both profess." The assembly of 1926 greeted this statement with applause and went on to adopt the special commission's report, recording only one negative vote.[27]

These events made a showdown at Princeton Seminary inevitable. Not only had the special commission begun during a heated dispute between two of the seminary's faculty, Machen and Erdman, but its repudiation of Machen bore heavily on another item of denominational business. In the spring of 1926, the board of directors at Princeton Seminary elected Machen to fill a vacancy in the department of theology by promoting him from assistant professor of New Testament to full professor of apologetics and ethics. According to Princeton's plan, such an appointment also had to be confirmed by the General Assembly. Ratification was typically only a formality. In the seminary's history none of the directors' choices had been vetoed. A different fate, however, awaited Machen.[28]

The same body, the 1926 General Assembly, that adopted the special commission's verdict heard two reports questioning Machen's qualifications. The first concerned his attitude toward Prohibition. At its spring meeting the New Brunswick (New Jersey) presbytery, of which Machen was a member, had adopted a resolution endorsing the Eighteenth Amendment and the Volstead Act. Machen voted "no" without comment and declined when asked whether he wanted his vote recorded. In an unpublished statement drafted to quiet suspicions at the General Assembly, he explained that while opposed to drunkenness he thought federal legislation was not a wise method of dealing with intemperance but actually caused moral harm. He also thought that the Westminster Confession prevented the church from entering "in its corporate capacity" into political affairs. His friends advised him not to publish his statement, while one of them reported that the General Assembly was "rabidly Prohibitionist" and would have vetoed Machen's election had it come to the floor. In fact, the 1926 assembly eventually adopted a resolution that opposed any modification of the Volstead Act and called upon all church members to support the Eighteenth Amendment vigorously.[29]

The second report concerned Machen's temperament. His election as professor was reviewed by the Advisory Committee on Theological Seminaries before going to the General Assembly. Testimony came before this committee that Machen was "temperamentally defective, bitter and harsh in his judgment of others and implacable to those who [did] not agree with him." Dr. George N. Luccock, chairman of the committee, concluded that such characteristics would "spiritually" disqualify an individual from holding a chair of apologetics and Christian ethics. The sources of these unflattering descriptions were Charles Erdman and J. Ross Stevenson, president of Princeton Seminary. Newspapers reported that Erdman charged Machen with "temperamental idiosyncrasies" while Stevenson told the assembly that Machen had "serious limitations." Undoubtedly, Machen's earlier contention that liberalism was un-Christian appeared to those who did not know him to be equally un-Christian. But few seemed to notice that Stevenson and Erdman were hardly charitable in their descriptions of Machen or that they may have had less than noble motives for denigrating their Princeton colleague. With Machen's reputation in question, the General Assembly took no action and, for all intents and purposes, rejected Machen's promotion.[30]

The General Assembly was not finished with affairs at Princeton, however. It granted Stevenson's request to form a committee to study conditions at Princeton Seminary and adjust and harmonize difficulties. After a year, the committee would report back to the General Assembly and only then could Machen's promotion be reconsidered. Unfortunately for Princeton conservatives, the composition of the committee did not seem favorable for an even-handed investigation. The chairman of this committee, William O. Thompson, president of Ohio State University and moderator of the 1926 General Assembly, was not predisposed to regard Machen favorably. He was a good friend and associate of Erdman and Stevenson and his religious views—evangelistic, activistic, and moralistic—were similar to moderates at the seminary. Furthermore, his first act as moderator had been to assert "approval and sympathy with the Eighteenth Amendment and the enforcement of the Volstead Act."[31]

When the committee to investigate Princeton met during November 1926 and January 1927, it focused on the antagonism between Erdman and Machen. For almost three years these professors had exchanged barbs on the front pages of New York, Trenton, and Philadelphia newspapers. Church officials obviously wanted to end bad publicity for the seminary and denomination. As the committee learned, tensions dated back to the months prior to the 1924 General Assembly. Erdman resented Machen's and other Princeton conservatives' opposition to his candidacy for moderator of the 1924 and 1925 assemblies. He felt especially wounded when the faculty, at the request of student representatives, replaced him as student adviser. Most of the acrimony stemmed from an incident in January 1925, when Erdman succeeded Machen as stated supply of First Church, Princeton. Upon Erdman's arrival, Henry Van Dyke, who with much fanfare had left the congregation because of Machen's preaching, returned to his pew. The editor of the *Presbyterian*, always on the lookout for ecclesiastical improprieties, pointed to Van Dyke's return as evidence that Erdman was a favorite of liberals.[32]

Erdman blamed Machen for the *Presbyterian*'s editorial in a letter to the *Presbyterian Advance*, a liberal weekly, and attributed Princeton's woes to the "unkindness, suspicion, bitterness and intolerance" of the faculty who were "editors of The Presbyterian." Machen was the only one who fit that description but had no prepublication knowledge of the editorial. When Erdman continued to question his motives, Machen wrote a letter to the *Presbyterian* publicly denying responsibility for the editorial. He insisted that he had opposed Erdman not from personal animosity but on principle. Machen explained that Erdman was unwilling to make doctrine a priority in denominational affairs. He also thought that Erdman had been treated unfairly by the *Presbyterian*, had Erdman's letter printed with his, and asked the *Presbyterian*'s editor to give both Van Dyke and Erdman a chance to respond to the original editorial. As these facts came to light before the Princeton committee Erdman became evasive and defensive about the specifics of the incident. His responses to questions even suggested that he had wanted to damage Machen's reputation.[33]

Nevertheless, throughout the hearings Erdman, Stevenson, and their supporters continued to blame Machen for discord at the seminary. One of the first pieces of testimony called Machen "queer" and wondered how he could "ever" inspire the seminarians since he lacked the gifts Erdman and Stevenson possessed. Stevenson told the committee that "suspicion, distrust, dissension, and division" were in the seminary and Machen was responsible. The Erdman-Machen controversy even divided the seminary's alumni association. Erdman's backers on the association's executive committee issued a statement endorsing Erdman. Machen lamented that the alumni's "pleasant social nature" had been compromised. "I am, indeed, not averse to controversy in the proper place," he explained, "but I also cherish pleasant social relationships even with ecclesiastical and theological opponents." When one of his own sympathizers wanted to use the alumni association to rally conservatives Machen warned that these associations were purely "social in character," were not representative, did not allow time for deliberation, and, consequently, were likely to be manipulated and of little value.[34]

When Machen testified he explained that his opposition to Erdman was not personal and that his colleague was overly sensitive to any form of opposition. Erdman's reaction to Machen's support for another candidate in the 1925 contest for moderator, he elaborated, would put a muzzle on all such endorsements because they could always be in-terpreted as a personal rebuke by the endorsee's opponent. Machen had backed Clarence Macartney instead of Erdman in 1924 because the Philadelphia pastor had been the first to speak out against Harry Emer-son Fosdick and because Erdman had consistently supported the pol-icy of "doctrinal indifferentism." Machen noted that the majority of Princeton's faculty were also profoundly opposed to such a policy and therefore did not support Erdman. To take the sting out of his remarks, Machen said he still held Erdman in high personal esteem and had never taken Erdman's unwillingness to support conservative tactics as a personal reproach.[35]

By the end of his testimony, Machen seemed to have convinced the committee that Erdman was actually responsible for bitterness at the seminary. Machen thought Erdman's response to the *Presbyterian*'s editorial was especially inflammatory. Newspaper reports, Machen ob-served, caused the full brunt of Erdman's remarks to fall upon him and still Erdman stood mute even when Machen had denied writing the editorial. He also noted that Erdman's and Stevenson's statements about his unfitness before the 1926 General Assembly exhibited per-sonal animosity and betrayed their unwillingness to hear the conser-vatives' side. He concluded by remarking on the irony of the situation. Because of the impression that Erdman had been treated unfairly and out of sympathy for him, Presbyterian commissioners in 1925 elected Erdman moderator. In contrast, because of his opposition to Erdman, Machen's promotion had been denied.[36]

When committee members pressed Erdman for an explanation, he again attributed the strife at Princeton to personal bitterness and com-plained that Machen had not done anything to shield him from the criticisms of the *Presbyterian*. Erdman nevertheless expressed remorse. "What has divided us is a bitter, intolerant spirit," he said. "I have no doubt shown it and regret it . . . I do want to get it out of my heart." Yet, he added, harmony would prevail if Machen would only acknowl-edge Erdman's sincerity in defending the evangelical faith.[37]

Then Machen made what many considered a truly Christian act. He declared that he would not let personal vindication get in the way of the seminary's welfare and that he was ready to resume "friendly re-lations" with Erdman, although he reserved the right to disagree with seminary colleagues. This was the moment for which many had been waiting. Erdman said that he was also willing to resume cordial rela-tions with Machen and other faculty. William Park Armstrong, Mach-en's mentor and friend, decided that he too could go along with his protégé. J. Ritchie Smith, professor of homiletics and Erdman sympathizer, applauded Machen's "fine statement" and J. Ross Stevenson called it "a great advance." Finally, the committee gave its blessing when George N. Luccock, the man who had recommended to the 1926 General Assembly that Machen's promotion be postponed, announced that Machen had reached a "spiritual victory" that demonstrated the gospel's powers of reconciliation.[38]

Despite these expressions of goodwill, harmony did not last long. When the committee convened for its final round of interviews in January 1927, new tensions surfaced that revealed the limits of unity based on good intentions. Erdman proposed a resolution that called for the faculty to affirm confidence in one another and loyalty to the seminary's historic theological outlook. Machen's Calvinistic colleagues immediately objected. Geerhardus Vos, professor of biblical theology, questioned whether the resolution would clarify matters since many ministers subscribed to the confession in an insincere manner. Caspar Wistar Hodge then complained that Erdman's proposal only highlighted the difficulties of defining the denomination's doctrinal standards, since all could subscribe to the Westminster Confession if interpreted in broad terms. Machen chimed in that the faculty's inability to agree on a definition of Princeton's historic position had been the source of trouble all along. After hearing these objections Chairman Thompson observed that Machen might be the root of the problem after all. He declared that Machen was "hot footed" in the "intellectual statement of controversy," whereas Erdman's proposal merely aimed to quiet the "mind of the church." The faculty "could go on forever with this analyzing of words" but the "man in the plowing field" did not see the importance of it. With his patience dwindling, the committee chairman ended the investigation.[39]

As Thompson learned, theological hairsplitting, not personalities, had been at the center of the struggle at Princeton. The origins of these tensions went back to curricular reforms carried out in the 1910s. During those debates two distinct parties had emerged that mirrored the divisions within the seminary of the late 1920s. On the one side were academic conservatives like Machen who wanted to retain the traditional curriculum with its stress upon Greek, Hebrew, and systematic theology. On the other side were Erdman and the newly elected president, Stevenson, who wanted to change the curriculum in favor of courses in English Bible and practical aspects of ministry. Ironically, although Erdman and Stevenson did not manifest the militancy against liberalism typical of fundamentalism, their educational policies resembled the vocational and pragmatic emphases of fundamentalist Bible institutes and colleges.[40]

These academic differences were closely connected to the theological leanings of Princeton's conservatives and moderates. Throughout the debates the Princeton faculty and administration split into two distinct camps. On the one side were strict Calvinists, a group that included Machen and the majority of professors (seven of eleven) and the majority of the board of directors (nineteen of twenty-eight), the body responsible for faculty and curriculum. On the other side were moderate evangelicals who were led by Erdman and Stevenson and included a majority of the board of trustees (seventeen of twenty-two), the officers responsible for finances. Contrary to the view that both sides at Princeton were conservative and therefore shared identical theological convictions, in fact, these groups held different views of the importance of theology and its role in the nature and mission of the church.[41]

Both sides claimed to be "evangelicals" but used the term in different senses. To conservatives associated with Machen, as his colleague Caspar Wistar Hodge explained, the Calvinism of the Westminster standards expressed a pure and consistent form of evangelicalism that was the only "impregnable barrier" against religious liberalism. Calvinism, Presbyterian traditionalists believed, was the most thorough understanding of humankind's absolute dependence upon divine grace. Doctrine, therefore, was inseparable from true faith. The indifference of Erdman and Stevenson to Calvinist theology, Machen and his colleagues thought, revealed a grave misunderstanding of the issues dividing the denomination and of the church's mission.[42]

Erdman and Stevenson, by contrast, were theologically tolerant, pragmatic, and evangelistic in their outlook. They held conventional views about the Bible and Christ as the sole means of salvation but were willing to overlook theological niceties. For Erdman true Christianity was best expressed in one's spirit or disposition. "A real believer," he wrote, rather than reciting orthodox creeds, "follows Christ and reflects the character of Christ." Having a correct understanding of Presbyterian theology was secondary to demonstrating Christian character. According to Erdman, a Christian minister should be "'gentle', sweetly reasonable, eager to show forbearance and kindly considerate; he must not be 'contentious' or quarrelsome, even as to matters of doctrine." Should theological concerns threaten to divide the church, doctrine would have to be sacrificed for the sake of effective outreach. A divided church, Erdman believed, was "always spiritually weak and impotent."[43]

Stevenson and Erdman disapproved of religious liberalism but believed that the special commission of 1925 had dealt with the matter adequately. Like the commission's report Princeton moderates never acknowledged the presence of liberals within the Presbyterian Church. Instead, they identified liberalism with an explicit denial of Christianity's basic tenets and failed to attend to the nuances and implications of theological discussion. Furthermore, because Machen had not attacked liberalism through ecclesiastical courts they thought his writings violated Presbyterian law, a charge that the Princeton committee rejected. Erdman and Stevenson were convinced, in contrast to Machen, that their tolerant policies upheld the principles of Presbyterian polity.[44]

When the Princeton committee reported to the General Assembly of 1927, the views of Erdman and Stevenson triumphed. Like the report by the special commission of 1925 the Princeton study demonstrated that the dominant outlook among Presbyterians, while mildly evangelical, veered from the concerns of Princeton's Calvinists. The report found little justification for Machen's opposition to Erdman and Stevenson. In two pages it cleared Princeton moderates of the charge of doctrinal indifferentism, citing their "definite statements to the contrary" as proof. From the committee's perspective Stevenson and Erdman represented the seminary's historic position "of sound, conservative and evangelical theology." Although committee members had been "greatly encouraged" by Machen's expression of willingness to work with Erdman, his subsequent remarks revealed that his gesture was only "academic and defensive." "Dr. Machen confesses no fault," the report added, "he accepts no forgiveness and offers none." His unwillingness to trust the affirmations of his colleagues was evidence that Christ's command to "be kindly affectioned one toward another" was not controlling the relations of Princeton's faculty. Although other Princeton conservatives had been more outspoken than Machen during the investigation, the report singled him out and concluded that his attitude left "much to be desired as a basis of brotherly relations."[45]

To resolve tensions at the seminary, the committee recommended a spirit of goodwill and trust, the consolidation of the boards of directors and trustees, and the enlargement of the president's power in academic and administrative affairs. When the 1927 General Assembly adopted the report by a vote of 503 to 323 the Presbyterian Church chose to overcome its internal divisions in the same way that other large Protestant denominations had, namely, by implementing administrative reforms that encouraged greater centralization and at the same time throttled dissent.[46]

Presbyterian procedure required such a decision be ratified by the following year's assembly. Due to efforts of Princeton conservatives this process became a bit unwieldy. Conservatives commissioned and wrote legal briefs that concluded that reorganization of the seminary was unconstitutional. Machen himself paid $1,000 in legal fees to the firms of Humes, Buck, and Smith (New York), and Lindabury, Depue, and Faulks (Newark). Machen's brother Arthur also volunteered his services. All opinions agreed that the seminary's constitution gave control to the conservative dominated board of directors and had been amended illegally by the General Assembly. To further their case, Machen also wrote *The Attack upon Princeton Seminary: A Plea for Fair Play*, a forty-eight-page pamphlet he had printed and distributed at his own expense, which opposed reorganization on legal, administrative, historical, and theological grounds. Whether legal or illegal, the reorganization, as conservatives correctly argued, clearly took power away from them and dispersed it among moderates sympathetic to Erdman and Stevenson by enhancing the scope of Stevenson's authority as president and by making conservatives a minority on the newly constituted board of directors.[47]

Nevertheless, Princeton conservatives were not popular figures within the denomination nor were they well connected to the centers of Presbyterian power. In fact, many Presbyterians, both moderates and fundamentalists, supported reorganization because Erdman backed it. If control of the seminary shifted to men like him, many reasoned, Princeton was hardly in danger of becoming liberal. Once again, conservative opposition to moderate evangelicals appeared to be vindictive and prevented a serious reckoning with the substance of conservative concerns. When the reorganization of Princeton was finally ratified at the General Assembly of 1929, Presbyterians both on the left and on the right were glad to put to rest what many believed was the last skirmish in the fundamentalist controversy.[48]

The reorganization of Princeton Seminary hurt Machen deeply. The seminary had been pivotal in his intellectual and personal development, enabling him to reconcile his academic interests and religious convictions. Now reorganization seemed to bring a fundamental change in the character of the institution with which he had so closely identified. He believed that Presbyterian officials had exchanged Princeton's Calvinistic and scholarly orientation for a moderate evangelicalism that would try to placate liberals and conservatives while maintaining the unity of the church. Machen's description of the change spoke poignantly of his own loss. "It is not merely an educational agency which is being destroyed," he wrote to one friend, "but a fine tradition of painstaking scholarship, courteous conviction and dignified conduct."[49]

As Machen considered his options, the thought of resignation did not come easily. He believed that Princeton was one of the only educational institutions remaining within old-line Protestantism that had retained its theological integrity. Princeton's longevity was especially important to Machen. He knew that younger seminaries could never approximate the rich holdings of Princeton's library. He wrote to his mother in the middle of June 1929 that he desired to "*live* at Princeton, say what I please, and write big, thick books." While Southern Presbyterian seminaries such as Columbia or Union (Richmond) may have been sufficiently conservative for Machen, moving south would have meant the abandonment of conservatives within the Northern church. Nevertheless, Machen confessed that he was "so sick of the uphill battle" that he was "almost willing to have it over." Life at the seminary would only have perpetuated the animosity of the past few years. Thus, in a spirit of fatigue rather than defiance, Machen tendered his resignation within a month after reorganization became official. Only three months later, in the fall of 1929, Machen, with the help of other conservatives in the Philadelphia area, founded Westminster Theological Seminary. When the new seminary opened at its downtown Philadelphia campus, Machen made clear that the cause of old Princeton was not forgotten. Although conservatives were sad to have lost Princeton, Machen declared that old seminary's "noble tradition" was alive and well at Westminster.[50]

Machen interpreted the passing of Princeton Seminary as the "end of an epoch in the history of the modern church." That view is certainly debatable. Throughout the seminary's history, many thought that Princeton's polemics were usually well informed, even if acerbic, and Machen was the last representative of this tradition. In the atmosphere of the twenties, Machen's polemics sounded shrill to the many Presbyterians who wanted to move beyond controversy and concentrate on the positive ministry and programs of the church. But Machen's perceptions about the significance of Princeton's reorganization were accurate to the extent that he sensed a shift within American mainstream Protestantism. Between 1870 and 1925, moderate evangelicals of a revivalistic persuasion like Erdman and confessionalists like Machen had coexisted somewhat peacefully within a diffuse Protestant consensus. Under the pressures of the 1920s, this center would no longer hold. Theological and scholarly questions took a backseat to organizational preservation and consolidation. The new consensus relied upon affirmations of denominational loyalty and Christian brotherhood, and was achieved through administrative reform.[51]

The reorganization of Princeton Seminary has not figured prominently in the history of fundamentalism but Machen's personality has. Most scholars presume that Princeton moderates and conservatives shared the same theological convictions but differed over procedural matters, and that while reorganization marked a shift from Calvinism to moderate evangelicalism the primary issue was personal acrimony among the faculty. In addition, most historians have tended to believe the winners in the Princeton struggle and attribute the controversy to Machen's mercurial personality. His temperament has also been used to explain the demise of the conservative movement within the Presbyterian Church. Machen's unwillingness to compromise in the give-and-take of ecclesiastical politics, so the argument runs, alienated many would-be supporters. According to Ernest Sandeen, "what Machen called faithful, militant witnessing for the truth was often nothing more than perverse obstinacy and a fatal lack of openness to the truth that might (however dimly) glow in some other heart." When crossed, Machen simply cut off his former friends with an "irreversible anathema and proceeded on his way uncompromised but more than ever the hermit saint." A more recent estimate concurs that "the great Machen" was "quite loony" and that his religious convictions do not explain his "curious" personality and behavior. (Few seem willing to grant that Machen's inability to compromise may have followed quite logically from the convictions he expressed in *Christianity and Liberalism*, a book that many have praised for its insightful critique of liberal Protestantism.)[52]

Various explanations have been offered for the quirks of Machen's personality. The most common that circulated during the Princeton investigation focused on his bachelorhood, a subject that also touches upon Machen's relationship to his mother. His lengthy and regular correspondence with her combined with his seemingly peevish behavior suggests to some that Machen was a spoiled child who always needed his mother's approval. Conversely, the companionship and responsibilities of a wife and children might have given him less time for ecclesiastical skirmishes and made him more willing to accept Presbyterian realities.[53]

No compelling evidence exists to suggest that Machen's reasons for not marrying had anything to do with an unusual relationship to his mother. He corresponded weekly with her (at a time when frequent letter-writing was the norm), paid regular visits to family in Baltimore, and vacationed most summers with his mother at the family cottage in Seal Harbor, Maine. Since both of Machen's brothers were married and had children, many of the responsibilities of caring for Minnie

Gresham Machen after her husband's death in 1915 naturally fell to the single son. Sometimes these duties—especially long stints in the summer—became a burden when Machen needed to travel abroad but did not want his mother to be alone in Maine. Still, their relationship was a good one. She was his confidante. In letters to her Machen revealed the frustrations, antagonisms, and personal feelings that he would not display in public or in formal correspondence. When she died in 1933 Machen lost the one person upon whom he could unburden himself and who always offered a sympathetic ear.[54]

Machen's reasons for not marrying are uncertain. Undoubtedly, he enjoyed the freedom of bachelorhood. He liked to travel, whether on speaking engagements or for pleasure. Machen was an avid mountain climber and visited Switzerland twice to enjoy its pleasures and challenges. He also paid regular visits to New York, Philadelphia, and Boston for a variety of cultural diversions. Machen did have a brief romance with Mildred B. Stearns that blossomed in the summer of 1920. He met her at Seal Harbor, where she also vacationed with her family. The major obstacle to their marriage was religion. Stearns was a Unitarian and even though Machen admired the intellectual integrity of Unitarians—he frequently advised liberals to exhibit such honesty— marriage to someone of such decidedly different religious views was out of the question. Machen corresponded with her throughout his life and visited her whenever in Boston. Members of Machen's family say she traveled alone from Boston to Baltimore to attend Machen's burial service at Greenmount Cemetery.[55]

Machen was on good terms with most of his colleagues at Princeton. He was a member of the Benham Club, one of Princeton's exclusive eating and social clubs that Woodrow Wilson opposed during his presidency at the university. Through the club Machen established many life-long friendships with other Presbyterian educators and ministers. Among his closest friends was Harold McAfee Robinson, who pastored churches in Philadelphia and eventually became an executive in the Presbyterian Board of Publications. One of the reasons why Machen held off in his criticisms of this agency, which was by no means in his mind a citadel of orthodoxy, owed to his friendship with "Bobbie." Machen also enjoyed the friendship of colleagues at the seminary, especially William Park Armstrong and Caspar Wistar Hodge. He socialized frequently with the Armstrong family, taking them to Princeton football games in return for the service that Armstrong often rendered to Machen's car.[56]

Machen's friends at the Benham Club gave him the nickname of "Das," which was derived from the article for the German word *madchen* ("maiden"). His students at Princeton and Westminster called him by that name or its derivative, "Dassie." It is no exaggeration to say that he was one of the most popular professors at Princeton. Part of Machen's appeal was his notoriety. Enrollment figures at the seminary show a marked increase during the years after the publication of *Christianity and Liberalism,* from 156 in 1919–20, and 224 in 1923–24, to 255 in 1928–29. Machen was also very accessible. He liked to spend his first class of every semester loosening the students up with many of the jokes and "stunts" that ingratiated him to members of the Benham Club. In addition to playing tennis with students, Machen also sponsored in his suite at Princeton or Philadelphia apartment an informal gathering of the "Checker Club," a time for students to enjoy large quantities of sweets, fruit, and soda, and to challenge Machen to a game of chess or checkers. When he moved to Philadelphia he often took students to college football games at the University of Pennsylvania or gave them his tickets to see the Philadelphia Athletics play at Shibe Park.[57]

Of course, Machen had enemies, especially in the Presbyterian Church. But his correspondence and personal dealings with antagonists were always courteous, even though in letters to his family he spoke of opponents in less flattering terms. A frequent response to hostile correspondence was to say that the writer's letter had caused "considerable regret" and then to explain his position. He often closed his letters to adversaries with statements about the importance of his being faithful to God. Yet Machen rarely let feelings of self-righteousness mask the theological or ecclesiastical point at issue. He frequently had to read or listen to sanctimonious rhetoric, believed that such language was a smokescreen for arguments without intellectual merit, and so tried to take the high road in public debate and private correspondence.[58]

Yet Machen was sensitive to even the smallest criticism or unintentional slight from family or close friends. Two examples, one from earlier and one from later in his career, bear out this trait. The first concerns Machen's hurt feelings upon learning secondhand that his colleague and friend Armstrong had received an honorary doctorate from Temple. He wrote to his mother that "a stranger would hardly judge that there was much intimacy between us if he found me ignorant of even so simple a matter as the proper title of my supposed friend." Thirteen years later, at the height of the controversy over Princeton Seminary, Machen was distressed by his older brother's offhand remark that some articles written by other conservatives made better arguments than he had. Gresham complained that Arthur seemed to be rejoicing in his inferiority and asked if the loyalty of a brother counted for nothing. These outbursts departed from the usual detachment and restraint he manifested when criticized in much more antagonistic ways by denominational foes or seminary colleagues and undoubtedly stemmed from the high esteem in which Machen held Armstrong and his older brother. Yet they also show someone who could be easily offended in his closest relationships.[59]

If Machen's personality does not adequately explain why he came to an impasse with Princeton moderates, his personal involvement with the seminary does. For Machen, the reorganization of Princeton was a profoundly personal matter, not simply because the seminary had nurtured him through times of religious doubt but also because his temperament had become the issue during debates leading up to reorganization. Machen's tactic had been to focus on Erdman's and Stevenson's policies and their effects upon the seminary and the church. As much as they frustrated him, Machen did not question their character or the sincerity of their motives. However, they interpreted his criticisms as a personal attack and responded in kind, calling him unkind, bitter, suspicious, intolerant, and divisive, both in print and before church councils.

Machen took the struggle over Princeton personally, then, because that struggle ended up being about him. If his character had not been so thoroughly questioned for the three years between his nomination for the chair of apologetics and the ratification of the Princeton committee's report, he might have been able to remain at Princeton and champion the conservative cause. Other conservatives stayed at Princeton, including Machen's friends Hodge and Armstrong. But they did not have to endure the hostility that he had. For Machen, remaining at Princeton would have meant working with Erdman and Stevenson and remembering the sting of their criticisms. A clean break was required not just to preserve Old Princeton, as Machen argued, but also to heal these personal wounds. Princeton moderates and church officials may have interpreted the seminary's reorganization as an organizational improvement, but Machen's experience suggested that the impersonal bureaucracy of large denominations could be ruthlessly personal.[60]

# CHAPTER SIX

# The Responsibility of the Church
# in the New Age

The choice before the American Protestant churches is plain. They must choose the [ultimate] frame of reference or the frame of reference supplied by American culture. If they choose the latter they will forfeit their right to speak in the name of the Christian faith. In so far as they continue to use that name they will be false witnesses who have betrayed their trust and are misleading people.   *Francis P. Miller (1935)*

When Machen decided to leave Princeton and found a small rival seminary it looked to some like the desperate move of an individual alienated from the religious and cultural mainstream. Coinciding as it did with the stock market crash of 1929, Machen's departure from Princeton also suggested a kind of religious militancy that would appeal to the socioeconomic dislocations of the 1930s. An otherworldly theology, with its assurance that the travails of this life are insignificant compared to the rewards that await the faithful in the next, some have thought, was a reassuring message for life during the Depression.[1]

The Great Depression did in fact contribute to the abandonment of old-line Protestant churches by fundamentalists. At least some conservatives interpreted America's financial ruin as a sure sign of God's judgment and in turn dedicated themselves to new evangelistic and missionary efforts. Economic hardship, many fundamentalists concluded, taught that the social gospel of the old-line churches was neither workable nor true. Instead of offering solutions to economic and political problems, fundamentalists insisted that saving individuals was the primary responsibility of Christians. Nevertheless, some could not abandon social responsibilities entirely and hoped that evangelism would restore the nation's moral foundation and eventually lead to prosperity.[2]

Fundamentalists were not alone in seeing religious meaning in the Depression. After the crash, a number of younger Protestant theologians reassessed liberal Protestant confidence in human nature and society. Reinhold Niebuhr of Union Seminary (New York), H. Richard Niebuhr of Yale Divinity School, Walter Marshall Horton of Oberlin College, Walter Lowrie, an Episcopal minister, and Wilhelm Pauck of Chicago Theological Seminary all contributed to a school of thought sometimes called "Neoorthodoxy" but perhaps more accurately labeled "theological realism." Whatever the name, these theologians' criticisms of Protestant liberalism echoed those of fundamentalists. Horton charged that Protestant ministers had too often studied social science rather than the Bible and had reduced Jesus to a moralist. Pauck accused liberals of abandoning Christianity for humanism, an "atheistic movement." Meanwhile, H. Richard Niebuhr concluded that liberalism taught no more than "a God without wrath" bringing "men without sin into a kingdom without judgment through the ministrations of a Christ without a cross." These theologians called upon the churches, in light of America's social crisis, to take their cues not from the progress of human history but from traditional Christian sources of truth.[3]

As much as Machen's move to Westminster echoed the cultural pessimism of Neoorthodoxy and fundamentalism, several aspects of the seminary's opening suggest that his decision did not entirely stem from feelings of desperation. For one thing, the new seminary's curriculum and aims did not repudiate the ideal of a learned ministry as many fundamentalist institutions did. Rather than founding a Bible institute that reduced educational requirements in order to hasten evangelistic activity before the end of the age, Machen established a seminary that required a liberal education, followed the traditional theological curriculum, and was designed to prepare Presbyterian ministers for routine parish work. The seminary's finances also revealed an important difference between Westminster and other fundamentalist operations. Despite rapid fluctuations on the New York Stock Exchange and the need to raise $50,000 to $60,000 in operating costs for the first year alone, Westminster opened its doors on September 25, 1929, only one month before the crash on Black Thursday, thanks in large part to Machen's own wealth. While many fundamentalist Bible schools depended on tuition and small donations from the faithful, Westminster still had sufficient contacts with privileged Protestantism to secure large contributions from wealthy donors.[4]

Nevertheless, Machen's move to Westminster and its repercussions for the Presbyterian Church did not take place independent of social realities. In fact, his decision stemmed from ideas about the relationship between the church and society that antagonized the leaders of mainstream Protestantism. As much as Machen had in common with fundamentalists and theological realists, his break with the Northern Presbyterian Church—a process that began with his move to Westminster and culminated in the founding of a new denomination, the Orthodox Presbyterian Church, in 1936—derived less from pessimism about America's future than from an alternative perspective on the place and function of religion in a liberal society. Since the time that he had moved to New Jersey as a student, Machen's affiliation with the Democratic party and his opinions about the role of the church in society put him at odds with Northern Presbyterians who were overwhelmingly Republican and believed the church had a right and responsibility to regulate public life. As a vocal civil libertarian Machen believed that Protestantism should not enjoy a privileged position in public affairs. As a Presbyterian confessionalist who defended the separation of church and state he also questioned the church's advocacy of specific political measures.[5]

In order to understand Machen's involvement in the Presbyterian struggles of the 1930s which culminated in his starting a new denomination, then, it is necessary first to examine his quirky political views. The Presbyterian controversy was intimately bound up with divergent ideas about the role of the church in American society. Although Machen's founding of a small, marginal Presbyterian denomination paralleled fundamentalist disillusionment with American society and the conservative exodus from mainline churches, it actually reflected his understanding of the relationship between religion and public life.

When H. L. Mencken first commented on Machen in the pages of the *American Mercury* he took some delight pointing out the fundamentalist's politics. Machen "is a Democrat and a wet," Mencken observed, "and may be presumed to have voted for Al in 1928." While Machen had never written publicly about his political preferences, his opposition to Prohibition would have been common knowledge in Baltimore. That city was the site of the 1926 Presbyterian General Assembly where denominational officials had used Machen's opposition to the Eighteenth Amendment to block his election to the chair of apologetics and ethics at Princeton Seminary. Mencken's newspaper, the *Baltimore Sun* had covered that controversy and noted the irony of the Presbyterian proceedings that pitted "dry modernists" against a "wet fundamentalist." Mencken would have also known of Machen's older brother's stand against Prohibition. Arthur W. Machen, Jr., was chairman of the Maryland branch of the National Association against the Prohibition Amendment and was the defense attorney in the much-publicized case of Congressman John Philip Hill, who was tried for the illegal manufacturing of liquor. Still, Machen's reasons for opposing Prohibition, as Mencken noted, were religious as well as political. Machen was a "wet," Mencken suspected, "simply because the Yahweh of the Old Testament and the Jesus of the New are both wet—because the whole Bible, in fact, is wet."[6]

Prohibition had been crucial to the 1928 presidential contest between the Republican Herbert Hoover and the Democratic nominee, Al Smith, who openly supported repeal of the Eighteenth Amendment, and it was the major reason why Machen voted for Smith. The politics of Prohibition, moreover, were closely tied to religious differences. Americans of British descent overwhelmingly chose Hoover, the Protestant, over Smith, the first Roman Catholic candidate for president. The 1928 election became a referendum on whether, in the words of the French observer André Siegfried, America would remain "Protestant and Anglo-Saxon." Protestants who normally avoided politics, Southern Baptists, Missouri Synod Lutherans, as well as fundamentalists, joined old-line Protestants in repudiating Smith. Machen's decision to vote for Smith was indicative of the divergence between his own social outlook and those of other Protestants.[7]

Civil libertarianism gave Machen additional reasons for supporting Smith. The Princeton professor had followed carefully and opposed strenuously educational reforms initiated during the late 1910s and early 1920s that eliminated foreign-language instruction in primary schools and made English mandatory. This legislation, which by 1919 had been passed in fifteen states, was just one prong of a more general effort by Americans of British descent to assimilate immigrants. Machen knew firsthand the value of an early acquaintance with classical languages and argued against the restriction of primary school instruction to English. Furthermore, he thought such legislation a direct challenge to civil and religious liberty. Such laws were an indication of the general "impoverishment of human life" and not substantially different from coercive measures in Germany and czarist Russia. State regulation of primary education constituted a threat not just to private but also to religious schools and violated a fundamental principle of religious liberty that extended "equal rights" to all religious and ethnic groups. When Al Smith led the initiative to repeal New York's laws regulating language instruction Machen wrote two letters of support to the New York governor. Smith responded that "in the humdrum of official life it is very pleasing to know that a man's efforts are appreciated."[8]

Opposition to Prohibition and primary school language legislation were just two examples of Machen's antistatist libertarianism. On a variety of issues he defended individual freedoms against the coercive power of government. Indeed, his defense of freedom was more typical of the noninterventionist variety of libertarianism that existed in the 1930s and 1940s rather than the defense of laissez-faire economic policies that has been typical of libertarianism since World War II. For instance, on the eve of America's entry into World War I Machen opposed military conscription as a permanent policy, arguing that it was a "radical step" against liberty. In 1925 he criticized a proposal requiring the registration of aliens for introducing into America a "full-fledged European police system." At the same time, Machen opposed legislation calling for the fingerprinting of suspected racketeers because its logical outworking would mean "police control of the movements of innocent people." So firm was his commitment to individual freedoms that in the midst of his hectic life during the 1930s he testified before Philadelphia's City Council against jaywalking laws.[9]

Still, Machen believed that civil liberties should be constrained by local institutions such as families and local government, a belief that showed some sympathy for the communitarian and spiritual concerns of social and cultural traditionalism. As much as Machen advocated civil freedoms and voluntary association, he did so primarily to defend families and religious groups, not just individuals, from the expansion of the state. His opposition to federal legislation, then, was not aimed simply at preserving personal freedom but also local communities and private initiative. Machen's defense of localism was most evident in his involvement with the Sentinels of the Republic, an organization founded to oppose Prohibition specifically and the growth of the federal government more generally. As an executive-committee member of the Sentinels, Machen spoke out against the child labor amendment, arguing that it put the family, "the formative and most important part of human life," under the "despotic control" of congressional bureaus. For similar reasons he contested the creation of a federal department of education and testified before Congress in 1926 under the Sentinel's auspices. While wary of flawed educational policies in individual states, Machen believed that consolidating power at the federal level would extend harmful reforms throughout the country and grant too much power to federal authorities. Competition between public and private schools and between different state systems, he believed, would improve education and make schools more responsive to local and family concerns.[10]

While Machen fought legislation that increased the size and power of federal government, he was also critical of the cultural Protestantism that often informed such reforms. Thus, while many viewed fundamentalist opposition to evolution as a threat to the freedom of public school instruction, Machen took aim at the Protestant moralism that pervaded government-sponsored education. He teamed up with Roman Catholics to oppose the introduction of character education into public school curricula and recommended that public schools stick to their proper function—"the impartation of knowledge." The only permissible form of moral guidance was the daily example of the teacher in the normal workings of the classroom. A religious or philosophical grounding for morality, however, violated the public character of government schools.[11]

By similar logic, Machen objected to prayer and Bible reading in public schools. Such practices, in his view, not only violated the separation of church and state but also obliterated real and significant differences between religions. Trying to find selected ethical teachings from the Bible upon which Protestants, Catholics, and Jews could agree was hopeless and resulted in making "even the best of books" to say "the exact opposite of what it means." The only satisfactory solution for religious instruction in public schools was a system of release time, where parents, if they chose, could provide for their children's religious upbringing. Even here, Machen cautioned that the state should not give credit nor should it attempt to regulate religious instruction imparted outside school.[12]

The admixture of public and religious interests was objectionable to Machen not just because it threatened the free exercise of religion but also because it corrupted belief itself. Thus, Machen extended his critique of the mainline churches to include Protestant assumptions about the Christian character of American society which often equated Protestantism with the ideals of liberty, equality, and civic virtue. He believed that historic Christianity was fundamentally narrow, exclusive, and partisan and, therefore, could not provide the basis for public life in a free society. To do so, he argued, was to mistake ethics for salvation. Using Christian morals to promote public duties gave the faulty impression that people could do good without grace. "When any hope is held out to lost humanity from the so-called ethical portions of the Bible apart from its great redemptive core, then the Bible is represented as saying the direct opposite of what it really says." This was precisely the danger that Machen perceived in the mainstream churches' support for social reform. Christians and churches could still endeavor to correct society but would have to do so from a basis upon which believers and nonbelievers could agree.[13]

Machen's opposition to a politics of morality stemmed from more than a concern to maintain proper boundaries between public and religious spheres. He objected to many initiatives, whether advocated by the church or state, because he believed the society they produced was fundamentally inhuman. Although he appreciated the scholarly and material benefits that science had yielded, he criticized the modern effort to solve individual and social problems through scientific methods. The modern world, Machen conceded, undoubtedly afforded enormous material and physical improvements, but in the realm of the human spirit there had been a "lamentable decline." Contemporary art and literature underscored the hollowness of modern life. Rather than celebrating improvements in the "external conditions of life" artists focused on the uncertainty of human existence. "Modern inventions in the material realm" were themselves valueless, drab, and empty unless used in the expression of spiritual reality.[14]

For Machen the "unprecedented" decline in art was only a symptom of the much deeper problem of utilitarianism. He lamented that the fundamental criterion for evaluating a particular policy, institution, or law was whether it contributed to social stability and physical well-being. Modern government was reducing idiosyncrasies of human personality and the range of individual freedom in the interest of the common good. Socialism was one example of utilitarianism. But such thinking was also evident in Western democracies where legislatures determined what was beneficial and forced their "'welfare' . . . ruthlessly upon the individual." Machen feared that "healthy hatred of being governed," formerly so strong in America, was being lost. "No interference is resented to day, no menace to family life, no government monopoly, if only it be thought to confer physical benefits."[15]

State control of primary and secondary education and the child labor amendment were two paternalistic programs, Machen thought, which regulated individual freedom and responsibility in the interest of an efficient and orderly society. Those who advocated standardizing public and private education, and desired greater regulation of children, he believed, whether consciously or not, were espousing views as old as Plato's *Republic*, ideas that made children the possession of the state and made the state's welfare the aim of education. In the short run standardization and efficiency might contribute to the stability of the state and yield an orderly life. But in the long run they would, as Machen believed was happening in Hitler's Germany, have the opposite effect. "A nation is the more stable the looser its control is over individual lives." For this reason, the life of any society ultimately depended on the "moral qualities of its individual citizens." Whereas bureaucracy destroyed moral fiber by narrowing individual choice, liberty ultimately provided the most stable society.[16]

For all of Machen's political convictions he lacked a coherent social philosophy beyond championing personal freedoms and a weak government. He rarely thought in terms of national or federal programs for fear of what those programs would do to local autonomy and customs. Machen believed the state's principle duty was to preserve the liberty of individuals, families, and private associations. In turn, families, communities, and voluntary organizations performed the lion's share of social services and preserved public order. Machen's political instincts were a throwback to the Jeffersonian republic where a hardworking and self-reliant middle class formed the backbone of society, and government was at best a crutch and potential source of tyranny. According to Machen, Jefferson may have been a freethinker, but he held "quite rightly . . . that the least governed people is the best governed." Machen even went so far as to say that "no people is fit to govern itself if it does not hate to be governed." Genuine freedom, therefore, involved the hatred of "restraint," "government interference," "inquisitorial measures of all kind," and the conviction that government was not intended to produce happiness but to prevent happiness from "being interfered with by wicked men."[17]

While libertarian views were unusual in a conservative Protestant, they make more sense when seen in the context of the broader cultural ferment of the 1920s and 1930s. Many Americans at this time were becoming increasingly uncomfortable with the expansion of the state. Efforts to create the federal department of education, for instance, elicited a sharp reaction against federal power that united such diverse constituencies as the Catholic Church, states' rights politicians, former Progressives, and Machen's own Sentinels of the Republic. Other education reforms as well as Prohibition, the child labor amendment, and the 1928 presidential election aroused antistatist sentiments and brought to the surface long-standing cultural divisions that ran along religious and ethnic lines. Machen was one of the few fundamentalists of British stock to be found consistently on the antistatist side of this divide. Even some of his closest allies in the Northern Presbyterian Church, whose Scotch-Irish heritage might have made them more sympathetic to minorities, endorsed Americanization. Had Machen grown up in the North he probably would have supported many of these measures. But his identification with the South prompted him to oppose the social agenda of nativist Protestantism.[18]

Ironically, despite his Southern sympathies and political affiliation, Machen joined the Sentinels of the Republic, an association that consisted largely of Massachusetts Republican business elites, as the primary outlet for his political views. This anomaly was not lost on Machen who confessed surprise that he would be "so close" to Yankees. Still, his membership in the Sentinels reveals another source of hostility to the state that transcended region. Other conservative intellectuals strongly opposed the expansion of the federal government because of fears about the tyranny of mass society. The New Humanist and Harvard classicist Irving Babbitt saw in many political reforms a departure from the system of checks and balances established by the U.S. Constitution and loathed the self-righteous moralism of progressive campaigns that appropriated the language of the kingdom of heaven to meddle in other people's privacy. So too, the debunker H. L. Mencken often noted the hypocrisy of "reformers" and "liberals" who in the name of freedom allowed "the inferior mass to pull down all men to their level." Similarly, Albert Jay Nock, essayist and civil libertarian, was critical of centralized government and believed that most if not all humanitarian reforms made physical existence paramount and gave people the illusion of security in exchange for freedom. The Southern Agrarian movement voiced another critique of mass society that attributed America's rootlessness and fragmentation to its materialistic and moralistic values. Although these intellectuals lacked a common political philosophy and disagreed about religious and aesthetic issues, they shared the belief that the most important aspects of human existence transcended physical well-being. Mass society and modern politics, in their view, had abandoned the higher ranges of human life for social utility and submerged ethnic, regional, and cultural differences into a homogeneous mass culture.[19]

Like these intellectuals, Machen objected to the increasing growth of the federal government under Franklin Delano Roosevelt, comparing it to Russia's "soul-crushing tyranny" and Germany's "fiendish wickedness." American government was treating civil liberty as if a "passing phase of life." The president's packing of the Supreme Court, moreover, was another example of the inalienable rights of the "humblest citizen" being superseded by economic and social programs. When it came to specific economic reforms, such as the contrasting merits of a managed currency or the gold standard, Machen charged Washington with dishonesty for failing to honor its debts and declare bankruptcy. Freedom had been forfeited for the security of "fed beasts in a stable" where all the higher ranges of human life were "crushed by an all-powerful State." Despite surface similarities between Machen's opposition to the New Deal and the hostility to big government associated with fundamentalists on the far right, such as William Dudley Pelley, Gerald B. Winrod, Gerald L. K. Smith, and William Bell Riley, there were important differences. While Machen defended local communities, voluntary associations, and religious freedom from the intrusion of federal regulations, fundamentalist politicians castigated the New Deal for abandoning Christian nationalism, harboring Jews, and not doing enough to redistribute America's wealth.[20]

One source of the political differences between Machen and other fundamentalists was economic. Most conservative Protestant politicians of the 1930s came from lower-middle-class backgrounds and represented the interests of small business. Machen, in contrast, lived comfortably as a bachelor on a salary of $2,500, inherited $50,000 (chiefly in stocks and other investments) from both sides of his family that continued to pay dividends throughout the 1930s (approximately $6,500 in 1936), and readily identified with the social status of the upper middle class. Nevertheless, he was generous with his wealth, giving to a variety of civic, cultural, and humanitarian institutions and organizations. The greatest outlet for Machen's generosity was the conservative cause in the Presbyterian Church and especially the seminary he helped to found. Machen used much of his inherited assets to finance Westminster. Receipts indicate that Machen contributed as much as $10,000 quarterly during the seminary's early years and that he underwrote over one-third of the seminary's budget during the first year alone.[21]

Furthermore, Machen was not unresponsive to poverty around him. He and another Princeton clergyman, Sylvester W. Beach, provided guidance and financial support from 1910 to 1933 to Richard Hodges, an elderly, unemployed alcoholic from Princeton. Machen found a Presbyterian family in rural southern New Jersey with whom Hodges could live and sent money to Hodges's landlords for rent, food, clothing, and spending money. When the older man died, Machen paid his funeral expenses and bought his cemetery plot. Machen and Hodges corresponded regularly during these years, an exchange that usually consisted of news of each other's lives, leavened with spiritual counsel from Machen. This was the kind of paternalism that Machen could stomach. It was free from bureaucratic red tape, involved a personal and sustained relationship, and most important, resulted from compassion, not coercion.[22]

Nevertheless, when speaking on social matters Machen could sound incredibly insensitive, especially in the context of the Depression. Just as the debunking of H. L. Mencken appeared to change from a liberating force for young intellectuals in the 1920s to a reactionary conservatism for those same intellectuals who in the 1930s embraced the left, so Machen's criticism of the moralism and paternalism of government, while echoing the cultural criticism of the 1920s, seemed naive if not heartless in the next decade. In fact, criticizing government programs designed to alleviate human suffering could easily be construed as a denial of the need for a strong state to check corporate and private interests. Machen acknowledged the good that a powerful central government might achieve by restraining big business but still advocated liberty and small government no matter how problematic. For him, the evils of uniformity and paternalism were far greater than any good the state might accomplish. Government programs in the end merely dealt with external and physical conditions while denying the importance of the "finer aspirations of humanity." The so-called impractical areas of life, thus, turned out for Machen to be vitally practical. What society needed was not more government programs but independent and self-reliant citizens who could think and act for themselves and see their own existence from a broader perspective. Machen's quixotic ideal was a factory worker who read Tennyson and Horace in his leisure time. Presumably that same worker would be consoled by literature while standing in line for soup and bread.[23]

Machen's social views, it should be noted, were not marginal. New York's newspapers regularly published his letters about politics and Machen continued to participate in a variety of academic networks. But his ideas did not escape criticism. One of his many missives despairing the loss of liberty and printed by the *New York Herald Tribune* responded to a petition from President Roosevelt to all ministers and church leaders for support of Social Security legislation. Machen argued that the president's program undermined a vital conviction of any healthy society—that the receiving of government aid "is a thing to be avoided with might and main." Compulsory government insurance would ultimately make slaves of the poor and paupers of all Americans. Machen also objected to the "low moral plane" on which the Roosevelt administration stood. Its monetary policy had broken down the sanctity of private and public contracts and encouraged the view that "solemn obligations" were to be kept only when "convenient." This amounted to nothing more than the principle that "might makes right."[24]

Machen's rebuke to Roosevelt caught the attentive eye of the popular syndicated New York columnist Heywood Broun. Broun thought it extraordinary that a Christian minister could oppose social security and "bridle" even at the mild form in which Roosevelt had presented it. He was even more amazed that Machen, a New Testament professor, had failed to heed Christ's advice in the story of the rich young ruler that the wealthy should give to the poor. Had Machen encountered the young man, Broun conjectured, he would have sent him away "rejoicing" because according to the professor the state's first duty was to protect "this admirable young fellow in his property rights" and to assure him that his own wealth would be "kept inviolate lest class distinctions be diminished." Broun's parting shot, ironically a form of argument Machen had used against liberal Protestants, cautioned Westminster students that they would someday have to choose between "the words of Jesus Christ and those of J. Gresham Machen."[25]

Machen responded to Broun and similar criticisms by noting the fundamental difference between the ethics of Christianity and those of socialism, whether the "complete" variety of the Soviet Union or the "partial" type of the New Deal. Jesus did not say to the rich young ruler, Machen noted, "Take the goods of that rich young ruler by force, sell them and distribute them among yourselves." Rather Jesus appealed to the wealthy to give freely to people in need. The fundamental difference between the Christian and the socialist was that the latter tried to accomplish by force what the former sought to accomplish by love. As Machen explained in a different forum, he was "dead opposed" to people who talked glibly about taking the profit motive out of industry. That motive, along with every other human ambition, should not be denied but consecrated. To seek success in business for its own sake was in Machen's estimate "highly un-Christian." But to seek profit for the good that it enabled an individual to do was "truly Christian." Rather than redistributing wealth by force, Christians should ask the rich to give to the poor as an act of compassion, thereby reducing the stigma usually associated with receiving aid.[26]

An invitation in 1932 to address the Academy of Political and Social Science on the church's responsibility during the Depression gave Machen the opportunity to make the connections between his religious and social views all the more explicit. On this occasion John A. Ryan, a Roman Catholic priest and professor of moral theology at Catholic University, and William H. Fineshriber, a Reformed rabbi from Philadelphia, gave alternative religious perspectives. The address that Machen delivered, "The Responsibility of the Church in the New Age," was significant because it revealed the connection between his social views and his opposition to liberal Protestantism.

In his remarks Machen hurried through the church's positive tasks. A true Christian church should be "radically doctrinal," "radically intolerant," and "radically ethical." The first two traits were standard fare. What Machen meant by being ethical was that the church should never be satisfied with "mere philanthropy." To be sure, it should respond to the physical needs of Christians and non-Christians alike. But the church should not be content with dispensing "creature comforts" or a "vague natural religion." Instead, it should seek to bring all people without exception, "high and low, rich and poor, learned and ignorant, compatriot and alien," into the "full warmth and joy" of the church.[27]

These positive tasks put direct limits on the mission of the church. First, the church could not be expected to participate with non-Christian religions in a program of ethical culture. "There is no such thing," Machen insisted, "as a universally valid fund of religious principles" upon which Christians and non-Christians could build. Against such programs, a true Christian church would seek from the state religious liberty for all parents to bring up their children according to the "dictates of their conscience." Second, the church should not make official pronouncements about political or social issues nor should it cooperate with the state in anything involving the use of force. Individual Christians could assist the state in a variety of ways. But the weapons of the church against evil were "spiritual, not carnal" and by becoming a "political lobby" the church turned aside from its proper tasks. The responsibility of the church in the new age, therefore, was the same as it always had been: to testify that the world was lost in sin and that salvation from such misery, whether for individuals or nations, could only come through Christ.[28]

Machen conceded that this was an unpopular and impractical message and that it was seldom heard in prominent Protestant churches, many of which he believed had become no more than agencies for the propagation of a vague moralism. The gospel rarely carried the weight of important institutions or the "pomp of numbers" and was often hidden away in "individual congregations resisting the central ecclesiastical mechanisms." Nevertheless, the message of sin and grace was precisely what the mechanical and metallic civilization of the modern age needed. The craze for efficiency and standardization as well as the desire to alleviate physical distress had led to the neglect of "unseen things." But the gospel restored a proper perspective on what was permanently valuable. For this reason, Machen thought the paradox of Christianity especially pertinent to modern life. "This world's problems can never be solved . . . if you think that this world is all. To move the world you must have a place to stand."[29]

This view of the church comported well with the Southern Presbyterian idea of the spirituality of the church, a concept forged during nineteenth-century debates over slavery. Many Southern Presbyterian divines taught that the church, because a spiritual entity, should not meddle in political affairs. Machen drew on this tradition when he stated that the church's tasks were strictly spiritual: to preach the word, administer the sacraments, and nurture believers. It had, as a corporate body, no obligation, except in extreme circumstances, to intervene in social matters. Yet this understanding of the church also reflected Machen's humanistic and political outlook. For him the fundamental aspect of human existence was spiritual and eternal, not temporal or material well-being. In the end, society could not be improved unless the religious needs of individuals, families, and communities became priorities. And with other established institutions attending to other aspects of human existence, the church, he reasoned, could hardly abandon the spiritual task.[30]

Thus, Machen's political views buttressed his Presbyterian confessionalism and put him outside the fold of both fundamentalists and mainstream Protestants who, while disagreeing on the means, shared a commitment to preserving Christian civilization in America. Machen's opposition to the social vision of the mainline churches was clear enough. By sanctioning political centralization, the social gospel minimized the importance of individual salvation, often abridged religious freedoms, and undermined the dignity, freedom, and responsibility of the individual, family, and voluntary association. Less clear were Machen's differences with fundamentalists. To be sure, Machen believed, as most conservatives did, that genuine social reform only began with the transformation of individuals. Yet most fundamentalists showed little hesitation to resort to politics in order to promote their beliefs in the public square. In contrast, Machen said that individuals, families, and private organizations of all faiths should have the freedom and responsibility to direct their own affairs. These differences with Presbyterians on the left and the right, as it turned out, were crucial to the denominational struggles of the 1930s that concluded his career.

By the time of his address before the American Academy of Political and Social Science Machen had become increasingly lonely and embittered. In the fall of 1931, his mother died. His relationship to her had been one of a close confidante as well as that of a dutiful son. Whatever obligations Machen felt as the only single son of his widowed mother, Minnie Gresham Machen had undoubtedly been a source of stability, affection, and joy. Her death—in one letter of bereavement Machen described her as "the wisest and best human being I ever knew"—left a vacuum in his life. Furthermore, Machen's move to Philadelphia removed him from warm friendships at Princeton, especially with William Park Armstrong and Caspar Wistar Hodge and their families. Machen still corresponded with his Princeton colleagues and visited them on trips to his old home, but the informal and unexpected contacts that came from living in close proximity to friends were gone. While his relations with faculty and students at Westminster were good, they obviously lacked the history and intimacy of family and Princeton friendships.[31]

Machen's loss fed feelings of antagonism toward the Presbyterian Church. His perception that Princeton Seminary had defected from the cause of orthodoxy because of meddling Presbyterian bureaucrats who were more concerned with image than substance predisposed him for a confrontation with the church. The move from Princeton, an institution he had labored to sustain for twenty-three years, made separation from the church likely if not inevitable. Throughout the 1920s Machen had followed the lead of his senior colleagues at the seminary who sought to preserve Princeton through proper channels. The lesson that Machen took away from Princeton was that the course of propriety had cost conservatives their sole institution and had obfuscated the issues dividing the church. From the Princeton reorganization on, Machen would be more willing to strike out on his own, both in the establishment of institutions and in voicing complaints not approved by his allies. Westminster Seminary was just one example of this secessionist impulse. If Machen had grown up in the Northern church or if conservatives had been able to retain control of Princeton, a different outcome might have resulted. As it happened, Machen came to believe that the same problems afflicting American society—the loss of personal freedom and intellectual integrity at the expense of bureaucratic centralization and efficiency—were destroying the Presbyterian Church. And as the denomination tried to recover from the controversies of the 1920s, Machen's contrary social views only aggravated the religious cleavage among Presbyterians.

The specific issue that led to a showdown between Machen and church authorities was foreign missions. In 1932 the controversial "Layman's Inquiry," *Re-Thinking Missions,* a one-volume condensation of a seven-volume study of world missions, suggested and financed by John D. Rockefeller, Jr., was published. For two years a fifteen-member commission surveyed missions in India, Burma, Japan, and China. The editor of the project and chief author of *Re-Thinking Missions* was William Ernest Hocking, Harvard professor of philosophy. His vision for missions—"world understanding on the spiritual level"—drew immediate fire from conservatives in several denominations. The aim of missions, according to Hocking, was to seek with people of other lands "a true knowledge and love of God" and express in life and word "what we have learned through Jesus Christ." He also believed that Christianity was the fulfillment of other religions, a view that greatly expanded the religious value of humanitarian services such as education and medicine. While the Institute for Social and Religious Research endorsed Hocking's conclusions, denominational missions boards tried to finesse the controversial nature of the report.[32]

Machen's reaction was predictable. From beginning to end, the report was an "attack upon the historic Christian Faith." The reaction of the Presbyterian Board of Foreign Missions was especially alarming. Although the report was not officially approved by the denomination, the original committee responsible for the study had two members from the Presbyterian board on it. When the report was issued, Machen argued, the church had a right to know whether the board rejected or accepted it. But rather than clarifying their attitude, they "dodged the issue." Presbyterian officials affirmed an "abiding loyalty" to missions and used Hocking's words to describe the aim of their calling: "loyalty to Jesus Christ, regarded as the perfect revelation of God and the only way by which men can reach a satisfying experience of Him." In one letter Machen wrote, "the sad thing" was that the board considered "such pitiful stuff" to be the gospel. The board also went on to declare confidence in Presbyterian missionaries and in their own ability to run the agency. Machen believed that the board should have condemned *Re-Thinking Missions*. "Did ever a trumpet in time of battle, in a time when the very citadel of the Faith had been attacked," he asked, "give forth a feebler sound?"[33]

Missions officials unwittingly provided conservatives with more ammunition when one of their prominent missionaries, the novelist Pearl Buck, lavished praise upon Hocking's report in an article for *Christian Century*. She called *Re-Thinking Missions* "a masterly statement" of religion's place in modern life, and of Christianity's relation to world religions. Then in early 1933, writing for *Harper's*, Buck labeled older ideas about salvation "superstitious" and concluded that traditional reasons for missions were "gone." What concerned Machen again was not Buck's statements as much as the missions board's reaction to them. He noted that she had raised "in the most definite and public way" the question whether the board would sanction views that were diametrically opposed to Presbyterian standards. The board's proper response should have been to say plainly that it was "irrevocably committed to the message which Mrs. Buck has attacked," that it would not "solicit a single penny from those who [agreed] with her," and that it could not tolerate among its missionaries "any such anti-Christian propaganda." Yet rather than condemning Buck's views, he said, the board kept silent. Such maneuvering was "dishonest" and destroyed whatever confidence conservatives might have in the board.[34]

Thus, the missions controversy of the 1930s replayed the same arguments and scripted a set of characters similar to the Presbyterian controversy from the preceding decade. This time the liberal role was played not by a New York preacher but by the Harvard professor Hocking. For Machen, again the conservative protagonist, *Re-Thinking Missions* was another clear instance of religious liberalism that deserved condemnation not just from local pulpits but from the church's central agencies. This situation left evangelical moderates uncomfortably trying to act out the role of mediator. Conservatives, like Machen, admitted that the Presbyterian mission board's failure to condemn Hocking's and Buck's remarks did not necessarily mean that all of its members were modernists. But it did suggest a willingness to tolerate deviant views in order to avoid controversy and to preserve the unity of the church. Consequently, just as in the 1920s when the moderately conservative Charles Erdman had been the object of Machen's ire, in the 1930s the popular, charismatic, and evangelical Robert E. Speer, secretary of the Board of Foreign Missions, served as the target for the Westminster professor's attacks.[35]

Although this controversy concerned the nature and rationale of missions, it was also personal. Several other Presbyterian agencies could also have been accused of the feeble witness that Machen saw in the missions board but none of them had both of the conservatives' nemeses. Charles Erdman was the board's president and, even though he kept a low profile during the controversy, no doubt his presence on the board was a factor in Machen's opposition. Speer, who because of his long career in missions became the denomination's spokesman, also had a history of conflict with Machen. In one letter Machen recalled how, as a young man, he had "almost worshipped the ground" on which the former Princeton football star had walked. In all likelihood, as a college student Machen, during a visit to the summer conferences at Northfield, Massachusetts, had been captivated by Speer, a gifted speaker and effective recruiter of undergraduates for the Student Volunteer Movement. However, his estimate of Speer soured during the 1920s. Speer served on the Special Commission of 1925 whose report denied the legitimacy of conservative criticisms, presided over the 1927 General Assembly where the Special Commission's report was approved, and as an influential trustee of Princeton Seminary had favored reorganization. For Machen, evangelical moderates like Speer were even more dangerous than theological liberals because they could reassure conservatives while cutting deals with modernists.[36]

Machen tried his hand at denominational politics for the first time in response to what he saw as the missions board's lubricity. At the April 1933 meeting of the New Brunswick presbytery, Machen submitted a four-point overture designed to overhaul the board's personnel and revive its theological zeal. He explained to a friend that it was not right for him to be "egging other people on" with his books when he took no "ecclesiastical step" himself. After he submitted the proposal, another minister suggested that Speer come to the presbytery's next meeting and answer Machen's charges. Machen had long wanted an open and frank discussion but as it turned out the debate, which some hoped would turn into a theological donnybrook, only fizzled.[37]

Machen's charges ranged from the board's pacifist stance on *Re-Thinking Missions* and Pearl Buck to a detailed list of the ways in which the board encouraged theological inclusivism and interdenominational cooperation. To some his charges seemed like nitpicking but Machen's specificity was an effort to compensate for his failure in the 1920s to name names and provide examples. In contrast, Speer wanted to avoid controversy. The important question, he said, was what action was "just and right" for the good of the church and in accord with "the mind of Christ." He read a prepared statement and responded to Machen's accusations only by saying they were "unfair and unjust at the present time." Speer also defended the board's integrity, declaring that it had shown itself a "bulwark" of Christian witness. After Speer's performance, Machen's overture was defeated and the presbytery adopted a resolution expressing confidence in the board.[38]

The Machen-Speer debate illustrated again the tension that had plagued the church throughout the 1920s between the confessionalism of Presbyterian traditionalists and the moderate evangelicalism of denominational leaders. As a proponent and example of Victorian Protestantism's sentimental piety, Speer tended to be content with vague Christian affirmations as long as they stemmed from wholesome motives and produced positive results. Such an outlook was well suited for a denominational administrator intent on preventing the church from splintering. Consequently, evangelical moderates such as Speer and Erdman were generally sympathetic to religious modernists as long as they avoided extreme views and displayed a cooperative spirit. Conservatives deserved rougher treatment because they were divisive and combative. Machen, who because of his academic training and religious outlook was aware of and underscored different theological perspectives within Presbyterian discourse, was just such a troublemaker. His hostility toward slippery or evasive language was another sign to moderates of his less-than-Christian temperament.[39]

After the 1933 General Assembly defeated a proposal similar to Machen's overture and vindicated Speer and the missions board, Machen and other conservatives decided to form a new missions agency, the Independent Board for Presbyterian Foreign Missions, which consisted of fifteen ministers, five elders, and five women. For one committed to Presbyterian order, Machen's decision was controversial. The new board took the unconventional step of conducting missionary activities without church supervision. Forming the new board was also an act of desperation. For even though Machen believed he had not violated church law, the renegade missions agency strained his own understanding of Presbyterian procedure. The board was clearly designed to expose the tyranny of the denomination's bureaucracy and divide the church between liberals and conservatives. As a result, he lost most of his credibility within the denomination. Even so, he saw no difference between an independent missions agency and an independent Presbyterian seminary. If denominational officials had not objected to Westminster, why was the independent board so offensive? Thus, while the missions controversy started out as a religious dispute, it became a legal and organizational battle where, by Machen's lights, the church again chose administrative over theological solutions.[40]

Yet, while irregular by denominational standards, the independent board revealed Machen's commitment to Presbyterian principles. He detested the "sickly interdenominationalism" of fundamentalism and stressed the new board's Presbyterian over its independent identity. The best way to guard against liberalism, he believed, was not through an interdenominational union of conservatives but rather through fidelity to historic Protestant creeds, reinforced by strong church ties. Thus, Machen had little sympathy for fundamentalist organizations that took a low view of the church. Instead, he identified most with Christian groups such as the Lutherans and the Christian Reformed who maintained their "ecclesiastical distinctness." He repeatedly counseled conservatives in all denominations not to abandon their confessional loyalties. For this reason the independent board's charter pledged to conduct and establish missions that propagated and defended the Westminster Confession and the "fundamental principles of Presbyterian church government." Machen was also convinced that the new board did not violate Presbyterian law. Even though it was not under denominational supervision, Presbyterian polity did not forbid the support of independent religious agencies.[41]

Despite the new board's independence, however, church officials correctly interpreted it as a rival to the old one. While the Presbyterian Church had allowed members and ministers to work in non-Presbyterian missions agencies, Machen's board, according to Lewis Mudge, the General Assembly's stated clerk, subverted Presbyterian law by undertaking "administrative functions within the church without official authorization." Mudge counseled various church agencies not to license or ordain Westminster Seminary graduates until they pledged to support the official work of the church. In September 1933, New Brunswick, Machen's presbytery, resolved that all ministerial candidates be examined on their loyalty to the regularly authorized boards and agencies of denomination, especially the Board of Foreign Missions. This action greatly weakened Machen's support among conservatives. Westminster had been founded to supply conservative ministers to the Presbyterian Church. Now the independent board was preventing the seminary from fulfilling its purpose. Eventually some conservatives, the most prominent of whom was Clarence Macartney, abandoned the seminary when Machen refused to sever his ties to the new missions board.[42]

Machen objected that the new pledges required of prospective ministers were unconstitutional. If it had been illegal in the 1920s for conservatives to demand the affirmation of specific doctrines taught by the denomination's confession of faith (the so-called five points), he argued, so was requiring a pledge of loyalty to the denomination. To obey the denomination's demands, Machen warned Westminster graduates, was to abandon the Reformation, the liberty guaranteed by the church's constitution and, above all, allegiance to Christ. Yet he saw the handwriting on the wall and decided to transfer to the more conservative Philadelphia presbytery. That presbytery received Machen in March of 1934 by a vote of seventy-nine to forty-eight despite the objections of those who contested his affiliation with the independent board.[43]

While Machen was transferring to Philadelphia, John McDowell, the General Assembly's moderator, issued a statement intimating that the new board was illegal. In May 1934 McDowell and two members of the General Council's administrative committee met with Machen. McDowell presented Machen with a document stating that the independent board was contrary to the denomination's constitution and that its members had violated either their ordination or membership vows, "or both." McDowell also told Machen that a study supporting this position was being circulated for the next General Assembly, less than a month away. When Machen asked for a copy of the study so he could respond, McDowell replied that the manuscript was already at the printer and a copy could not be obtained.[44]

The study duly appeared as *Studies of the Constitution of the Presbyterian Church in the U.S.A.* It placed the broadest possible construction upon the General Assembly's powers and centralized the workings of the denomination. It also declared that anyone who would not give to the officially authorized missions board was in "exactly the same position" with regard to church law as a church member who refused "to take part in the celebration of the Lord's Supper or any other of the prescribed ordinances" of the denomination. Furthermore, *Studies* stipulated that monetary gifts only be given to organizations approved by the General Assembly. This report was the basis for the Assembly's "Mandate of 1934," which ordered independent board members to resign from their positions or else be brought to trial.[45]

Presbyterian conservatives, whether members of the board or not, were outraged, but Machen did not respond until December 1934, when the New Brunswick presbytery summoned him before its judicial committee. His objections ranged from the mandate's implication that church benevolences were a tax to its outright illegality in giving the General Assembly, the highest court of appeal, the power to make such a ruling without ever hearing a case that had come to it from a lower court. The mandate, he said, had originated surreptitiously from within denominational headquarters, contravened the lawful rights of individuals and lower judicatories, and violated due process by declaring independent board members guilty without a trial. The same destructive forces, Machen wrote, that were at work in the state—"the centralization of power under an arbitrary bureaucracy"—were also at work in the church.[46]

In his own defense, Machen argued that he was entirely within his legal rights. The charge that the new board was exercising ecclesiastical functions was "utterly baseless"; the board had no more connection to the Presbyterian Church than any other independent organization. Although the independent board used the word "Presbyterian," Machen reminded his colleagues that their denomination did not have an exclusive right to the name. One of the board's members was a minister in the Southern Presbyterian Church. He further explained that his actions, though controversial, were still proper. Presbyterian ministers who were convinced that the church was engaged in wrongful practices were obligated by their ordination vows and by the principle of freedom of conscience to try to reform such practices, even if it meant disobeying the General Assembly. The church's only remedy for such disobedience was an impartial trial that examined the case on its merits. Until that step was taken, dissenting ministers were free to remain in the church and make their views known.[47]

As it turned out, Machen received his trial but was never given the opportunity to defend his actions. First, the New Brunswick presbytery ruled that he had incorrectly transferred to Philadelphia and so was still under its jurisdiction. Apparently, Philadelphia's clerk had not filed the proper paperwork. Yet this procedural slip-up could not hide the fact that Philadelphia's conservative majority either would have refused to try Machen or would have made matters messy for the denomination. Next, the New Brunswick commission that tried Machen ruled it would not hear any evidence concerning liberalism in the church, the missions controversy, or even the legality of the 1934 mandate. It concluded the proceedings on March 29, 1935, finding Machen guilty and recommending his suspension from the ministry.[48]

Machen interpreted the trial as a victory for modernism. His response to the decision, while self-righteous, was nonetheless understandable given the rough treatment by his old peers. The entire case, he said, came down to whether he would obey the church's order to support the "modernist propaganda" of the official Board of Foreign Missions. "Being a Christian man," he said, "I cannot do so." From Machen's perspective the church was modernist. Any ecclesiastical body that did not actively seek to eliminate error from its ranks was guilty of that same error.[49]

Machen's other reaction to his trial was more to the point. In the same statement to the press quoted above, he called the 1934 mandate a "purely arbitrary administrative order" and said that his church had simply condemned him without a hearing. Although he insisted that the problems facing his denomination were theological, by the time his trial had concluded so much ink had been spilled over legal and constitutional matters that the conflict had become a struggle for power that rested upon divergent understandings of the church and society. That is why throughout these religious debates Machen so often repeated his fears about the perilous effects of political centralization. His views of the church, as well as those of his Presbyterian opponents, did not stand isolated from but were very much shaped by a particular political outlook.[50]

For Machen the church was not an assimilative or unifying institution but instead contributed to national diversity. It was just one part of a specific group's identity. Christianity, he argued, made exclusive claims about the nature of reality and morality and so was hardly capable of providing a common reference for the diversity of American society. Yet the exclusiveness of the church did not prevent Christians from promoting religious freedom and cultural pluralism. Machen believed that in a free society composed of distinct subgroups with different interests liberty guaranteed considerable autonomy to these groups to decide local and private affairs. A free society rich in diversity was optimal because it prevented the tyranny of the majority and allowed religious groups to practice their faith without fear of repression. Machen's politics thus reinforced his insistence on the particularity of the church and prompted him to argue that religion was a local and private matter, not an instrument for achieving broader social purposes. He repudiated older American Protestant notions that the church should shape public life. Rather, Presbyterianism was one particular religious expression in a free and pluralistic society.

In contrast, moderate Presbyterians and some conservatives who still believed that the church undergirded social order and stability viewed religious diversity as a threat. A certain amount of heterogeneity might be tolerable, but the need for order required cultural uniformity. As a fundamental feature of human experience, religion provided the basis for social unity. Whether through individual conversion or wholesome influences upon public and cultural institutions, Protestantism was indispensable to the public good. Christianity was not incompatible with liberty because it ultimately promoted the good of all. The church's cultural mandate, then, was to bring all aspects of life, as Robert Speer put it, "under Christ's Lordship." Machen would not have disagreed with Speer's sentiments but would have restrained the church's reach. While Speer advocated a national Christian culture, Machen preferred local expressions of Christian influence. Thus, the differences between Machen and the leaders of the Presbyterian Church were, from one angle, a religious variation on the debates over cultural pluralism and assimilation.[51]

These different political outlooks were evident in the struggle over missions. In keeping with his Southern loyalties, Machen insisted on the prerogatives and authority of lower judicatories (presbyteries) and freedom of conscience. He believed that the only way to resolve the legality of the new missions board was first through a trial at the local level with provision for appeals to higher courts. Even then, obedience to the decisions of higher courts was not necessary if a lower court or individual believed such judgments contradicted the denomination's constitution or the Bible. In his view, the General Assembly was "just as much subject" to the church's constitution as the "humblest" Presbyterian. "All our liberties as Presbyterians," he wrote, "are based upon the great principle that we cannot be deprived of even the least of our rights . . . by a simple majority vote of the General Assembly, but only . . . through judicial process."[52]

Machen was also more willing than his opponents to acknowledge irreconcilable differences in the church and to insist that the composition of committees and judicial councils reflect these competing perspectives. For instance, during the proceedings that led up to his trial he had to ask repeatedly for the presence of a stenographer so that the statements of both sides would not be distorted in secondhand reports. He also asked that the trial be open to the public in order to guarantee a fair hearing. The ministers responsible for trying Machen, however, were reluctant to grant his requests. They saw themselves as impartial even though they were following the ruling of the General Assembly which said that Machen had violated church law. So Machen scored the committee as well as other church judicial bodies for failing to have conservative representation. The church's "policy of secrecy and bureaucratic tyranny," he said, made secession by conservatives a necessity if true Presbyterianism were to be preserved.[53]

Denominational officials contested Machen's judgments but they also had difficulty convincing themselves and others that denominational proceedings against him had followed Presbyterian procedures. The study that condemned the new missions board had been commissioned by denominational executives, and had been adopted by the General Assembly without the consent of local assemblies. Moreover, New Brunswick did not allow Machen the chance to defend himself. The resolution to the missions controversy in fact signaled a shift toward "administrative centralization and theological decentralization." These bureaucratic reforms would continue into the late 1930s when the church reorganized the Chester and Philadelphia presbyteries, the area where conservatives were strongest, in order to minimize conflicts within the denomination.[54]

In contrast to Machen's secessionist perspective, Presbyterian moderates favored bureaucratic centralization as a way to resolve conflict. They echoed the political arguments of an older generation of Republicans that from a Southern perspective sacrificed constitutional principles for national unity. What mattered most to denominational officials such as Speer and Erdman was not resolving the differences between competing theologies but maintaining the unity of the church. Machen's endless carping about theological integrity and administrative regularity were only disruptive and hindered the positive work of the church. As Speer declared in his debate with Machen, "There *are* dangers in union enterprises . . . but . . . the safety of union is greater than its dangers." Speer went on to compare the unity of the Presbyterian Church to the union of states in America. In what Machen must have considered an extremely powerful expression of the differences between himself and Speer, the latter added how proud he was of his great-great-grandfather who had voted in Pennsylvania's delegation for the adoption of the U.S. Constitution "in the face of opposition of his constituents who feared the great dangers that lurked in the American union." Differing visions of America, then, corresponded closely to divergent ideas about the church and its mission.[55]

Machen's views differed so dramatically from most Northern Presbyterians that he had little chance of winning the day. Yet one of the curious features of the Presbyterian controversy is why the denomination devoted so much energy to silencing what was at best a small and peripheral movement. Even though the economy of the 1930s may have made mission funds scarce, in 1936 Machen's independent board only supported 11 missionaries compared to the Presbyterian Church's 1,356. And when Machen eventually formed a new denomination in 1936 he could only rally thirty-four ministers and seventeen elders. Westminster Seminary, with an average of eight graduates per year throughout the 1930s, was hardly a threat to established Presbyterian seminaries. Also, conservatives were rarely a factor in General Assembly elections for moderator. The peak of conservative strength came in 1924 when Clarence Macartney garnered 464 votes (51%). By 1933 and 1934, the conservative candidates received only 118 (13%) and 90 (10%) votes respectively. To be sure, establishmentarian inclinations made the Presbyterian Church's choice during the missions controversy between the cantankerous Machen on one side and the respectable Hocking, the wealthy Rockefeller, and the popular Buck on the other a relatively easy one even if veiled in equivocation. Still, support for Machen never became so great that it threatened the church's resources and stability. A policy of ignoring Machen may have actually forced him out of the church more quickly and with less publicity.[56]

Machen's failure to attract a larger following also remains something of a puzzle. Here was a nationally respected, articulate, and forceful scholar who was regularly invited to speak at churches and conferences. But he could only win 5,000 members to his new denomination compared to the old church's membership of close to 2 million. One explanation may be that Machen's concerns were too Calvinistic and Presbyterian for the greater fundamentalist constituency. Within the Presbyterian Church the conservative movement in the 1930s became basically a regional phenomenon with Philadelphia offering Machen the greatest support. In all likelihood, his concerns did not make much difference in the normal routine of ministers and laity outside the Northeast. No doubt, some Presbyterians also perceived Machen's guilt-by-association tactics and the missions agency he established as a rear-guard action that obviated the need for a new kind of conservatism, one made attractive by Neoorthodox thinkers like the Niebuhr brothers. Yet, while the missions controversy may have showed the need for new thinking, from Machen's perspective new organizational structures were essential if confessionalism were to survive. Neo-orthodoxy, though critical of mainline Protestantism's capitulation to cultural respectability, did not alter the configuration of power in American Protestantism's large-scale religious organizations. Machen believed that the Presbyterian Church had become increasingly centralized and unresponsive to dissent. Secession, not criticism from within, was the only way for conservatism to prevail.[57]

Thus, it was with a profound sense of relief that Machen declared on June 11, 1936, before the first General Assembly of his new denomination, "we became members, at last, of a true Presbyterian Church." The contentment that Machen experienced was short-lived, however. Only a few months later theological controversies were dividing the new denomination while the old church was taking Machen's followers to court over property disputes and over the original name Machen had chosen for his denomination—the Presbyterian Church of America—a designation Presbyterian leaders thought too similar to the older church. The years of contention finally took their toll on Machen. In late December of 1936, he traveled to North Dakota to rally support from members of the new church who had been receiving reports from the mainline denomination that he was an "unsavory and troublesome person." Machen, whose mission was to quiet these fears, was tired from a hectic pace, and unprepared for the upper Midwest's bitter cold. During the trip he came down with pneumonia and on January 1, 1937, died in Bismarck.[58]

Machen's death in North Dakota was filled with irony. A Presbyterian scholar who enjoyed the East Coast's urban culture and spent his life addressing the well educated, Machen died in the Catholic hospital of a small and remote town on the Northern Plains trying to rally a few Presbyterians of modest means. Yet Bismarck was also an appropriate place for Machen's death; the town's cultural isolation fit well with his religious convictions and social views. For Machen, Christianity was not to be a national presence that shaped culture. The quest for a Christian civilization, he believed, had severely weakened the church's witness and had greatly abetted the centralization of political power and the homogenization of cultural life in America. The church should only be one voice in the cacophony of American creeds and its influence should be limited to Christian homes and schools, local communities, and voluntary organizations. Machen's cultural stance first took root in his decision to leave Princeton for Westminster, grew stronger during the missions controversy of the 1930s, and finally bore fruit in the new denomination he helped to found. By establishing rival institutions and building alternative networks, Machen hoped to preserve a Christian witness that was cautious about the church's cultural involvement and fully attuned to the reality of religious freedom. That hope made Machen too Christian for most intellectuals and too marginal for most Protestants. But it did approach the problem of the relationship between church and society in a way that grasped well the possibilities and perils of modern America.

# Confessional Protestantism in

# Modern America: The Legacy of

# J. Gresham Machen

> From the beginning, in truth, we have sought to foster *Presbyterianism*,
> the Presbyterianism, as we believe, of the Bible and of the historic
> creeds, not merely what might happen currently to go under the name
> of Presbyterianism . . . We have not been able to go along with the throngs
> who capitalize on the unbelief and doctrinal indifference of our day to
> deprecate denominationalism and to join in all kinds of union movements.
> *Ned B. Stonehouse on the Orthodox Presbyterian Church, 1948*

When J. Gresham Machen died on January 1, 1937, the prospects for
a resurgence of conservative Protestantism within American society
looked bleak. Fundamentalist campaigns had been defeated within
mainline Protestant denominations, conservative views about the Bible
and theology were widely discredited within academic circles, and
popular perceptions continued to associate fundamentalism with big-
otry, ignorance, and social backwardness. Where fundamentalism
thrived, it did so as a subculture far removed from the institutions
central to the development of twentieth-century American culture.[1]

 Yet within a decade after Machen's death fundamentalism experienced a remarkable transformation. A combination of revivalistic fervor, academic ambition, and social awareness produced a series of
organizations and institutions that laid the foundation for a resurgence
of evangelicalism which by most assessments has altered the dynamics
of American religion since World War II and has become a significant
force in current debates about the direction of American society. Looking strictly at evangelistic activity, the hallmark of the evangelical tradition, the new movement was important for spawning the career of
Billy Graham whose first rallies attracted thousands of teenagers under

the auspices of Youth for Christ. This renewal of evangelicalism accomplished more than gaining new converts. It was also notable for bringing together a group of leaders who broke the revivalist mold by pursuing Ph.D.s at mainstream American universities and by producing a body of thoughtful writing on a wide range of intellectual, social, and religious matters that singlehandedly gave the new evangelical movement greater visibility and respectability within ecclesiastical and academic communities.[2]

Although Machen's premature death prevented him from participating in the evangelical renewal of the 1940s, his influence upon the movement was readily discernible. Many of the leaders of the new evangelicalism had studied with Machen either at Princeton or at Westminster. In other cases, where his influence was less direct, Machen's own scholarship and learned conservatism became benchmarks for the kind of intellectual endeavors that a new generation of evangelicals would pursue. And even though some of the new evangelicals would balk at Westminster Seminary's Calvinistic theology, the school itself retained a reputation for solid scholarship, especially in the fields of biblical studies and theology, which provided intellectual ballast to the evangelistic fervor of conservative Protestantism.[3]

Nevertheless, despite Westminster's academic stature, the seminary remained on the sidelines of the post–World War II evangelical resurgence because of its close ties to the Orthodox Presbyterian Church. During the 1940s, as evangelicals constructed a number of national organizations designed to coordinate and consolidate the activities and resources of conservative Protestantism, Machen's followers in the Orthodox Presbyterian Church refused to participate and the faculty at Westminster provided a theological rationale for the Orthodox Presbyterian's isolation. This unwillingness to join the emerging conservative coalition dismayed evangelical leaders who believed that Orthodox Presbyterians had abandoned the vision of their founder and succumbed to a fundamentalist conception of ecclesiastical purity.[4]

As it happened, however, the cleavage between the new evangelical movement and Orthodox Presbyterians reflected historic tensions within American Protestantism. Although both sides appeared to be conservative in their opposition to religious modernism, each held different rationales for that opposition. These differences had important implications for the way each group would relate to the broader culture and to other Protestants. To explore the differences between the new evangelicals and Orthodox Presbyterians is useful not only for solving the riddle of Machen's limited influence within the later evangelical movement, but also for understanding his legacy.

Machen's premature death caused considerable grief within the ranks of Protestant traditionalists. Leaders from a variety of denominations mourned the loss of one whom many regarded as the most articulate and capable spokesman for conservative views. The *Southern Methodist Advocate* remarked that with Machen's passing evangelicalism had lost "its ablest exponent and defender." The editor of *The Banner*, the organ of the Christian Reformed Church, agreed that the "cause of orthodoxy" had lost "its most prominent champion." Albert C. Dieffenbach, a Unitarian and the religion editor for the *Boston Evening Transcript*, eulogized that Machen was as "learned and valiant" a theologian as the Protestant church had produced in modern times. Princeton Seminary's Caspar Wistar Hodge said of his long-time friend and colleague that evangelical Christianity had lost "the greatest theologian in the English-speaking world."[5]

These tributes from religious leaders outside the Orthodox Presbyterian Church, however appropriate, could not quell the storm of controversy that engulfed the small denomination Machen had helped to establish. Even though his religious identity as a champion of strict confessionalism and Presbyterian procedures had become clearer during the missions controversy of the 1930s, Machen still held considerable appeal for a broad range of fundamentalists who otherwise would have been repelled by his Presbyterian particularism. Despite the fact that Machen himself was not drawn into the fray over evolution, the high view of the Bible's truthfulness that was implicit in his defense of Christian supernaturalism appealed powerfully to antievolutionists who believed that modern science denied divine intervention into the natural order. His insistence that Christianity was first and foremost a message to the individual soul won support from many who suspected that the older denominations had abandoned evangelism for social reform. And, in a movement that thrived on controversy, Machen's willingness to challenge church officials pleased fundamentalists who rarely let denominational loyalty hamper the cause of evangelism.[6]

As a result, some who followed Machen into the Orthodox Presbyterian Church did not fully share his Presbyterian views. The problem of diversity within the ranks of Machen's supporters became apparent even before Machen's fatal trip to North Dakota. At Westminster Seminary, where Machen was popular with the students, complaints could be heard that the Presbyterianism of the faculty was almost unbearable. Methodists, who comprised roughly 20 percent of the student body, thought Westminster professors presented Calvinism too belligerently. Meanwhile, premillennialists, who outnumbered other views four to one by one estimate, complained that faculty too readily denounced dispensationalism. Fundamentalist students also protested that the faculty condoned the use of cigarettes and alcohol. Some even grumbled that the curriculum was irrelevant to soul-winning. According to one administrator, "The image of the Seminary is Allis [professor of Old Testament] belaboring the critics, Van Til [professor apologetics] soaring in the skies of philosophic thought, and Murray [professor of systematic theology] drilling them on the decrees of God and privately denouncing California excursionists for driving cars on the Sabbath."[7]

Disagreements between fundamentalist and traditionalist Presbyterians had also surfaced within the Independent Board for Presbyterian Foreign Missions and the Orthodox Presbyterian Church. The issue generating the most debate was the use and popularity of the Scofield Reference Bible, an edition of the King James Version first published in 1909 that included extensive notes and comments from a dispensationalist perspective. Presbyterian traditionalists like Machen and the majority of faculty at Westminster opposed the Scofield Bible because they thought its teachings undermined Calvinistic conceptions of sin and grace. Some fundamentalist Presbyterians, for example, James Oliver Buswell, president of Wheaton College, tolerated dispensationalism in the interest of solidarity while others, such as Carl McIntire, an obstreperous minister in southern New Jersey, defended the use of the Scofield Bible. Machen tried to close the widening breach by backing Buswell as moderator at the new church's second General Assembly.[8]

His conciliatory efforts, however, could not satisfy disgruntled fundamentalists, like McIntire, who eventually took control of the Independent Board for Presbyterian Foreign Missions. For Machen, even though the board was established to be independent of the mainline church, its Presbyterian identity was critical. He was committed to Presbyterian theology and polity and believed that the board should only support missionaries of like mind. Fundamentalists on the board in early November 1936, contrary to Machen's impassioned requests, succeeded in ousting Machen as president and elected a minister of a nondenominational church. Close associates and family members believed that Machen was so hurt by this action that his physical strength was seriously depleted, making him an easy prey for his fatal illness. His sister-in-law Helen Woods Machen later reported in a sworn affidavit what Machen had told her over the telephone on the night of the independent board's elections. "They kicked me out as President, its the hardest blow I've had yet, I'm done for now . . . Now everything is in the hands of men who haven't the slightest notion of the issues at stake . . . everything I've worked for, loved and suffered for has been kicked out too. I feel it's the end for me, this time they've finished me." Nevertheless, in his last letter to Buswell, written only two weeks after the independent board's elections, Machen avoided personal animus while declaring that the independent board was "at the parting of the ways between a mere fundamentalism, on the one hand, and Presbyterianism on the other."[9]

The final issue that split fundamentalist and traditionalist Presbyterians concerned personal morality. In Buswell's estimation this was the proverbial straw that would break the camel's back. Those in the church who sided with him, Buswell wrote (in what turned out to be his last letter to Machen), were concerned about reports that Westminster students used liquor in their rooms "with the approval of some members of the faculty." The use of alcohol, even in the celebration of the sacrament, he added, was "far more likely" to divide the church than "any question of eschatology." Buswell and other fundamentalists in the church were also "shocked" by leaders of the new denomination who defended "the products of Hollywood," a "useless, . . . waste of energy." Machen never responded to Buswell but his opposition to Prohibition provides a clue to his views on alcohol. In addition to opposing the expanded powers of the federal government that the Eighteenth Amendment granted, Machen also thought the Bible allowed moderate use of alcohol. This was also the position of the majority of faculty at Westminster who came from ethnic churches where the idea of total abstinence within American evangelicalism was foreign. As for Buswell's reference to Hollywood, Machen did enjoy going to the movies and commented favorably on Charlie Chaplin but did not make any remarks about film in his published writings.[10]

Although Machen died before these debates were settled, the Orthodox Presbyterian Church emerged firmly in the hands of Presbyterian traditionalists. As an index of its Calvinistic identity, when it adopted the Westminster Confession of Faith as its theological standard, the denomination eliminated chapters on the love of God and missions that in 1903 had been amended by the old-line denomination. The new church considered these revisions antithetical to Calvinism. The Orthodox Presbyterian Church also decided to cancel its support for the independent board and to set up its own agency for missions. Last, the church chose not to establish any policy about consumption of alcohol or movies. Rebuffed by the traditionalists, a small group of fundamentalists in May 1937 withdrew from the Orthodox Presbyterian Church to form the Bible Presbyterian Synod.[11]

This split paralleled almost exactly the division a century earlier between Old and New School Presbyterians. The Presbyterian split of 1837 had also concerned the meaning of Calvinism, cooperation with non-Presbyterians in evangelism and missions, and personal behavior. Presbyterian fundamentalists such as Buswell and McIntire were closer to the outlook of nineteenth-century New England evangelicals who minimized denominational differences in order to convert individuals and reform society. Presbyterian traditionalists, most of whom taught at Westminster and were now in control of the Orthodox Presbyterian Church, paralleled the Scotch-Irish Presbyterians who resisted the tide of revivalism and reform in order to preserve old-world patterns of faith and practice.[12]

In the give-and-take of these debates the Orthodox Presbyterian Church became the institutional manifestation of the faith Machen had labored to defend. Unlike fundamentalists who stressed biblical inerrancy and dispensationalism, the new denomination adhered carefully to Presbyterian polity and the Westminster Confession. The church also shunned respectability in the broader culture, not by adhering to the mores of the fundamentalist subculture, but by insisting that the institutional church's mission was narrowly religious, not social or moral. In further pursuit of a strict Presbyterianism, the Orthodox Presbyterian Church valued a well-educated ministry and leaned heavily upon the conservative and well-informed scholars who taught at Westminster Seminary and served on a variety of denominational committees. The preservation of Old School Presbyterianism through a Calvinist seminary and a confessional church free from the constraints of establishmentarian Protestantism—this was Machen's legacy and Westminster Seminary and the Orthodox Presbyterian Church clearly embodied those ideals. Although the size and influence of his church and seminary was small, Machen had managed to sustain a religious tradition that otherwise may have become extinct.[13]

Yet in the climate of evangelical resurgence during the 1940s the new church's Old School Presbyterianism began to look like a betrayal of Machen's vision. Wartime fears and activities prompted a number of evangelical leaders, some of whom had studied with Machen, to sponsor and establish institutions and organizations that would unite conservative Protestants of all denominations in a campaign to restore evangelical Christianity in America. The leaders of this enterprise, while still fundamentalist in orientation, repudiated the negative and defensive tactics of the 1920s and strove to be more engaged in social and intellectual matters. The National Association of Evangelicals, founded in 1942, headed the list of agencies connected to this cooperative conservative Protestantism, also called "new evangelicalism." It was designed to coordinate evangelical activities and to provide a voice for all evangelical Protestants whom the mainline Federal Council of Churches did not represent. The Orthodox Presbyterian Church, however, refused to join the new initiative over fears that affiliation would compromise the denomination's Presbyterian identity.[14]

This decision appeared to be another instance of the prideful quest for purity that so often characterized fundamentalism. Orthodox Presbyterian narrowness, however, looked back to Old School Presbyterian practice rather than fundamentalist belligerence. A self-conscious Calvinism no doubt was one barrier between orthodox Presbyterians and most other evangelicals and fundamentalists. Both sides perceived that the theology of the Westminster Confession and the revivalism of American evangelicalism were not easily reconciled. But as Machen had argued, theology and church organization were intimately connected. Because orthodox Presbyterians believed that local churches and denominational agencies should oversee and regulate religious activities, they were wary of interdenominational cooperation in any endeavors that were properly the task of the church. For similar reasons, the Orthodox Presbyterian Church decided not to join the American Council of Christian Churches, a fellowship of fundamentalist individuals, churches, and organizations founded in 1941 by Carl McIntire. Thus, just as the Old School Presbyterian Church had refused to support the interdenominational voluntary organizations founded by revivalists during the Second Great Awakening, so too the Orthodox Presbyterian Church remained separate from the cooperative endeavors of 1940s whether evangelical or fundamentalist. In the 1920s such Presbyterian conservatism was readily linked to the protests of fundamentalists. But throughout the 1930s and 1940s, as different coalitions of conservative Protestantism emerged, confessional Presbyterian concerns proved to be markedly different from those of fundamentalists and the new evangelicals.[15]

Nevertheless, as Machen had demonstrated, Presbyterian particularism, while narrow in religious affairs, could be tolerant in cultural and social matters. By tightly prescribing the nature and function of the institutional church, Old School Presbyterianism leaned toward a strict separation of church and state and, as a result, was more tolerant of religious and cultural diversity than the revivalist tradition. This difference was also evident in orthodox Presbyterian decisions not to join the new evangelical initiatives of the 1940s. A large theme in the post–World War II resurgence of evangelicalism as well as the revivalist crusades of the antebellum era was the belief that evangelism would correct social ills and reconstruct Christian civilization in America. Because they did not construe the relationship between Christianity and American society in the same way or were foreign to Anglo-American Protestantism, confessional and ethnic religious groups throughout American history have been leery of supporting evangelical campaigns, especially when such efforts were aimed, whether explicitly or implicitly, at Americanizing religious and ethnic outsiders. Thus, while evangelical leaders set their sights on winning the nation's soul, the Orthodox Presbyterian Church established links with other ethnic confessional communions in America, most notably the Dutch Calvinists in the Christian Reformed Church, and with Reformed churches in other countries. According to Paul Woolley, professor of church history at Westminster Seminary, the new church could either have "many members and much money and read about itself in the newspapers" or it could retain its Reformed identity, but it could not have both.[16]

The splintering of conservatives during the 1940s, therefore, highlighted historic tensions within American Protestantism. The National Association of Evangelicals reflected the outlook of antebellum revivalism while the Orthodox Presbyterian Church embodied the attitudes of nineteenth-century confessional groups who sought to preserve their own particular identity against the inclusive and expansive evangelical empire of revivalism and voluntary associations. Theologically, the message of evangelicals was well adapted to the forces of modernization while confessionalists strove to retain Old World beliefs. By calling upon rational, autonomous individuals to make personal decisions for Christ, revivalists revealed a higher estimate of human nature than many confessionalists who affirmed traditional conceptions of human sinfulness and relied upon the institutional church for spiritual sustenance. Revivalists stressed Christianity's ethical demands and looked for a highly disciplined and morally responsible life as evidence of genuine faith. For confessionalists, theological distinctions were crucial. They equated correct doctrine with religious faithfulness. Furthermore, evangelicals and confessionalists disagreed about the nature of the church. Revivalists did not have clear definitions of the church; their communions minimized the distinction between clergy and laity while evangelical support for religious and benevolent voluntary agencies blurred differences between religious doctrines. Confessionalists, in contrast, defended a high view of church offices and government, and believed that the spiritual tasks of preaching and performing the sacraments limited what the church as an institution could do and provided a proper perspective on human suffering.[17]

These religious differences also had social and political consequences. In the first half of the nineteenth century the conflicting
beliefs of evangelicals and confessionalists, sometimes designated
"pietists" and "liturgicals" respectively, were significant in determin-
ing political affiliation. The evangelicals, who refused to compartmen-
talize religion and politics, identified first in the 1830s with the Whigs
and then after 1854 with the Republicans. These parties drew their
strength from New England, championed Anglo-Protestant mores,
and viewed government positively as the proper means for establishing divine law. Confessionalists, however, resisted evangelical efforts
at Anglo conformity and invariably joined the Democratic party, a loose
coalition of traditionalists, Southerners, anticlericals, and freethinkers,
which advocated libertarian and secularist aims. Rather than viewing
government positively, Democrats sought to protect individuals from
undue governmental interference and to keep the state free from
church control. Such an outlook was obviously attractive to immigrant
Catholics but also appealed to some Protestants who sought protection
from what they perceived as the religious and cultural imperialism of
Northern evangelicals. Thus the Republican party championed cultural conformity while the Democratic party stood for cultural and ethnic diversity.[18]

To be sure, by the 1940s religious differences between conservative
Protestants were less likely to predict party affiliation than they had in
the nineteenth century. Especially in the wake of the political realign-
ment fostered by the New Deal, orthodox Presbyterians, evangelicals,
and fundamentalists were overwhelmingly Republican. But religious
differences still accounted for divergent attitudes toward American society and divided twentieth-century evangelicals and confessionalists
in ways remarkably similar to the antebellum era. The Protestants af-
filiated with the National Association of Evangelicals were still committed to the notion that America was a Christian nation and believed
that an outpouring of revivals would restore the country to its religious
roots. While this approach relied more on the powers of persuasion
than on governmental policy, evangelicals saw little wrong with laws
and policies that privileged Protestant mores and values. In contrast,
like confessionalists of the nineteenth century, orthodox Presbyterians
were suspicious of the civil religion lurking in Anglo-American Protestantism and threw their energies into the church and denominational
agencies as the proper means for expanding Christian influence. Although few orthodox Presbyterians wholeheartedly endorsed Mach-
en's libertarianism, their understanding of Christianity did restrict
the church's involvement in social matters and so, like Machen, the

new denomination implicitly acknowledged the cultural diversity that Machen had defended.[19]

Despite older affinities between confessionalism and religious pluralism, Machen's pose of insisting upon ecclesiastical uniformity while also accepting cultural diversity seems strikingly awkward. Especially in the case of a state church tradition such as Presbyterianism, the normal expectation would be that confessionalists like Machen would favor policies of religious uniformity. But the disestablishment of religion in America reversed Old World patterns of church-state relationships. In nineteenth-century America the advocates of revival functioned virtually as the established church while confessionalists occupied the cultural periphery. Such a position forced religious traditionalists, who normally would have desired a religious establishment, to defend pluralism. Thus, just as Old School Presbyterians joined with freethinkers in the antebellum era to oppose evangelical efforts to create a uniform culture, so Machen and the Orthodox Presbyterian Church sided with secularists and ethnic groups to block the Protestant establishment's attempts to build a Christian civilization in America. Even though mainstream Protestantism had by the early twentieth century abandoned much of its revivalist heritage, it consisted largely of groups that had come to prominence through revivals (Baptists, Methodists, New School Presbyterians, Congregationalists), and it perpetuated the older evangelical ideal of providing moral and religious guidance to the nation.[20]

As it turns out, the alliance between Machen, the defender of Presbyterian orthodoxy, and Mencken, the debunker of all orthodoxy, was not as farfetched as it first seemed. Fundamentalists, who were appalled by Mencken's infidelity, supported Machen as long as he attacked mainline churches. But once they saw the larger implications of confessional Presbyterianism as manifested in the Orthodox Presbyterian Church and Westminster Seminary, fundamentalists first and then evangelicals backed away. Most conservative Protestants believed just as strongly as mainstream Protestants in the idea of a Christian America. Fundamentalist and evangelical criticism of liberalism in the historic Protestant denominations hinged on the perception that the mainline had abandoned revivalism, not on the belief that churches should provide moral and spiritual leadership for the nation. Thus the fragmentation of conservatives in the 1940s actually revealed four different camps within American Protestantism, fundamentalists, evangelicals, mainline Protestants, and confessionalists. The first three groups agreed on the necessity of a cultural consensus informed by Anglo-American Protestantism but disagreed over the means for achieving that consensus. Confessionalists, which in addition to the Orthodox Presbyterian Church included the Christian Reformed Church, Missouri Synod Lutherans, and some ethnic Anabaptists, dissented, although sometimes only implicitly, from the idea of a Christian America and sought autonomy to preserve their own faith and practice.[21]

The splits among fundamentalists, evangelicals, and traditionalist Presbyterians during the 1930s and 1940s, thus, bring Machen's thought and career into bolder relief. His purpose throughout the fundamentalist controversy had been to preserve a seminary that would train ministers in Old School Presbyterian theology and a church where those seminarians could minister. It had not been to reestablish Christian civilization as was the case for many American Protestants. In fact, Machen's narrow religious aims severely limited the authority and responsibility of the church in public life.

 In the end, Machen's thought and career is a reminder that the relationship between religion and modern culture is not as clear-cut or unambiguous as commonly thought. In the sense that he defended historic Christianity at a time when much of the intellectual world was turning secular, Machen by all means displayed "anti-modern" views. But according to a definition that makes modernity inherently antithetical to religious faith, any belief, no matter how well adapted to the modern world, is "anti-modern." The larger sense of modernity, the assumed *bête noire* of Protestant conservatives, entails tolerance of cultural and religious diversity. Here Machen showed a remarkable willingness to defend religious freedom and cultural pluralism while fundamentalist and modernist Protestants continued to cling, though differing over specifics, to the idea of a Christian America. Indeed, at the same time that secular intellectuals attacked the Protestant ethos of American culture, Machen argued that the churches' involvement in cultural and social life was harmful because it undermined faithful witnessing to Christian truth. Unfortunately for Machen, that twin commitment—to Presbyterian orthodoxy and religious pluralism— went largely unheeded in fundamentalist and evangelical circles. Yet his outlook may still prove instructive to believers and secularists in America today who through a series of culture wars struggle to reconcile the demands of faith with the realities of modernity.[22]

# NOTES

## Preface

1. Stanley Coben, *Rebellion against Victorianism: The Impetus for Cultural Change in 1920s America* (New York, 1991).

## Introduction

1. Lewis Perry, *Intellectual Life in America* (New York, 1984), 385; Frederick Lewis Allen, *Only Yesterday* (New York, 1931), 234, 235, 236, 230, 232; Lippmann quoted on 232.

2. Walter Lippmann, *A Preface to Morals* (New York, 1929), 12, 4, 14; H. L. Mencken, *A Treatise on the Gods* (New York, 1930), 296–97.

3. Reinhold Niebuhr, review of *Treatise on the Gods, Atlantic Bookshelf* (June 1930): 20, quoted in Mary Miller Vass and James L. West III, "The Composition and Revision of Mencken's 'Treatise on the Gods,'" *Menckeniana* 88 (Winter 1983): 12; George A. Gordon, "A Review of Mr. Lippmann's *A Preface to Morals*," *Congregationalist* 114 (Nov. 14, 1929): 636, and Harry Emerson Fosdick, *New York Evening Post*, April 27, 1929, both quoted in William R. Hutchison, *The Modernist Impulse in American Protestantism* (Cambridge, 1976), 286.

4. Lippmann, *Preface to Morals*, 46, 47; Mencken, *Treatise*, 307. For a discussion of fundamentalist and secular perceptions of liberal Protestantism, see Hutchison, *Modernist Impulse*, chap. 8.

5. Lippmann, *Preface to Morals*, 32; H. L. Mencken, "Doctor Fundamentalis," *Baltimore Evening Sun*, January 18, 1937; Mencken, "The Impregnable Rock," *American Mercury* 9 (1931): 411.

6. Mencken, "The Impregnable Rock," 411.

7. Daniel Joseph Singal, "Towards a Definition of American Modernism," in *Modernist Culture in America*, ed. Singal (Belmont, Calif., 1991), 12–13. For the variety of perspectives on cultural modernism, see idem, *The War Within* (Chapel Hill,

N.C., 1982); Henry May, *The End of American Innocence* (New York, 1959); T. J. Jackson Lears, *No Place of Grace* (New York, 1981); Marshall Berman, *All That Is Solid Melts Into Air* (New York, 1981); and David A. Hollinger, "The Canon and Its Keepers: Modernism and Mid-twentieth-century American Intellectuals," *In the American Province* (Bloomington, Ind., 1985), 74–91.

8. See, for instance, Singal, "Towards a Definition"; Morton White, *Social Thought in America* (1947; rev. ed., New York, 1976); James T. Kloppenberg, *Uncertain Victory: Social Democracy and Progressivism in European and American Thought, 1870–1920* (New York, 1986); Robert H. Wiebe, *The Search for Order* (New York, 1967), chaps. 5–7; and Grant Wacker, *Augustus H. Strong and the Dilemma of Historical Consciousness* (Macon, Ga., 1985). Tensions within modernist culture between the cognitive aims of scientists and other academics and the experiential strategies of writers and artists are seldom addressed in the secondary literature. David A. Hollinger, "The Knower and the Artificer" (*Modernist Culture in America*, ed. Singal, 42–69), points out this tension and endeavors to resolve it.

9. R. Lawrence Moore, *Religious Outsiders and the Making of Americans* (New York, 1986), 165. On fundamentalism's inherently antimodernist posture, see George M. Marsden, *Fundamentalism and American Culture* (New York, 1980); Samuel Hayes, *American Political History as Social Analysis* (Knoxville, Tenn., 1980), 280–83; William Appleman Williams, *America in a Changing World* (New York, 1978), 171–72; Sydney E. Ahlstrom, *A Religious History of the American People* (New Haven, 1972), 779–84, 909–15; and Martin A. Marty, *Modern American Religion*, Vol. 1: *The Irony of It All* (Chicago, 1986), chap. 11.

10. Hollinger, "The Knower and the Artificer," 62, points out the distance between Protestant and cultural modernism. For the dominance of the modernist outlook within modern American culture, see Singal, "Towards a Definition," 3. On Protestantism's "second disestablishment," see Handy, *A Christian America*, 159–84.

11. On the continuing influence of mainline Protestantism, see William R. Hutchison, "Preface: From Protestant to Pluralist America," and idem, "Protestantism as Establishment," in *Between the Times*, ed. Hutchison (Cambridge, 1989), x, viii, 3–18; and Martin A. Marty, *Modern American Religion*, Vol. 2: *The Noise of Conflict* (Chicago, 1991).

12. J. Gresham Machen, "Christianity in Conflict," in *Contemporary American Theology*, vol. 1, ed. Vergilius Ferm (New York, 1932), 245.

### Chapter 1. Between Culture and Piety

*Epigraph:* David Starr Jordan, "The Religion of the Sensible American," *Hibbert Journal* 6 (1907–8): 868.

1. William R. Hutchison, "Cultural Strain and Protestant Liberalism," *American Historical Review* (hereafter *AHR*) 76 (1971): 386–411; David A. Hollinger, "Inquiry and Uplift: Late Nineteenth-century American Academics and the Moral Efficacy of Scientific Practice," in *Authority of Experts*, ed. Thomas L. Haskell (Bloomington, Ind., 1984), chap. 5; Samuel Haber, *The Quest for Authority and Honor in the American Professions, 1750–1900* (Chicago, 1991), chap. 7; Robert M. Crunden, *Ministers of Reform* (1982; Urbana, Ill., 1984), 3–15; Burton J. Bledstein, *The Culture of Profession-*

alism: *The Middle Class and the Development of Higher Education in America* (New York, 1976), 248–86.

2. Everett T. Tomlinson, *World's Work* 9 (1904): 5635–40, quotation on 5639, col. 1.

3. H. L. Mencken, "Sahara of the Bozart," *Prejudices, Second Series* (New York, 1920), 137; idem, "The Agonies of Dixie," *American Mercury* 27 (1933): 251–53. On the realities of the Old South and Mencken's myth, see Fred C. Hobson, Jr., *The Serpent in Eden: H. L. Mencken and the South* (Chapel Hill, N.C., 1974), 14–20; and Joseph L. Morison, "Colonel H. L. Mencken, C.S.A.," *Southern Literary Journal* 1 (1968): 42–43.

4. *Letters of Arthur W. Machen*, ed. Arthur W. Machen, Jr. (Baltimore, 1917), 354–55.

5. On the classical tradition in the South, see Edwin A. Miles, "The Old South and the Classical World," *North Carolina Historical Review* 48 (1971): 258–75. On the importance of the classics for legal training and for belles lettres in antebellum America, see Robert A. Ferguson, *Law and Letters in American Culture* (Cambridge, 1984). When Machen died, the Baltimore Bar adopted a memorial that noted that a primary feature of his practice had been the cultivation of the "reasoning faculties."

6. *Letters of Arthur W. Machen*, 101; Machen, "Christianity in Conflict," 246; *Baltimore Sun*, December 22, 1915; Arthur W. Machen, Sr., to Machen, February 12, 1906, Machen Archives, Westminster Theological Seminary, Philadelphia (hereafter MA). *Letters of Arthur W. Machen*, ed. Machen, 359.

7. Ned B. Stonehouse, *J. Gresham Machen: A Biographical Memoir* (Grand Rapids, Mich., 1954), 28–35.

8. Mary Gresham Machen, *The Bible in Browning* (New York, 1903), is an homage to Henry Van Dyke's *Poetry of Tennyson*. Arthur W. Machen, Jr., to Patton, February 26, 1926, MA. On Machen's religious upbringing, see Stonehouse, *J. Gresham Machen*, 40–43.

9. Stonehouse, *J. Gresham Machen*, 43–46; Machen, "Christianity in Conflict," 249; Machen to Arthur W. Machen, Sr., January 18 and June 29, 1902; Machen to Minnie Gresham Machen, October 5, 1913; and Machen, "Mountains and Why We Love Them," in *What Is Christianity?* ed. Ned Bernard Stonehouse (Grand Rapids, Mich., 1951), 304–14.

10. Allen Tate, "A Southern Mode of the Imagination," in *Collected Essays* (Denver, 1959), 557–58; Machen to Thomas Machen, January 12, 1904, MA; Paul Woolley, *The Significance of J. Gresham Machen Today* (Nutley, N.J., 1977), 2–3; Machen to Minnie Gresham Machen, April 2, 1905, and January 21, 1906; Machen to Thomas Machen, May 13 and July 15, 1906; and Machen to Arthur W. Machen, Sr., July 31, 1901, MA. On patrician manners, see Edwin Harrison Cady, *The Gentleman in America* (Syracuse, N.Y., 1949), 146–59; Stow Persons, *The Decline of American Gentility*, 276–85; John Higham, "The Reorientation of American Culture in the 1890s," *Writing American History* (Bloomington, Ind., 1970), 86–87.

11. Mencken, "Sahara of the Bozart," 138; Machen to Minnie Gresham Machen, MA. On Victorian sentimentality, see Ann Douglas, *The Feminization of American Culture* (New York, 1977); and Daniel Walker Howe, "Victorian Culture in America," in *Victorian America*, ed. Howe (Philadelphia, 1976), 22–27. On the formality of the Genteel Tradition, see Martin Green, *The Problem of Boston* (New York, 1966),

and Persons, *The Decline of American Gentility,* 274–304. Machen confessed that Sydney Lanier's "Marshes of Glynn" was his favorite poem in a letter to his mother, April 7, 1910, MA. His literary tastes were eclectic. During one summer, he read Victor Hugo, George Eliot, Freussen (a contemporary German novelist), Tennyson, and Goethe; Machen to Thomas Machen, October 16, 1904; Arthur W. Machen, Jr., to Machen, March 25, 1905; and Machen to Minnie Gresham Machen, April 30, 1910, MA.

12. On Johns Hopkins's significance, see Hugh Hawkins, *Pioneer: A History of the Johns Hopkins University* (Baltimore, 1960); and Laurence R. Veysey, *The Emergence of the American University* (Chicago, 1965). On Gildersleeve, see *Dictionary of American Biography,* 6:277–82 (quotation is on 280, col. 2); *Basil Lanneau Gildersleeve: An American Classicist,* ed. Ward W. Briggs, Jr., and Herbert W. Benario (Baltimore, 1986).

13. Gildersleeve, "Grammar and Aesthetics," *Essays and Studies,* 127–57; quotations on 133 and 157; idem, "University Work in America," *Essays and Studies,* 120–23. For Gildersleeve's defense of the traditional curriculum, see "Limits of Culture," and "Classics and Colleges," *Essays and Studies,* 3–85. On the dominance of philology in American academics and at Johns Hopkins, see Gerald Graff, *Professing Literature* (Chicago, 1987), chap. 4, and 99–102. For the strictures against religious modernism made by students of ancient literature, see below, chaps. 3 and 5.

14. Henry Van Dyke, "Christianity and Literature," *Essays of Application* (New York, 1905), 160; and idem, quoted in Tertius Van Dyke, *Henry Van Dyke* (New York, 1935), 235; W. R. Castle, Jr., "Barrett Wendell—Teacher," in *Essays in Memory of Barrett Wendell* (Cambridge, 1926), 5, 7, quoted in Veysey, *Emergence of the American University,* 222. On the literary criticism of the period, see Graff, *Professing Literature,* chap. 6; May, *The End of American Innocence,* 30–79; William Van O'Connor, *An Age of Criticism* (Chicago, 1952), 3–18; Robert F. Falk, "The Literary Criticism of the Genteel Decades: 1870–1900," in *The Development of American Literary Criticism,* ed. Floyd Stovall (Chapel Hill, N.C., 1955), 113–58; "Defenders of Ideality," in *Literary History of the United States,* Vol. 1: *History* (1946; 4th ed., rev., New York, 1974), 809–26; Robert T. Self, *Barrett Wendell* (Boston, 1975), 53–68; George Kennedy, "Gildersleeve, The Journal, and Philology in America," *American Journal of Philology* (hereafter *AJP*) 101 (1980): 1–11; E. Christian Kopff, "Gildersleeve in American Literature: The Kaleidoscopic Style," in *Basil Lanneau Gildersleeve,* ed. Briggs and Benario, 56–61; and J. David Hoeveler, Jr., *The New Humanism* (Charlottesville, Va., 1977), 81–106.

15. Quotation from Henry Ward Beecher, *Yale Lectures on Preaching* (1872), 225–26. On Victorian attitudes toward religion, see D. H. Meyer, "American Intellectuals and the Victorian Crisis of Faith," in *Victorian America,* ed. Howe, 59–77; Hutchison, *Modernist Impulse,* 43–46, 77–144; Marsden, *Fundamentalism and American Culture,* 11–39; James Turner, *Without God, Without Creed: The Origins of Unbelief in America* (Baltimore, 1985), 187–202; and Grant Wacker, "The Holy Spirit and the Spirit of the Age in American Protestantism, 1880–1910," *Journal of American History* (hereafter *JAH*) 72 (1985): 45–62. On Beecher and Brooks, see Paul A. Carter, *The Spiritual Crisis of the Gilded Age* (DeKalb, Ill., 1971), 1–20, 43–62, 109–32; and William G. McLoughlin, *The Meaning of Henry Ward Beecher* (New York, 1970). On Moody, see James F. Findlay, Jr., *Dwight L. Moody* (Chicago, 1969), 176, 225.

16. First quotation comes from Kirk's obituary, *Baltimore Sun,* November 7, 1953; Harris E. Kirk, *The Spirit of Protestantism* (Nashville, 1930), 184, 190–91; Kirk, "The

Soul's Arabia," in *The Southern Presbyterian Pulpit*, ed. Charles Haddon Nabers (New York, 1928), 154–55. See also Harris E. Kirk, *The Religion of Power* (New York, 1916), 238–65, 301–5; and Donald G. Miller, *The Scent of Eternity: A Life of Harris Elliott Kirk of Baltimore* (Macon, Ga., 1989). On Franklin Street Presbyterian Church, see Harold M. Parker, Jr., "Much Wealth and Intelligence: The Presbytery of Patapsco," *Studies in Southern Presbyterian History* (Gunnison, Ga., 1979), 24–38; Ernest Trice Thompson, *Presbyterians in the South*, Vol. 2: *1861–1890* (Richmond, 1973), 183–84; and Miller, *Scent of Eternity*, chaps. 7, 8. Although Old School Presbyterianism has attracted little scholarly attention, *The Princeton Theology, 1812–1921: Scripture, Science, and Theological Method from Archibald Alexander to Benjamin Warfield*, ed. Mark A. Noll (Grand Rapids, Mich., 1983), and George M. Marsden, *The Evangelical Mind and the New School Presbyterian Experience* (New Haven, 1970), provide useful material on that tradition.

17. Henry Van Dyke, "A Divine Impossibility," and "Salt," in *The Open Door* (Philadelphia, 1903), 55–56, 75–76.

18. Arthur W. Machen, Jr., to Machen, March 25, 1906, MA. On Protestant efforts to recruit businessmen, see Gail Bederman, " 'The Women Have Had Charge of the Church Work Long Enough': The Men and Religion Forward Movement of 1911–1912 and the Masculinization of Middle-class Protestantism," *American Quarterly* 41 (1989): 432–65.

19. Machen to Arthur W. Machen, Sr., July 17, 1902, MA.

20. Ibid.; Machen, "Christianity in Conflict," 249. See especially pages 246–49 for Machen's high regard for his parents. Not only was Machen's father a prominent Baltimore attorney but his older brother, Arthur, was fast becoming an authority on tax law. See Arthur Webster Machen, Jr., *A Treatise on the Modern Law of Corporations* (Boston, 1908); and idem, *A Treatise on the Federal Corporation Tax Law of 1909* (Boston, 1909).

21. Machen to Minnie Gresham Machen, September 15 and 21, 1902; and Machen to Arthur W. Machen, Sr., October 5, 1902, MA. On Machen's attention to Princeton's tennis courts, see Machen to Minnie Gresham Machen, August 22, October 3 and 10, and November 10, 1909, MA.

22. Machen to Arthur W. Machen, Sr., October 5 and 13, 1902; and Machen to Arthur W. Machen, Jr., October 13, 1902, MA.

23. Machen to Minnie Gresham Machen, January 11, 1903, April 9, and May 1, 1904, MA. Machen to Thomas Machen, February 1, 1903; and Machen to Arthur W. Machen, Sr., February 15, 1903, MA.

24. Machen to Minnie Gresham Machen, April 9 and May 1, 1904. Machen's prize-winning essay appeared as "The New Testament Account of the Birth of Jesus," *Princeton Theological Review* (hereafter *PTR*) 3 (1905): 641–70, and 4 (1906): 37–81. Basil Gildersleeve wrote several letters of recommendation and introduction for Machen before he left for Germany. Gildersleeve to Machen, May 30, 1904, MA.

25. On Ritschl and Herrmann, see Bernard M. G. Reardon's introduction in *Liberal Protestantism* (Stanford, Calif., 1968), 20–40; Robert T. Voekel's introduction to Wilhelm Herrmann, *The Communion of the Christian with God* (Philadelphia, 1971), xxii–xlii; Van A. Harvey, "On the Intellectual Marginality of American Theology," in *Religion and Twentieth-century Intellectual Life*, ed. Michael J. Lacey (Cambridge, 1989), 186–90; and Claude Welch, *Protestant Thought in the Nineteenth Century*, vol. 2 (New Haven, 1985), 42–54, and chap. 8.

26. The place of religion in American higher education, specifically biblical

scholarship, is discussed in greater detail below in chapter 2. On the divorce between academics and religious life in America, see Bruce Kuklick, *Churchmen and Philosophers: From Jonathan Edwards to John Dewey* (New Haven, 1985); and Turner, *Without God, Without Creed.*

27. Machen to Minnie Gresham Machen, October 24, 1905; and Machen to Arthur W. Machen, Jr., November 2 and December 10, 1905, MA.

28. Machen, "Christianity in Conflict," 261; Machen to Arthur W. Machen, Jr., April 18, 1906, MA. For interpretations that regard Machen's study in Germany as a showdown between conservative and liberal views of the Bible, see George M. Marsden, "J. Gresham Machen, History, and Truth," *Westminster Theological Journal* (hereafter *WTJ*) 42 (1979): 167–68; Dallas Roark, *J. Gresham Machen and His Desire to Maintain a Doctrinally True Presbyterian Church* (Ann Arbor, Mich., 1963), 67–97; and Bradley James Longfield, *The Presbyterian Controversy* (New York, 1991), 41–49.

29. Machen to Arthur W. Machen, Jr., April 18, 1906; Machen to Arthur W. Machen, Sr., February 4, January 21, 1906; and Bill Munson to Machen, January 22, 1906, MA.

30. Machen to Arthur W. Machen, Jr., December 10, 1905; Machen to Minnie Gresham Machen, July 22 and 29, 1906, MA.

31. Machen to Arthur W. Machen, Jr., April 18, 1906, MA.

32. Machen to Arthur W. Machen, Jr., April 18, and June 3, 1906, MA.

33. Machen to Minnie Gresham Machen, July 29, 1906, MA. For a more detailed account of the events that led to Princeton's hiring of Machen, see Stonehouse, *J. Gresham Machen*, 130–35.

34. Charles Hodge, *Systematic Theology*, vol. 1 (1872; Grand Rapids, Mich., 1975), 10; Benjamin Breckinridge Warfield, "Introduction to Beattie's *Apologetics*," reprinted in *Selected Shorter Writings of Benjamin B. Warfield, II*, ed. John E. Meeter (Phillipsburg, N.J., 1973), 99. On Princeton Theology and Scottish Realism, see Theodore Dwight Bozeman, *Protestants in an Age of Science* (Chapel Hill, N.C., 1977); John C. Vander Stelt, *Philosophy and Scripture* (Marlton, N.J., 1978); *The Princeton Theology*, ed. Noll, 30–33; and Mark A. Noll, "Common Sense Traditions and American Evangelical Thought," *American Quarterly* 37 (1985): 216–38. For Princeton's efforts to integrate living piety with their rational theology, see W. Andrew Hoffecker, *Piety and the Princeton Theologians* (Phillipsburg, N.J., 1981).

35. The phrase "apodictic certitude" comes from "Christianity in Conflict," 263, where Machen describes the impact of Patton's reasoning on his own doubts. For criticism of Princeton's apologetics, see Cornelius Van Til, *The Defense of the Faith*, 2d ed. (Philadelphia, 1955), 260–66; Vander Stelt, *Philosophy and Scripture*; and Jack B. Rogers and Donald K. McKim, *The Authority and Interpretation of the Bible* (San Francisco, 1979).

36. Machen to Minnie Gresham Machen, October 16, November 18, and September 11, 1906, MA.

37. Machen to Minnie Gresham Machen, September 14, 1906; and Minnie Gresham Machen to Machen, September 17, 1906, MA. Although Mrs. Machen's initial reply to her son's plans has been lost, the references to it in these two letters make its substance clear.

38. Machen to Minnie Gresham Machen, October 4, 1908. For similar sentiments, see Machen to Minnie Gresham Machen, September 15, 1906, March 24,

June 9, and October 13, 1907, and March 22, 1908; and Machen to Arthur W. Machen, Sr., January 20 and November 11, 1907, MA.

39. "Princeton Theologues Protest against Some Courses and Demand Others in Seminary," March 6, 1909. On student riots, see Veysey, *Emergence of the American University,* 277, 295, 315.

40. Machen to Minnie Gresham Machen, February 21 and March 14, 1909, MA. For more details on the revolt and its background, see Ronald Thomas Clutter, *The Reorientation of Princeton Theological Seminary, 1900–1929* (Ann Arbor, Mich., 1982), chaps. 2–3.

41. See "Personal Reminiscences of J. Gresham Machen," *Presbyterian Journal* 44 (Nov. 27, 1985): 6–10, 13; and Woolley, *Significance of J. Gresham Machen,* 6.

42. Machen to Minnie Gresham Machen, May 21 and June 13, 1909, MA. For a defense of Kirk, see Minnie Gresham Machen and Arthur W. Machen, Sr., to Machen, June 14, 1909, MA. For Kirk's perspective on this episode, see Miller, *Scent of Eternity,* 403–12.

43. Machen to Minnie Gresham Machen, April 16, 1911, and January 14, September 21, and October 19, 1912; Machen to Arthur W. Machen, Sr., September 25, 1913, MA.

44. The original title was "Scientific Preparation of the Minister." See Machen to Minnie Gresham Machen, March 3, June 23, and September 21, 1912, MA.

45. Machen, "Christianity and Culture," *PTR* 11 (1913): 1–15. I am using the reprint of the address from *What Is Christianity?* ed. Stonehouse, 156–58.

46. Machen, "Christianity and Culture," 156, 158, 159, 160. On the growth of fundamentalism in the 1910s, see Marsden, *Fundamentalism and American Culture,* 118–32.

47. George Santayana, "The Genteel Tradition in American Philosophy," in *The Genteel Tradition* (Cambridge, 1967), 37–64; Van Wyck Brooks, *America's Coming-of-Age* (New York, 1975), 30. On Pragmatism, see David A. Hollinger, "The Problem of Pragmatism in American History," *In the American Province* (Bloomington, Ind., 1985), 24–43; and John Dewey, "The Influence of Darwin on Philosophy," *The Influence of Darwin on Philosophy* (New York, 1910). On the "New History," see James Harvey Robinson, *The New History* (New York, 1912); and John Higham, *History* (Baltimore, 1983), 104–16. On Lippmann and Croly, see Charles Forcey, *The Crossroads of Liberalism* (New York, 1961). Singal, "Towards a Definition," stresses the "integrative mode" of modernism. For other assessments of the demise of Victorianism, see May, *The End of American Innocence;* White, *Social Thought in America;* and Wiebe, *The Search for Order.*

48. "Rejoice with Trembling," sermon delivered June 23, 1914, manuscript in MA.

49. "Spiritual Culture in the Theological Seminary," reprinted in *Selected Shorter Writings of Benjamin B. Warfield, II,* ed. Meeter, 468–96, quotation on 495.

50. Ibid., 469. On Warfield's life, see *The Princeton Theology,* ed. Noll, 15–16; and the introduction to Warfield's *Biblical and Theological Studies,* ed. Samuel G. Craig (Philadelphia, 1968), xi–xviii.

51. Machen, "Christianity and Culture," 161–62.

## Chapter 2. The Double-edged Sword of Biblical Criticism

*Epigraph:* William Newton Clarke, *The Use of the Scriptures in Theology* (Edinburgh, 1907), 146, 147.

1. Quotations come from Crunden, *Ministers of Reform,* 200, 213, 217.

2. Gaius Glenn Atkins, *Religion in Our Times* (New York, 1932), 156. For religious influences upon Woodrow Wilson, see John M. Mulder, *Woodrow Wilson: The Years of Preparation* (Princeton, 1978), and upon politics during the Progressive era more generally, see Robert T. Handy, "Protestant Theological Tensions and Political Styles in the Progressive Period," in *Religion and American Politics,* ed. Mark A. Noll (New York, 1990), 281–301.

3. Mark S. Massa, *Charles Augustus Briggs and the Crisis of Historical Criticism* (Minneapolis, 1990), 13. On Machen's scholarship, see, for instance, Wacker, *Augustus H. Strong,* 21–24; George M. Marsden, "Understanding J. Gresham Machen," in *Understanding Fundamentalism and Evangelicalism* (Grand Rapids, Mich., 1991), 182–201; and Longfield, *Presbyterian Controversy,* chap. 2. For the broader impact of biblical criticism, see Carter, *The Spiritual Crisis of the Gilded Age;* Hutchison, *Modernist Impulse;* Kuklick, *Churchmen and Philosophers,* chap. 15; and Grant Wacker, "The Demise of Biblical Civilization," in *The Bible in America,* ed. Nathan O. Hatch and Mark A. Noll (New York, 1982), 121–38.

4. Machen, "History and Faith," in *What Is Christianity?* ed. Stonehouse, 170, 172–73.

5. Protestants continued to insist, for instance, as the 1909 General Assembly of the Presbyterian Church put it, that "our continent was not settled by bands of atheists or infidels . . . but by colonies of Christian people acknowledging Jesus Christ as Lord." Quoted in David Little, "Reformed Faith and Religious Liberty," in *Major Themes in the Reformed Tradition,* ed. Donald K. McKim (Grand Rapids, Mich., 1992), 210. On the continuing influence of Protestant mores upon American life, see May, *The End of American Innocence;* Crunden, *Ministers of Reform;* Marty, *The Irony of It All;* and Robert T. Handy, *Undermined Establishment* (Princeton, 1991).

6. Machen, "History and Faith," 183, 184.

7. Quotation from George M. Marsden, *Religion and American Culture* (San Diego, 1990), 127. On the rise of biblical criticism in America and its threatening implications, see Wacker, "Demise of Biblical Civilization"; Jerry Wayne Brown, *The Rise of Biblical Criticism in America* (Middletown, Conn., 1969); Mark A. Noll, *Between Faith and Criticism* (San Francisco, 1986); and Ferenc Morton Szasz, *The Divided Mind of Protestant America* (University, Ala., 1982). On debates about biblical revision, see Kenneth Cmiel, *Democratic Eloquence* (New York, 1990), 206–23.

8. Benjamin W. Bacon, "Ultimate Problems of Biblical Science," *Journal of Biblical Literature* (hereafter *JBL*) 22 (1903): 11. See Ernest DeWitt Burton, "The Place of the New Testament in a Theological Curriculum," *American Journal of Theology* (hereafter *AJT*) 16 (1912): 181–95; Curtis Howe Walker, "The Trend in the Modern Interpretation of Early Church History," *AJT* 20 (1916): 614–16; Gerald Birney Smith, "What Shall the Systematic Theologian Expect from the New Testament Scholar?" *AJT* 19 (1915): 388–90; and Arthur Cushman McGiffert, "Theological Education," *AJT* 15 (1911): 1–19. On the influence of German methods on American learning, see Noll, *Between Faith and Criticism,* 33–36, 51–54; Veysey, *The Emergence of the American University,* 121–79, 264–341; Bledstein, *The Culture of Professionalism,* 287–331; Jurgen

Herbst, *The German Historical School in American Scholarship* (Ithaca, N.Y., 1965); John Higham, "The Matrix of Specialization," Laurence Veysey, "The Pluralized Worlds of the Humanities," and Dorothy Ross, "The Development of the Social Sciences," all in *The Organization of Knowledge in Modern America, 1860–1920*, ed. Alexandra Oleson and John Voss (Baltimore, 1979), 3–18, 51–106, 107–38.

9. Warfield and A. A. Hodge, "Inspiration," *Presbyterian Review* 2 (1881): 225–60; Green and Harper, on "The Pentateuchal Question," *Hebraica* 5 (1888–89): 18–73, 243–91; 5 (1889): 137–89; 6 (1889–90): 1–48, 241–95; 6 (1890): 109–38, 161–211; 7 (1890–91): 1–38, 104–42; and Briggs, "Critical Theories of the Sacred Scriptures in Relation to Their Inspiration," and "A Critical Study of the Higher Criticism with Special Reference to the Pentateuch," *Presbyterian Review* 2 (1881): 550–79, and 4 (1883): 69–130, respectively. On nineteenth-century American biblical scholarship, see Noll, *Between Faith and Criticism*, 15–49; Warner M. Bailey, "William Robertson Smith and American Biblical Studies," *Journal of Presbyterian History* (hereafter *JPH*) 51 (1973): 285–308; Walter F. Peterson, "American Protestantism and the Higher Criticism, 1870–1910," *Transactions of the Wisconsin Academy of Sciences, Arts, and Letters* 50 (1961): 321–29; and Brown, *The Rise of Biblical Criticism in America*.

10. *Minutes* of the General Assembly of the Presbyterian Church, U.S.A., 1892, 179–80 (hereafter G.A. *Minutes*).

11. Lefferts A. Loetscher, *The Broadening Church: A Study of Theological Issues in the Presbyterian Church since 1869* (Philadelphia, 1954), chaps. 6–8; Massa, *Charles Augustus Briggs*, chap. 4. On the issues separating Old and New School Presbyterians and their troubled 1870 reunion, see Marsden, *The Evangelical Mind and the New School Presbyterian Experience*. On these controversies, see Noll, *Between Faith and Criticism*, 27–29; and for Presbyterian developments specifically, see Loetscher, *Broadening Church*, chaps. 6–8; and Massa, *Charles Augustus Briggs*, chap. 4.

12. Daniel Coit Gilman, "Centennial of the British and Foreign Bible Society," *Annual Report. American Bible Society* 58 (1904): x. Szasz, *Divided Mind*, 31; Noll, *Between Faith and Criticism*, 40, 67–75; and W. Ward Gasque, "Nineteenth-century Roots of Contemporary New Criticism," in *Scripture, Tradition, and Interpretation*, ed. W. Ward Gasque and William Sanford LaSor (Grand Rapids, Mich., 1978), 146–56, suggest reasons why the New Testament generated less controversy than the Old. For an alternative perspective, see Wacker, "Demise of Biblical Civilization."

13. William Newton Clarke, *Sixty Years with the Bible* (New York, 1909), 253; Shirley Jackson Case, *The Historicity of Jesus* (Chicago, 1912), 281; and Lyman Abbott, "The Right Use of the Bible," *Outlook* (May 28, 1904): 210, and "The New Bible," *Outlook* (May 13, 1911): 59.

14. Machen, "The New Testament Account of the Birth of Jesus"; idem, "The Hymns of the First Chapter of Luke," *PTR* 10 (1912): 1–38; idem, "The Origin of the First Two Chapters of Luke," *PTR* 10 (1912): 213–77; and idem, "The Virgin Birth in the Second Century," *PTR* 10 (1912): 533–84. Machen's efforts compare favorably with those in other journals. See, for instance, Robert T. Kerlin, "Virgil's Fourth Eclogue—An Overlooked Source," *AJP* 29 (1908): 449–60; Basil L. Gildersleeve, "A Syntactician among the Psychologists," *AJP* 31 (1910): 74–79; B. L. Ullman, "Horace and Tibullus," *AJP* 33 (1912): 450–55; Benjamin W. Robinson, "An Ephesian Imprisonment of Paul," *JBL* 29 (1910): 181–90; Henry A. Sanders, "The Genealogies of Jesus," *JBL* 32 (1913): 184–93; and Benjamin W. Bacon, "The Order of Lukan 'Interpolations,'" *JBL* 34 (1915): 166–79.

15. Machen to Minnie Gresham Machen, January 14, 1912, MA. Machen, "The

Hymns of the First Chapter of Luke," and "The Origin of the First Two Chapters of Luke" (quotations on 271). Machen could not determine whether Luke had used an oral tradition, translated an Aramaic document, or edited a written Greek source. The exact debate into which Machen entered was one dominated by the German scholars, Adolf von Harnack, H. Zimmermann, and Friedrich Spitta who had tried to account for the difference between the prologue of Luke's Gospel (Luke 1:1–4) and the birth narrative (Luke 1:5–2:52). For conservative concerns, see James M. Gray, "The Inspiration of the Bible—Definition, Extent and Proof"; L. W. Munhall, "Inspiration"; and George S. Bishop, "The Testimony of the Scriptures to Themselves," in *The Fundamentals: A Testimony to the Truth*, 4 vols. (1910–15; rpt.: Los Angeles, 1917), 2:9–43, 44–60, and 80–97.

16. J. Gresham Machen, "The Virgin Birth in the Second Century," *PTR* 10 (1912): 580; review, "The Hymns of the First Chapter of Luke and the Origin of the First Two Chapters of Luke," *Theologische Literaturzeitung*, no. 1 (Jan. 4, 1913): 8. These conclusions were pivotal to *The Virgin Birth of Christ*, published in 1930 by Harper and Brothers. On the Presbyterian Church's doctrinal affirmations, see Loetscher, *Broadening Church*, 97–99.

17. My argument here is based upon a comparison of Machen's work with the citations in n. 15 above.

18. William Park Armstrong, "Gospel History and Criticism," *PTR* 12 (1914): 427–53, quotations on 435, 443, 444. Armstrong's outline resembles the methods set out by University of Chicago scholar Ernest DeWitt Burton in "The Place of the New Testament in a Theological Curriculum."

19. Noll, *Between Faith and Criticism*, 75–78. For Princeton's views on inerrancy, see Warfield and Hodge, "Inspiration"; and Warfield, "The Divine and Human in the Bible," in *Selected Shorter Writings of Benjamin B. Warfield, II*, ed. Meeter, 542–48. For different assessments of Princeton's biblical scholarship, see Ernest R. Sandeen, *The Roots of Fundamentalism* (Chicago, 1970), 103–31; Rogers and McKim, *The Authority and Interpretation of the Bible*, 264–97; Moisés Silva, "Old Princeton, Westminster, and Inerrancy," in *Inerrancy and Hermeneutic*, ed. Harvie M. Conn (Grand Rapids, Mich., 1988), 47–66; and Thomas H. Olbricht, "Intellectual Ferment and Instruction in the Scriptures: The Bible in Higher Education," in *The Bible in American Education*, ed. David L. Barr and Nicholas Piediscalzi (Chico, Calif., 1982), 97–119.

20. On the importance of Protestantism for American thought after the rise of research universities, see May, *The End of American Innocence*; Handy, *A Christian America*; Marsden, *Religion and American Culture*, chap. 3; and D. G. Hart, "Faith and Learning in the Age of the University: The Academic Ministry of Daniel Coit Gilman," in *The Secularization of the Academy*, ed. George M. Marsden and Bradley J. Longfield (New York, 1992), chap. 4.

21. Machen to Minnie Gresham Machen, January 10, 1915, April 6 and October 6, 1916; and Faris to J. Gresham Machen, August 4, 1914, MA.

22. Machen to Minnie Gresham Machen, April 16 and October 6, 1916; Faris to J. Gresham Machen, August 4, 1914, MA.

23. Machen to Minnie Gresham Machen, June 30, 1915, MA.

24. Machen to Minnie Gresham Machen, May 10 and August 15, 1917, MA. For more detail on the steps leading up to Machen's service in the war and on his wartime experience, see Stonehouse, *J. Gresham Machen*, 240–97.

25. Machen to Minnie Gresham Machen, March 25, 1917; letter to congressmen quoted in Stonehouse, *J. Gresham Machen*, 248; Machen to Minnie Gresham Machen, September 17, 1914 and May 29, 1918, MA.

26. Pershing quoted in *Service with Fighting Men*, vol. 1 (New York, 1922), 574. See also Harold C. Warren, *With the Y.M.C.A. in France* (New York, 1919).

27. Machen to Minnie Gresham Machen, June 29, 1918, MA.

28. Machen to Minnie Gresham Machen, September 16 and May 29, 1918, MA.

29. Machen to Minnie Gresham Machen, December 5, 1918, and January 12, 1919, MA.

30. Machen to Minnie Gresham Machen, January 19, 1919, and July 15, 1920, MA.

31. Machen, *The Origin of Paul's Religion* (New York, 1921), 44, 17–19. For Machen's earlier interest in Paul, see his "Jesus and Paul," in *Biblical and Theological Studies* (New York, 1912), 545–77. On the affinities between the study of the classics and Pauline scholarship, see F. F. Bruce, "The New Testament and Classical Studies," *New Testament Studies* 22 (1976): 229–42; and Robert M. Grant, "American New Testament Study, 1926–56," *JBL* 87 (1968): 48–49.

32. Moore to Minnie Gresham Machen, January 15, 1920, and Machen to Minnie Gresham Machen, January 13, 1921, MA; "The Origin of Paul's Religion," *The Literary Supplement* (Oct. 28, 1922): 513. For a comparison of previous Sprunt lectures, see Kirk, *The Religion of Power*.

33. See William Newton Clarke, *The Ideal of Jesus* (Edinburgh, 1911); Charles Augustus Briggs, *The Ethical Teaching of Jesus* (New York, 1904); and on European developments, Welch, *Protestant Thought in the Nineteenth Century*, vol. 2, chap. 5.

34. Johannes Weiss, "The Significance of Paul for Modern Christians," *AJT* 17 (1913): 366; Arthur Cushman McGiffert, "Was Paul or Jesus the Founder of Christianity?" *AJT* 13 (1909): 1–20; Rudolph Knopf, "Paul and Hellenism," *AJT* 18 (1914): 497–520; Archibald M. Hunter, *Interpreting the New Testament, 1900–1950* (Philadelphia, 1951), 68–76; Johannes Munck, "Pauline Research since Schweitzer," W. D. Davies, "Paul and Judaism," and Helmut Koester, "Paul and Hellenism," in *The Bible in Modern Scholarship*, ed. J. Philip Hyatt (Nashville, 1965), 166–77, 178–86, 187–95.

35. Machen, *Origin of Paul's Religion*, 24.

36. Ibid., 20, 7. Representative conservative reactions to higher criticism can be found in *The Fundamentals*.

37. Ibid., 8, 16, 17, 19.

38. Ibid., chap. 5, 234–90, chap. 8, quotations on 24, 9, and 238.

39. Ibid., 316, 317. Machen recognized the inherent tension between the supernaturalistic assumptions of the biblical writers and the naturalistic premises of modern critics. See especially, *Origin of Paul's Religion*, 205–7, and 288–90. Still, he focused almost exclusively upon the historical dimension of the problem. For a philosophical approach to these issues by a Princeton scholar, see Armstrong, "Gospel History and Criticism," and "The Resurrection of Jesus," *PTR* 8 (1910): 586–616.

40. The epistemological interpretation of the modernist-fundamentalist controversy follows the insights of Thomas S. Kuhn, *The Structure of Scientific Revolutions* (Chicago, 1970). For appropriations of Kuhn, see Wacker, *Augustus H. Strong*, 16, 152–59; idem, "Demise of Biblical Civilization"; and Marsden, "Understanding

J. Gresham Machen"; idem, *Fundamentalism and American Culture*, 176–77, 212–21; Timothy P. Weber, "The Two-edged Sword: The Fundamentalist Use of the Bible," in *The Bible in America*, ed. Hatch and Noll, 101–20; Noll, *Between Faith and Criticism*, 67–68; Vander Stelt, *Philosophy and Scripture;* and Darryl G. Hart, "The Princeton Mind in the Modern World and the Common Sense of J. Gresham Machen," *WTJ* 46 (1984): 1–25. For a philosophical approach to these issues by a Princeton scholar, see Armstrong, "Gospel History and Criticism," and "The Resurrection of Jesus."

41. Wacker, *Augustus H. Strong*, 16. On the emergence of the historical consciousness, see H. Stuart Hughes, *Consciousness and Society* (New York, 1958); White, *Social Thought in America*; David W. Noble, *The Paradox of Progressive Thought* (Minneapolis, 1958); and David A. Hollinger, "William James and the Culture of Inquiry," in *In the American Province* (Bloomington, Ind., 1985), 3–22. On fundamentalism and Common Sense Realism, see works cited in note 40, above.

42. Gerald Birney Smith, Shirley Jackson Case, and D. D. Luckenbill, "Theological Scholarship at Princeton," *AJT* 17 (1913): 94–102, quotations on 95 and 100. The Princeton volume was entitled *Biblical and Theological Studies*. For a similar criticism of Princeton, see George Holley Gilbert, "A Critique of Professor Warfield's Article, 'The Christology of the New Testament Writings' in the July Number of this *Journal*," *AJT* 15 (1911): 609–13.

43. Henry J. Cadbury, "An Outstanding New Book," *The Congregationalist*, January 19, 1922; James Moffatt, review in *Hibbert Journal* 21 (1922): 807; Rudolf Bultmann, review of *The Origin of Paul's Religion*, *Theologische Literaturzeitung* 49 (1924): 13; and Edgar Whitaker Work, "The Origin of Paul's Religion," *Biblical Review* 7 (1922): 303. See also Adolf Jülicher, review of *The Origin of Paul's Religion*, *Die Christliche Welt* 33 (Aug. 17, 1922): 626.

44. Lyman Abbott, "Paul," *The Outlook* 132 (1922): 104; George A. Barton, "Paul's Religion Clearly Traced to First Source," *Philadelphia Public Ledger*, September 12, 1922; Benjamin W. Bacon, "The Divine Jesus," *Literary Review* (April 1922): 217; Cadbury, "Outstanding New Book"; Bultmann, *Theologische Literaturzeitung*, 14; and Work, "Origin of Paul's Religion," 303. On Bacon and Cadbury, see Roy A. Harrisville, *Benjamin Wisner Bacon* (Missoula, Mont., 1976); and Margaret Hope Bacon, *Let This Life Speak* (Philadelphia, 1987).

45. For evidence of shared methods and divergent theological convictions, compare Burton, "The Place of the New Testament in a Theological Curriculum"; McGiffert, "Theological Education"; idem, "The Progress of Theological Thought during the Past Fifty Years," *AJT* 20 (1916): 321–32; Benjamin W. Bacon, "The Problem of Religious Education and the Divinity School," *AJT* (1904): 690–701; Weiss, "The Significance of Paul for Modern Christians," 352–67; Smith, "What Shall the Systematic Theologian Expect?" B. B. Warfield, "The Emotional Life of Our Lord"; William Park Armstrong, "The Place of the Resurrection Appearances of Jesus"; and Machen, "Jesus and Paul," *Biblical and Theological Studies*, 35–89, 307–55, 545–77, respectively.

46. Bacon, "Ultimate Problems," 10–12; Smith, "What Shall the Systematic Theologian Expect?" 387; Robinson, *The New History*, 24; and Shirley Jackson Case, "The Historical Study of Religion," *Journal of Religion* 1 (1921): 14.

47. For evidence of this static outlook in humanistic scholarship, see George Burton Adams, "History and the Philosophy of History," *AHR* 14 (1909): 235–51; William A. Dunning, "Truth in History," *AHR* 19 (1914): 217–29; Basil L. Gildersleeve, "Thucydides," and "English and German Scholarship," in *Selections from the*

*Brief Mention of Basil Lanneau Gildersleeve*, ed. C. W. E. Miller (Baltimore, 1930), 146–48, 364–76; Paul Shorey, "Fifty Years of Classical Studies in America," *Transactions and Proceedings of the American Philological Association* 50 (1919): 55–58; Jefferson B. Fletcher, "Our Opportunity," *Publications of the Modern Language Association of America* (hereafter *PMLA*) 31 (1916): xxxiv–lvi; T. Atkinson Jenkins, "Scholarship and the Public Spirit," *PMLA* 29 (1914): lxxxvii–cxvi; and Julius Goebel, "The New Problems of American Scholarship," *PMLA* 30 (1915): lxxiv–lxxxiv. See also Laurence Veysey, "The Pluralized Worlds of the Humanities," 51–106, especially 93 n. 2; and Bruce Kuklick, "The Emergence of the Humanities," *South Atlantic Quarterly* 89 (1990): 194–206.

48. For the influence of the social sciences on the study of classical thought and religion, see F. M. Cornford, *From Religion to Philosophy* (1957; New York, 1915); Jane Ellen Harrison, *Themis* (Cambridge, 1912); and Stanley Edgar Hyman, *The Armed Vision* (New York, 1948). These studies should be compared to the traditional approach found in Paul Shorey, *The Unity of Plato's Thought* (Chicago, 1903); Clifford Herschel Moore, *The Religious Thought of the Greeks* (Cambridge, 1916); and R. D. Hicks, *Stoic and Epicurean* (New York, 1910). On connections between social thought and biblical studies, see William J. Hynes, *Shirley Jackson Case and the Chicago School* (Chico, Calif., 1980), especially chap. 5; James P. Wind, *The Bible and the University* (Atlanta, 1987); and Robert W. Funk, "The Watershed of American Biblical Tradition: The Chicago School, First Phase, 1892–1920," *JBL* 95 (1976): 4–22.

49. Machen, "Christianity in Conflict," 253. On Armstrong's lectures and student reactions, see Edwin H. Rian, "Theological Conflicts of the 1920s and 1930s in the Presbyterian Church and on the Princeton Seminary Campus," *Princeton Seminary Bulletin* 5 (1984): 219; and Clutter, *Reorientation of Princeton*, chaps. 2–3. During the rebellion of 1909 students objected especially to Armstrong's teaching. For Armstrong's arguments, see "Gospel History and Criticism," and "The Resurrection of Jesus."

50. Floyd V. Filson, "The Study of the New Testament," in *Protestant Thought in the Twentieth Century*, ed. Arnold S. Nash (New York, 1951), 60. See also Ernest W. Saunders, *Searching the Scriptures* (Chico, Calif., 1982), 53–55.

51. Machen, *Origin of Paul's Religion*, 3.

52. Ibid., 168, 169.

53. Machen, *Origin of Paul's Religion*, 7; David S. Kennedy, *Presbyterian* 91 (Nov. 10, 1921): 4; and Samuel G. Craig, "Dr. Machen on the Origin of Paul's Religion," *Presbyterian* 91 (Dec. 1, 1921): 15. Kennedy wrote that Machen's contribution would help to comfort those grieving the recent deaths of the reformed theologians B. B. Warfield, and Dutchmen Abraham Kuyper and Hermann Bavinck. For the influence of Kennedy and Craig among conservative Presbyterians, see Edwin H. Rian, *The Presbyterian Conflict* (Grand Rapids, Mich., 1940).

## Chapter 3. Highbrow Fundamentalism

*Epigraph:* Mencken, "Doctor Fundamentalis."

1. See, for instance, Coben, *Rebellion against Victorianism*; Singal, "Towards a Definition of American Modernism," chap. 1; and Hollinger, "The Canon and Its Keepers," 74–91.

2. For interpretations of fundamentalism as an effort to preserve Victorian val-

ues, see Marsden, *Fundamentalism and American Culture;* Singal, "Towards a Definition," 20–21; Hayes, *American Political History as Social Analysis,* 280–83; Williams, *American in a Changing World,* 171–72; Preston William Slosson, *The Great Crusade and After* (New York, 1930), 140, 355–57, 430–31; Winthrop S. Hudson, *Religion in America* (1965; 3d ed., New York, 1981), 365–79; and Ahlstrom, *A Religious History of the American People,* 779–84, 909–15.

3. Machen to Minnie Gresham Machen, June 5, 1923, MA; and "The Issue in the Church," in *God Transcendent,* ed. Ned Bernard Stonehouse (1949; Carlisle, Pa., 1982), 47, 49. Eight of the sermons that Machen preached during his tenure as stated supply have been reprinted in the anthology, *God Transcendent,* 15–73.

4. *Trenton Evening Times,* January 4, 1924, 1, col. 2. A scrapbook that Machen's mother prepared carries newspaper clippings on the Van Dyke incident from the *Trenton Evening Times,* January 4, 1924, the *Philadelphia Public Ledger,* January 5, 1924, the *Newark Evening News,* January 5, 1924, and the *New York Times,* January 4, 1924. See also, "Van Dyke's Pew," *Time,* January 14, 1924, 18.

5. Van Dyke quoted in Van Dyke, *Henry Van Dyke,* 405; and Lewis quoted in *After the Genteel Tradition,* ed. Malcolm Cowley (New York, 1936), 12, 13–14.

6. H. L. Mencken, "Protestantism in the Republic," in *Prejudices, Fifth Series* (New York, 1926), 111, 115. On Mencken's influence upon public perceptions and on press coverage of fundamentalism in general, see Paul M. Waggoner, "The Treatment of the Fundamentalist Movement in Major American Periodicals: 1918–1941," M.A. thesis, Trinity Evangelical Divinity School, 1982, esp. 82–85.

7. Rollin Lynde Hartt, "The War in the Churches," *World's Work* 46 (1923): 472, 473; idem, "Is the Church Dividing?" *World's Work* 47 (1923/24): 169. For Hartt's other articles, see "Down with Evolution," *World's Work* 46 (1923): 605–14; and "Fighting for Infallibility," *World's Work* 47 (1923/24): 48–56. On the importance of Bible institutes to the movement, see Marsden, *Fundamentalism and American Culture,* 129–31; and Virginia Lieson Brereton, *Training God's Army* (Bloomington, Ind., 1990). Marsden (pp. 184–95) attributes the decline of fundamentalists' respectability to the Scopes trial. For another perspective, see Paul M. Waggoner, "The Historiography of the Scopes Trial: A Critical Reevaluation," *Trinity Journal* 5, n.s. (1984): 155–74.

8. Hartt, "The War in the Churches," 470, 473, 474. Norris's use of guns seems to pervade his career. His supporters, according to Hartt (p. 473), said he carried a gun while his detractors claimed he carried two guns. Hartt also asked Norris about a rumor that the minister and his followers had defended against a possible eviction with machine guns. Norris replied, "All we had was sawed-off shot guns." On Norris's shooting a man in self-defense, see Marsden, *Fundamentalism and American Culture,* 190.

9. Machen was asked to contribute articles and reviews to the *Woman's Home Companion,* the *Philadelphia Public Ledger,* the *New York Post Literary Review, Religious Education,* and *Forum.* See "My Idea of God," *Woman's Home Companion* 52 (1925): 15, 124; review of Edward Gordon Selwyn's *The Approach to Christianity* in the *Public Ledger,* January 16, 1926; review of Douglas Clyde Macintosh's *The Reasonableness of Christianity* in the *New York Evening Post Literary Review,* January 30, 1926; "Criticism and Comments on Professor Cole's Article," *Religious Education* 22 (1927): 118–20; and manuscript prepared for *Forum*'s symposium on "Are Religion and Science Irreconcilable?" with letter from Henry Goddard Leach to Machen, July 25, 1927, MA. Machen's contribution was not used. See *Forum* 78 (1927): 328–42.

10. Machen, "Christianity versus Modern Liberalism," *Moody Monthly* 23 (1923): 349–52. The Moody Bible Institute advertisement is in the *Christianity and Liberalism* "Scrapbook," MA. *Sunday School Times*, December 8, 1923, quoted in J. M. Stanfield, *Modernism: What It Is, What It Does, Whence It Came, Its Relation to Evolution* (New York, 1927), 36.

11. See Charles Clayton Morrison, "Fundamentalism and Modernism: Two Religions," *Christian Century* (Jan. 2, 1924): 5–6; Lippmann, *Preface to Morals*, 32–34; William R. Hutchison, *Modernist Impulse*, 262–67; Marsden, *Fundamentalism and American Culture*, 174–75; and Claude Welch, "Theology," in *Religion*, ed. Paul Ramsey (Englewood Cliffs, N.J., 1965), 224–27; and Ahlstrom, *A Religious History of the American People*, 912, who calls Machen's book "the chief theological ornament of American fundamentalism."

12. Machen, "What Fundamentalism Stands for Now," in *What Is Christianity?* ed. Stonehouse, 253; "Dr. Machen Declines the Presidency of Bryan University," *Presbyterian* 97 (July 7, 1927): 8; "Does Fundamentalism Obstruct Social Progress? The Negative," *Survey Graphic* 5 (1924): 391–92, 426–27; and "What Fundamentalism Stands for Now," *New York Times*, June 21, 1925. For Machen's speaking engagements, see Machen to Minnie Gresham Machen, February 29, 1924, January 20 and March 24, 1929, and April 6, 1930; Horace Bridges to Machen, February 29, 1924; Robert S. Dawe to Machen, June 20, 1924; Henry P. Van Dusen to Machen, January 30, and March 29, 1929, MA.

13. For the historiography of fundamentalism, see Stewart G. Cole, *The History of Fundamentalism* (New York, 1931); H. Richard Niebuhr, "Fundamentalism," *Encyclopedia of Social Sciences* (New York, 1937), 6:526–27; Norman F. Furniss, *The Fundamentalist Controversy, 1918–1931* (New Haven, 1954); Ray Ginger, *Six Days or Forever? Tennessee v. John Thomas Scopes* (Boston, 1958); Richard Hofstadter, *Anti-Intellectualism in American Life* (New York, 1962); Paul A. Carter, "The Fundamentalist Defense of the Faith," in *Change and Continuity in Twentieth-century America: The 1920s*, ed. John Braeman, Robert Bremmer, and David Brody (Columbus, 1968), 179–214; Sandeen, *Roots of Fundamentalism*; Timothy P. Weber, *Living in the Shadow of the Second Coming* (New York, 1979); and Marsden, *Fundamentalism and American Culture*. Machen had two interesting exchanges with one of the first historians of fundamentalism, Stewart G. Cole, who regarded Machen as a Neo-Calvinist, not a fundamentalist. See Cole, "The Place of 'Religious Education' in the Seminary Curriculum," and Machen, "Criticism and Comments on Professor Cole's Article," *Religious Education* 22 (1927): 105–17, 118–20, respectively. Cole to Machen, March 1, and Machen to Cole, March 3, 1927, MA.

14. *God Hath Spoken: Twenty-Five Addresses Delivered at the World Conference of Christian Fundamentals* (Philadelphia, 1919), 25; Marsden, *Fundamentalism and American Culture*, 158–63. On Riley, see William Vance Trollinger, Jr., *God's Empire: William Bell Riley and Midwestern Fundamentalism* (Madison, Wis., 1990).

15. Riley to Machen, April 29, 1929; and Machen to Riley, April 30, and May 1, 1929; Machen to Milton, May 25, 1923, MA. Machen, *Christianity and Liberalism* (New York, 1923), 49. For Machen's later opposition to premillennialism, see chap. 6 below. On fundamentalism in the Southern Baptist Church and Machen's appeal in that denomination, see William E. Ellis, "*A Man of the Books and a Man of the People*": *E. Y. Mullins and the Crisis of Moderate Southern Baptist Leadership* (Macon, Ga., 1985); and James J. Thompson, Jr., *Tried as by Fire: Southern Baptists and the Religious Controversies of the 1920s* (Macon, Ga., 1982).

16. *God Hath Spoken*, 11; Noll, *Between Faith and Criticism*, 36–39; Sandeen, *Roots of Fundamentalism*, 103–31; and Marsden, *Fundamentalism and American Culture*, 51–58, 107–13.

17. Noll, *Between Faith and Criticism*, 40. On scientific naturalism, see William Jennings Bryan, *In His Image* (New York, 1922), chap. 4; and Stanfield, *Modernism*, 88–103. On premillennialism and the Bible, see I. M. Haldeman, *How to Study the Bible* (New York, 1904); and James M. Gray, *Synthetic Bible Studies*, rev. ed. (New York, 1923). For premillennial pessimism, see Isaac M. Haldeman, *The Signs of the Times* (New York, 1912); and Philip Mauro, *The Number of Man: The Climax of Civilization* (New York, 1909). The one Princeton biblical scholar whose work fundamentalists cited was the Old Testament scholar Robert Dick Wilson. His books, *Is the Higher Criticism Scholarly?* (Philadelphia, 1922), and *A Scientific Investigation of the Old Testament* (Philadelphia, 1926), were both published by The Sunday School Times Company.

18. Machen, *Christianity and Liberalism*, 1.

19. Machen to Minnie Gresham Machen, January 4 and 16, 1924, MA. The quotation comes from the latter. See also Stonehouse, *J. Gresham Machen*, 341. On Machen's dealings with Macmillan, see his correspondence with John Murray for the years 1922 and 1923; and Machen to Minnie Gresham Machen, February 27 and December 6, 1922, MA. Machen's *New Testament Greek for Beginners* is still in print and has gone through more than fifty printings.

20. Harry Emerson Fosdick, "Shall the Fundamentalists Win?" in *American Protestant Thought in the Liberal Era*, ed. William R. Hutchison (1968; Lanham, Md., 1984), 179; Machen, "The Issue in the Church," 45. For background on Fosdick's sermons, see Robert Moats Miller, *Harry Emerson Fosdick* (New York, 1985), chap. 7; and Longfield, *Presbyterian Controversy*, chap. 1.

21. See, for example, Marsden, *Fundamentalism and American Culture*, 165–67; Loetscher, *Broadening Church*, 100–102; and Longfield, *Presbyterian Controversy*, 26–27.

22. Samuel McCrea Cavert, *Church Cooperation and Unity in America* (New York, 1970), 325–29; Eldon G. Ernst, "Presbyterians and the Interchurch World Movement—A Chapter in the Development of Protestant Unity in Twentieth-century America," *JPH* 48 (1970): 231–48; and Handy, *A Christian America*, 184–97.

On the traditional conservatism of Philadelphia Presbyterianism, see Loetscher, *Broadening Church*, 110–14; Marsden, *The Evangelical Mind and the New School Presbyterian Experience*, chap. 3; Elwyn Smith, *The Presbyterian Ministry in American Culture* (Philadelphia, 1962); and Leonard J. Trinterud, *The Forming of an American Tradition: A Re-examination of Colonial Presbyterianism* (Philadelphia, 1949).

23. Machen's articles for the *Presbyterian* were "The Proposed Plan of Union," 90 (June 10, 1920): 8, 9; "For Christ or Against Him," 91 (Jan. 20, 1921): 8–9; and "The Second Declaration of the Council on Organic Union," 91 (March 17, 1921): 8, 26. The full citation for "Liberalism or Christianity?" is *PTR* 20 (1923): 93–117. On the origins of *Christianity and Liberalism*, see Machen to Minnie Gresham Machen, May 30, 1920, January 14, and December 6, 1922; John H. Cole to Machen, November 8, 1921, and March 1, 1922; and Machen to Cole, January 11, 1922, MA.

24. G.A. *Minutes*, 1923, 2:212, quoted in Longfield, *Presbyterian Controversy*, 74; Machen to Minnie Gresham Machen, May 25, 1923, MA; Loetscher, *Broadening Church*, 98–99, 109–14. On Bryan's activities as a churchman, see Longfield, 72–76;

and Lawrence W. Levine, *Defender of the Faith, William Jennings Bryan* (New York, 1965), 282–86. For Machen's views on evolution and Prohibition, see chaps. 4 and 5 below. The Philadelphia overture was largely the creation of Clarence E. Macartney, minister of Arch Street Presbyterian Church, a member of Princeton Seminary's board of directors, and the acknowledged leader of conservatives. On Macartney's leadership, see Longfield, *Presbyterian Controversy*, chap. 5; C. Allyn Russell, *Voices of American Fundamentalism* (Philadelphia, 1976), chap. 8; and Macartney, "Shall Unbelief Win? An Answer to Dr. Fosdick," *Presbyterian* 92 (July 13, 1922): 8.

25. Loetscher, *Broadening Church*, 102–3, 116–17, and Roark, *J. Gresham Machen*, chap. 2, argue that Machen's book, although well conceived, missed the mark because it did not address the American situation. Machen believed, however, that the implications of American liberalism were just as radical as those of German liberalism. See especially his review of *Christian Ways of Salvation*, PTR 21 (1923): 482–86, an evaluation of the theology of George W. Richards, the author of the preamble to the plan for organic union. On Richards, see Michael C. Romig, "George Warren Richards: Architect of Church Union," *JPH* 55 (1977): 74–99.

For Bryan's similarities to other fundamentalists and for the effects of premillennialism on fundamentalist conceptions of the church, see Marsden, *Fundamentalism and American Culture*, 134–35, 68–71; and Weber, *Living in the Shadow*, 172–76. On the importance of ecclesiology to the 1920s controversy among Presbyterians, see Ki Hong Kim, *Presbyterian Conflict in the Early Twentieth Century: Ecclesiology in the Princeton Tradition and the Emergence of Presbyterian Fundamentalism* (Ann Arbor, Mich., 1983). On Canadian struggles, see N. Keith Clifford, *The Resistance to Church Union in Canada, 1904–1939* (Vancouver, 1985). Clifford (pp. 1–8) notes that some conservatives had fundamentalist sympathies, but inerrancy and premillennialism were not at issue. Interestingly enough, Machen had cordial relations with Canadian Presbyterians and was invited in 1926 to be the principal of Knox College, the denomination's institutions. On Machen's interest in Canadian affairs, see his correspondence with Robert S. Grant from 1921 to 1930, MA; and Stonehouse, *J. Gresham Machen*, 478.

26. Machen, *Christianity and Liberalism*, 160, 52. Marsden, *Fundamentalism and American Culture*, 4, 225, 228, regards this kind of doctrinal militancy as essential to fundamentalism.

27. Machen, *Christianity and Liberalism*, chap. 4. Machen (pp. 72–79) addressed inerrancy only implicitly in his discussion of inspiration. Compare with Princeton's elaborate formula in Benjamin Breckinridge Warfield, "The Real Problem of Inspiration," in *The Inspiration and Authority of the Bible*, ed. Samuel G. Craig (Phillipsburg, Pa., 1948), 169–228; and Warfield, "Inspiration," *The International Standard Bible Encyclopedia* (Chicago, 1915), 3:1473–83. On the importance of the Bible to the fundamentalist controversy, see, for instance, Harry Emerson Fosdick, *The Modern Use of the Bible* (New York, 1924); Lippmann, *Preface to Morals* chaps. 1 and 2; and Bryan, *In His Image*. On the theology vacancy at Princeton, see Machen to Minnie Gresham Machen, April 13, 1921, and to Maitland Alexander, April 13, 1921, MA.

28. Machen, *Christianity and Liberalism*, 62–63, 67–68.

29. Ibid., 81, 86.

30. Ibid., 104–5. On the place of miracles in Princeton apologetics, see Archibald Alexander, "Inaugural Address, 1812," in *The Princeton Theology*, ed. Noll, 73–91;

and Hodge, *Systematic Theology*, 1:202–40, 633–36. For background on this line of argument, see Mark A. Noll, "The Founding of Princeton Seminary," *WTJ* 42 (1979): 72–110; Bozeman, *Protestants in an Age of Science*; and Herbert Hovenkamp, *Science and Religion in America, 1800–1860* (Philadelphia, 1978).

31. Machen, *Christianity and Liberalism*, 117, 124, 128, 132.

32. Frederick J. Hoffman, *The Twenties: American Writing in the Postwar Decade* (New York, 1949); Perry, *Intellectual Life in America*, 324–30.

33. Ernest Hemingway, *A Farewell to Arms* (New York, 1929), 196. On the postwar temper, see Hoffman, *The Twenties*, chap. 2.

34. Machen, *Christianity and Liberalism*, 64, 180, 68, 133, 134.

35. Machen, "The Church in the War," in *What Is Christianity?* 214; idem, *Christianity and Liberalism*, 138. For the reactions of Protestant clergy to the war, see Marsden, *Fundamentalism and American Culture*, chap. 16; Hutchison, *Modernist Impulse*, chap. 7; and John F. Piper, Jr., *The American Churches in World War I* (Athens, Ga., 1985).

36. See Marsden, *Fundamentalism and American Culture*, 141–53; and Weber, *Living in the Shadow*, chap. 5. For Machen's views of the war, see chap. 2 above.

37. Lyman P. Powell, "Real Cooperation of the Churches," *The American Review of Reviews* 59 (1919): 633; "Report of the Committee of Twenty," in Interchurch World Documents, 1:6; and "Interchurch World Movement Report," *New Era Magazine* 1 (1919): 522, all quoted in Eldon G. Ernst, *Moment of Truth for Protestant America* (Missoula, Mont., 1972), 55, 52, 121. On the Interchurch World Movement hymns and on the organization's business practices, see Ernst, 60 and chap. 5. See also the essays in *The Problem of Christian Unity*, ed. The Christian Unity Foundation (New York, 1921); and The Commission on the War and the Religious Outlook, *Christian Unity: Its Principles and Possibilities* (hereafter *Christian Unity*) (New York, 1921).

38. Machen, *Christianity and Liberalism*, 180.

39. Ibid., 149, 151; Machen to Minnie Gresham Machen, January 28 and April 17, 1920, MA.

40. For a fuller treatment of Machen's ideas about church and society, see chap. 6 below. On Machen's Southernness, see Longfield, *Presbyterian Controversy*, 44–49.

41. Machen, *Christianity and Liberalism*, 112.

42. Machen, "The Issue in the Church," 47.

43. Machen, "The Proposed Plan of Union," 8, 9. See also idem, "The Second Declaration of the Council on Organic Union," *Presbyterian* 91 (March 17, 1921): 8, 26.

44. Panthea Reid Broughton, *William Faulkner: The Abstract and the Actual* (Baton Rouge, La., 1974), 12, 14. On literary developments, see Hoffman, *The Twenties*, chap. 5; Graff, *Professing Literature*, 145–51; and John McCormick, *The Middle Distance* (New York, 1971).

45. Machen, *Christianity and Liberalism*, 70.

46. Review of *Christianity and Liberalism*, *Sunday School Times*, December 8, 1923, as quoted in Stanfield, *Modernism*, 36; Massee to Machen, December 12, 1922, MA; and Samuel G. Craig, review of *Christianity and Liberalism*, *Presbyterian* 93 (April 5, 1923): 13–14.

47. Reviews of *Christianity and Liberalism*, *Herald Tribune*, March 23, 1924, and *Globe*, January 19, 1924, reviews in *Christianity and Liberalism* "Scrapbook," MA.

"The Parsons' Battle," *New Republic* 37 (Jan. 9, 1924): 162. "The Case of the Fundamentalists," *Nation* 117 (Dec. 26, 1923): 729.

48. William P. Merrill, *Liberal Christianity* (New York, 1925), 14; *Presbyterian Advance*, August 16, 1923, in *Christianity and Liberalism* "Scrapbook"; Nolan R. Best, "Professor Machen's Christianity and Liberalism," *Continent* 54 (Dec. 12, 1923): 679; and Gerald Birney Smith, "A Short and Easy Way of Dealing with Liberals," *Journal of Religion* 3 (1923): 542.

49. Machen, *Christianity and Liberalism*, 52. Best considered Machen's explanations to be "unctuous cant," but Hutchison (*Modernist Impulse*, 264) believes that Machen was sincere.

50. Machen to Victor Masters, October 10, 1924, MA. See Machen, "A Debate: Is the Teaching of Dr. Harry Emerson Fosdick Opposed to the Christian Religion? Yes," *Christian Work* 117 (1924): 686–88. On Machen's strategy in attacking liberals, see Machen to Best, April 5, 1923; Machen to Albert Dale Gantz, April 13, 1923; Machen to Henry Bird, February 20, 1924; Machen to Walter Duncan Buchanan, November 21, 1923, and December 7, 1923; and Machen to Herbert A. Gibbens, May 3, 1924, MA. Fosdick quoted in Miller, *Harry Emerson Fosdick*, 142.

51. Shailer Mathews, *Faith of Modernism* (New York, 1924), 22; Merrill, *Liberal Christianity*. While Merrill explicitly refuted Machen, Mathews did not. Still, Hutchison (*Modernist Impulse*, 277) argues that Mathews's book offered "an extended response to the question of legitimacy" that Machen's book had raised.

It should be noted that Merrill defended liberalism while Mathews defended modernism. Mathews (pp. 34–35) believed that modernism was an "evangelical" movement whose starting point was "inherited orthodoxy," while liberalism tended "toward the criticism and repudiation of doctrines *per se*." For a distinction between modernism and liberalism, see Hutchison (pp. 2–9), and Kenneth Cauthen, *The Impact of Religious Liberalism* (New York, 1962). I have decided for convenience's sake to refer to Mathews and Merrill as liberals. This designation is justifiable since Merrill understood liberalism in much the same way that Mathews understood modernism. For Merrill, liberalism did not carry the connotation of denial and repudiation that it did for Mathews. See Merrill, chap. 2, especially 141, where he affirms his continuity with evangelicalism and the Westminster Confession of Faith. Machen himself was uncertain about which term to use. See Machen, *Christianity and Liberalism*, 2; and Machen to Minnie Gresham Machen, April 13, 1923, MA.

52. Mathews, *Faith of Modernism*, 162, 121, 80, 121.

53. Merrill, *Liberal Christianity*, 61, 147, 168, 152.

54. Mathews, *Faith of Modernism*, 117, 182, 117; Merrill, *Liberal Christianity*, 33; and Lippmann, *Preface to Morals*, 42–45.

## Chapter 4. Science and Salvation

Epigraph: Robert Andrews Millikan, *Science and Religion* (Boston, 1924), 51.

1. The Darrow and Bryan quotations come from Paul A. Carter, *Another Part of the Twenties* (New York, 1977), 44. On fundamentalism as a popular reaction against academic elites, see Szasz, *Divided Mind*, 131–35; and Carter, *Another Part of the Twenties*, 52–56.

2. Bryan to Machen, June 23, 1925; Machen to Bryan, July 2, 1925, MA. For Machen's involvement at the Mount Desert Congregational Church, see Rockefeller to Machen, September 20 and November 12, 1926, and September 5, 1927; Machen to Rockefeller, October 28, 1926, and September 9, 1927; William Adams Brown to Machen, March 31 and April 2, 1924; and Machen to Brown, April 1 and 3, 1924, MA. On the significance of Mount Desert Island and informal networks for mainline Protestantism, see Hutchison, "Protestantism as Establishment," 9–13. According to Rollin Lynde Hartt, "The War in the Churches," 473, Bryan's "Bible Talks" reached between 20 and 25 million people through 110 newspapers.

3. Carter, "The Fundamentalist Defense of the Faith," 210.

4. See Albert Edward Wiggam, "The Religion of the Scientist," World's Work 50 (1925): 391–99; Harry Emerson Fosdick, "Science and Religion," Harper's 152 (1926): 296–300; Edwin Grant Conklin, "Science and the Faith of a Modern," Scribner's Magazine 78 (1925): 451–58; Charles A. Ellwood, The Reconstruction of Religion (New York, 1922); William E. Hammond, The Dilemma of Protestantism (New York, 1929); Shailer Mathews, The Contributions of Science to Religion (New York, 1924); and Jabez T. Sunderland, Evolution and Religion (Boston, 1925). On challenges coming from physics, see Erwin N. Hiebert, "Modern Physics and Christian Faith," in God and Nature, ed. David C. Lindberg and Ronald L. Numbers (Berkeley, 1986), 424–47; and Stephen Kern, The Culture of Time and Space, 1880–1918 (Cambridge, 1983). For a good overview of the encounter between Christianity and science, see the essays in God and Nature.

5. Durant Drake, The New Morality (New York, 1928), 253, 255; Mather, "The Psychology of the Anti-evolutionist," in Controversy in the Twenties: Fundamentalism, Modernism, and Evolution, ed. Willard B. Gatewood (Nashville, 1969), 194, 196. See also Fosdick, "Science and Religion," 299–300; J. Macbride Sterrett, Modernism in Religion (New York, 1922), chap. 7; Eldred C. Vanderlaan, "Modernism and Historic Christianity," Journal of Religion 5 (1925): 225–38; Robert Andrews Millikan, Science and Life (Boston, 1924), 53–54; and H. G. Wells, The Outline of History (New York, 1921), 499–505.

6. Mathews, Faith of Modernism, 16–17. See also W. S. Rainsford, "The New Religious Reformation," World's Work 50 (1925): 391–99; Roy Wood Sellars, Religion Coming of Age (New York, 1928), 122–32; Charles A. Dinsmore, Religious Certitude in an Age of Science (Chapel Hill, N.C., 1924); Kirby Page, Jesus or Christianity: A Study in Contrasts (New York, 1929); and Halford E. Luccock, Jesus and the American Mind (New York, 1930). On the anticonfessional character of American evangelicalism, see Nathan O. Hatch, "Sola Scriptura and Novus Ordo Seclorum," and George M. Marsden, "Every One's Own Interpreter? The Bible, Science, and Authority in Mid-nineteenth-century America," in The Bible in America, ed. Hatch and Noll, 59–78, 79–100. For the influence of philosophical idealism on American Protestantism, see Kuklick, Churchmen and Philosophers, chaps. 13–15; and Turner, Without God, Without Creed, chaps. 6–9.

7. This is basically the argument of Carter, "Fundamentalist Defense"; Marsden, Fundamentalism and American Culture; and Sandeen, Roots of Fundamentalism.

8. George McCready Price, Back to the Bible or The New Protestantism (Takoma Park, Wash., 1916), chap. 3; Harry Rimmer, The Facts of Biology and the Theories of Evolution (Glendale, Pa., 1929), 10–13, 26. On Price and Rimmer, see Ronald L. Numbers, The Creationists: The Evolution of Scientific Creationism (New York, 1992), chaps. 4–5.

9. Rimmer, *The Harmony of Science and the Scriptures* (Glendale, Pa., 1927), 3; Price, *The Phantom of Organic Evolution* (New York, 1924), 9; Price, *Back to the Bible*, 6.

10. Machen hints at this argument in his letter to Bryan, July 2, 1925, MA.

11. Noll, *Between Faith and Criticism*, 56. For the way other Protestants handled the virgin birth, see William Bell Riley, "The Faith of the Fundamentalists," *Current History* 26 (1927): 334–36; Fosdick, "Shall the Fundamentalists Win?" 174–77; Frederic Palmer, *The Virgin Birth* (New York, 1924); Leighton Parks, *What Is Modernism?* (New York, 1924), 76; and Shirley Jackson Case, *Experience with the Supernatural in Early Christian Times* (New York, 1929).

12. W. H. Murray to Machen, April 16, 1930, and Machen to Murray, April 17, 1930, MA.

13. Machen to Eugene Exman, Feb. 21, 1931; and Machen to Minnie Gresham Machen, July 21, 1929, MA. *The Times Literary Supplement*, April 10, 1930; *New York Herald Tribune*, August 17, 1930; Cadbury, "The Virgin Birth of Christ," *Christian Century* (March 4, 1931), in *The Virgin Birth "Scrapbook,"* MA. For other reviews, see *Expository Times* (1930); *Biblical Review* (1930); *Anglican Theological Review* (1930); *Die Christliche Welt* (March 14, 1931); *Theologische Studien und Kritizen* (Sept. 4, 1930); *Journal of Religion* (1930); *Deutsche Literatureseitung* (Jan. 24, 1932); all in *The Virgin Birth "Scrapbook."*

On the appeal of dispensationalism, see Noll, *Between Faith and Criticism*, 57–61; and Weber, *Living in the Shadow of the Second Coming* (New York, 1979). For a recent estimate of Machen's book, see Stephen Farris, *The Hymns of Luke's Infancy Narratives: Their Origin, Meaning, and Significance* (Sheffield, 1985), 22–23, 27, 109. Machen's relationship with his publisher can be followed in his correspondence with W. H. Murray beginning in 1920, MA.

14. Machen, *The Virgin Birth of Christ*, 43, vii–viii, 320–23, 379. *Baltimore Southern Methodist*, March 27, 1930, *The Virgin Birth "Scrapbook"*; Machen, *The Virgin Birth of Christ*, x.

15. Machen, *The Virgin Birth of Christ*, 219, 384–94. On the place of revelation in modernist thought, contrast Kenneth Cauthen's distinction between evangelical and modernistic liberals, in *Impact of Religious Liberalism*, 27, 29, with Hutchison's definition of modernism, in *Modernist Impulse*, 4–9. Machen detected in D. C. Macintosh's *The Reasonableness of Christianity* (New York, 1925) an attempt to circumvent historical criticism.

16. For Machen's objections to modernist biblical scholarship in the 1920s, see "He Opened to Us the Scriptures" (review of Benjamin W. Bacon), *PTR* 21 (1923): 640–42; "Inspiration: A Study of Divine Influence and Authority in the Holy Scripture" (review of Nolan R. Best), *PTR* 21 (1923): 672–79; "Jesus of Nazareth: A Biography" (review of George A. Barton), *PTR* 22 (1924): 665–67; and "The Character of Paul" (review of Charles Edward Jefferson), *PTR* 22 (1924): 667–70. He was especially critical of Fosdick's *The Modern Use of the Bible* and Edgar Johnson Goodspeed's translation of the New Testament, *The New Testament: An American Translation* (New York, 1923). See Machen, "The Modern Use of the Bible," *PTR* 23 (1925): 66–81, reprinted in *What Is Christianity?* ed. Stonehouse, 185–200; and Machen, *What Is Faith?* (New York, 1925), 24–26. For his appreciative comments of a liberal scholar who recognized the problems of modern scholarship, see Machen's review of Arthur Cushman McGiffert's *The God of the Early Christians* (New York, 1924), "The God of the Early Christians," *PTR* 22 (1924): 544–88. On Machen's general

assessment of the state of New Testament scholarship, see his "Forty Years of New Testament Research," *Union Seminary Review* (Richmond) 40 (1928): 1–11.

17. Machen, *What Is Faith?* 27, 144–48. Machen's thought here follows that of older Princeton theologians. See *The Princeton Theology*, ed. Noll. For a perceptive analysis of the rationalistic assumptions informing American Protestant theology, see Mark A. Noll, "The Rise and Long Life of the Protestant Enlightenment in America," paper presented at the Symposium on Knowledge and Belief in America, The Wilson Center, Washington, D.C., April, 1991.

18. Machen, *What Is Faith?* 26.

19. Ibid., 149, 98–102, 157, 159. Machen had a good deal of respect for American Lutherans. He wrote to Clarence Macartney that the Lutheran's "healthy denominational consciousness" and catechetical instruction had prevented modernism from making inroads into their churches, February 28, 1924, MA.

20. *What Is Faith?* 27, 35.

21. Ibid., 235, 238.

22. Ibid., 52, 30, 32.

23. Ibid., 16, 75–78, 33, 131, 249.

24. Ibid., 249–50, 135.

25. Ibid., 20, 23, 27.

26. On the democratic character of American evangelicalism, see Nathan O. Hatch, *The Democratization of American Christianity* (New Haven, 1989). For the implications of popularization on evangelical intellectual life, see, Mark A. Noll, "The Evangelical Mind in America," paper presented at the Religion and American Culture Seminar, Institute for the Study of American Evangelicals, Wheaton College, April, 1991.

27. Machen, "The Relation of Religion to Science and Philosophy" (review of *Christianity at the Cross Roads*, by E. Y. Mullins), PTR 24 (1926): 38, 51, 47. For Mullins's critique of Machen, see his review of *What Is Faith?* in *Review and Expositor* 23 (1926): 198–205. On this Baptist tradition of apologetics, see Wacker, *Augustus H. Strong*, chap. 7; Ellis, "*A Man of Books and a Man of the People*," chap. 4; and Marsden, *Fundamentalism and American Culture*, 107–8, 122, 216–17.

28. Machen, *Christianity and Liberalism*, 6.

29. Machen, "What Fundamentalism Stands for Now," 255.

30. Machen to Bryan, July 2, 1925, MA. Machen, "Against Phi Beta Kappa Resolution on Free Speech in Colleges" (letter to editor), *New York Times*, September 18, 1925.

31. On that controversy, see Thompson, *Presbyterians in the South*, Vol. 2: *1861–1890*, 442–90.

32. Warfield, "Calvin's Doctrine of Creation" [1915], in *Works of Benjamin B. Warfield*, vol. 5 (New York, 1927), 305. Machen to George S. Duncan, February 18, 1924; Machen to Edward J. Russell, February 20, 1924; and Machen to Lloyd Shippen, February 22 and 27, 1929, MA.

33. Machen, *The Christian View of Man* (1937; Edinburgh, 1965), 145. This point is also made by David N. Livingstone, *Darwin's Forgotten Defenders* (Grand Rapids, Mich., 1987), 64–65.

34. Ibid., 114–20.

35. Ibid., 120–23.

36. Machen, "What Fundamentalism Stands for Now," 255; Vernon Kellogg, "What Evolution Stands for Now," *New York Times*, June 21, 1925.

37. See, for instance, Marsden, *Fundamentalism and American Culture*, 212–21; Wacker, *Augustus H. Strong*, 24–31, 111–20; and Noll, "Common Sense Traditions and American Evangelical Thought," 216–38. Modernists offered a similar interpretation. See Mathews, *Faith of Modernism*, 16–18; and Henry Sloane Coffin, "Fundamentalists and Modernists Should Work Together Amicably," in *The Real Issue* 1 (1924): 3–4.

38. Harry Emerson Fosdick, *Christianity and Progress* (New York, 1922), 154. See also Gerald Birney Smith, "Can Christianity Welcome Freedom of Teaching?" *Journal of Religion* 2 (1922): 245–62; Mathews, *Contributions of Science to Religion*, chap. 16; Maynard Shipley, *The War on Modern Science: A Short History of the Fundamentalist Attacks on Evolution and Modernism* (New York, 1927), 3–8; *The Summarized Proceedings of the American Association for the Advancement of Science, 1921–1925* (Washington, D.C., 1925), 66–67 (hereafter *Summarized Proceedings*); and Henry Fairfield Osborn, *Evolution and Religion in Education* (New York, 1925). For the persistence of inductive or Baconian methods in American conceptions of science, see David A. Hollinger, *Morris R. Cohen and the Scientific Ideal* (Cambridge, 1975), 143–52.

39. *Summarized Proceedings*, 67, reprinted in *Controversy in the Twenties*, ed. Gatewood, 170; Bryan to Machen, June 23, 1925, MA; Machen to Bryan, July 2, 1925, MA; Machen, *What Is Faith?* 219–20. See A. C. Dixon, "The Root of Modern Evils," in *Controversy in the Twenties*, ed. Gatewood, 123; John W. Porter, *Evolution—A Menace* (Nashville, 1922), 29; John Roach Straton, *The Famous New York Fundamentalist-Modernist Debates: The Orthodox Side* (New York, 1925), 59–61; Robert Andrews Millikan, *Evolution in Science and Religion* (New Haven, 1927); Harry Emerson Fosdick, "A Reply to Mr. Bryan in the Name of Religion," *New York Times*, March 12, 1922, in *Evolution and Religion: The Conflict between Science and Theology in Modern America*, ed. Gail Kennedy (Boston, 1957), 30–34; and Mathews, *Contributions of Science to Religion*, 397–402.

40. John Dewey, *A Common Faith* in *John Dewey: The Later Works, 1925–1935*, Vol. 9: *1933–34*, ed. Jo An Boydston (Carbondale, Ill., 1981). See also Henry Nelson Wieman, Douglas Clyde Macintosh, and Max Carl Otto, *Is There a God? A Conversation* (Chicago, 1932), originally published in the *Christian Century* from February to August 1932; and Dewey's response, "Dr. Dewey Replies," *Christian Century* (March 22, 1933). William R. Hutchison (*Modernist Impulse*, 5–9) defines modernism by its desire to expand Christianity beyond traditional categories. For connections among Protestantism, social science, and progressivism, see Dorothy Ross, *The Origins of American Social Science* (Cambridge, 1991); Daniel T. Rodgers, "In Search of Progressivism," in *The Promise of American History*, ed. Stanley I. Kutler and Stanley N. Katz (Baltimore, 1982), 121–27; David B. Danbom, *"The World of Hope": Progressives and the Struggle for an Ethical Public Life* (Philadelphia, 1987); John Higham, "Hanging Together: Divergent Unities in American History," *JAH* 61 (1974): 20–27; and Gary Scott Smith, "The Men and Religion Forward Movement of 1911–1912," *WTJ* 49 (1987): 91–118.

41. Mathews, *Faith of Modernism*, 10–11.

42. Machen, *What Is Faith?* 115, 71ff.; and idem, *Christianity and Liberalism*, 153ff.

43. Paul Elmer More, *The Christ of the New Testament* (Princeton, 1924); John Crowe Ransom, *God without Thunder* (1930; New York, 1965), 328; Paul Elmer More, *On Being Human* (Princeton, 1936), 153. For a similar perspective, see T. S. Eliot,

"Second Thoughts about Humanism," in *Selected Essays* (New York, 1932), 429–38. On antiformalism in American social thought, see White, *Social Thought in America*; and Kloppenberg, *Uncertain Victory.*

Liberal Protestants denied these charges and countered that religious experience was a proper remedy to the impersonal universe offered by science. See Merrill, *Liberal Christianity*, 41–58; Fosdick, *The Modern Use of the Bible*, 244–51; and Mathews, *Contributions of Science to Religion*, chap. 17.

44. On the religious concerns of New Humanists, the Southern Agrarians, and T. S. Eliot, see Hoeveler, *The New Humanism*, 162–81; and Singal, *The War Within*, chap. 7. On the differences that academic specialization encouraged among humanistic scholars, see Veysey, "The Pluralized Worlds of the Humanities," 51–106. On the appeal of scientific methods and assumptions to American Protestants, see Noll, "The Rise and Long Life of the Protestant Enlightenment."

45. A good overview of the impact of science upon Christian thought is Turner, *Without God, Without Creed.*

46. Hutchison, *Modernist Impulse*, 8; Frederick Gregory, "The Impact of Darwinian Evolution on Protestant Theology," in *God and Nature*, ed. Lindberg and Numbers, 369–90; and Numbers, "The Creationists."

47. Mathews, *Faith of Modernism*, 112–13; and quotation in Carter, *Another Part of the Twenties*, 47. For similar explanations of the miraculous, see Fosdick, *The Modern Use of the Bible*, 131–69; Parks, *What Is Modernism?* chap. 2; and Merrill, *Liberal Christianity*, 24–29.

48. William Jennings Bryan, *Orthodox Christianity versus Modernism* (New York, 1923), 29; and J. E. Conant, *The Church, The Schools and Evolution* (Chicago, 1922), in *Controversy in the Twenties*, ed. Gatewood, 115. On the importance of evolution to fundamentalism, see Marsden, *Fundamentalism and American Culture*, 212–21; Gatewood's introductions in *Controversy in the Twenties*, 31–36, 113–16; Szasz, *Divided Mind*, chap. 9; and Numbers, "The Creationists," 394–403.

49. Machen, "What Fundamentalism Stands for Now," 253. See also *Christianity and Liberalism*, 105; *The Virgin Birth of Christ*, 381; and Machen to Bryan, July 2, 1925, MA.

50. Robinson quoted in Stonehouse, *J. Gresham Machen*, 425. J. H. Dickinson to Machen, April 4, 1929; Biederwolf to Machen, June 19, 1929; and Gray, July 7, 1929; and Chafer to Machen, July 3, 1929, MA.

51. Bryan to Machen, June 23, 1925, and Machen to Bryan, July 2, 1925, MA. The best treatment of fundamentalist higher education is Brereton, *Training God's Army.*

52. Machen, "Criticism and Comments on Professor Cole's Article," 119; and idem, *What Is Faith?* 15, 19, 21. For a conventional treatment of Progressive educational reforms, see Lawrence A. Cremin, *The Transformation of the School* (New York, 1961). For the views of humanistic scholars on higher education, see Hoeveler, *The New Humanism*, chaps. 4 and 5; and Laurence Veysey, "Stability and Experiment in the American Undergraduate Curriculum," in *Content and Context*, ed. Carl Kaysen (New York, 1973), 1–63.

53. "Criticism and Comments on Professor Cole's Article," 120. For changes in mainstream Protestant theological education during the 1920s, see Robert Kelly, *Theological Education in America* (New York, 1924); William Adams Brown and Mark A. May, *The Education of American Ministers*, 4 vols. (New York, 1934); and

Stephen A. Schmidt, *A History of the Religious Education Association* (Birmingham, 1983), chaps. 2 and 3. For the training fundamentalists offered, see Brereton, *Training God's Army.*

## Chapter 5. A Question of Character

*Epigraphs:* Orisen Swett Marden, *Masterful Personality* (New York, 1921), 41–42; Charles Erdman, *The Doctrine of the Spirit* (New York, 1926), 100.

1. On the organizational transformation of American Protestantism, see Ben Primer, *Protestants and American Business Methods* (Ann Arbor, Mich., 1979); Louis Weeks, "The Incorporation of American Religion: The Case of the Presbyterians," *Religion and American Culture* 1 (1991): 101–18; the essays in *The Organizational Revolution: Presbyterians and American Denominationalism*, ed. Milton J Coalter, John M. Mulder, and Louis Weeks (Louisville, 1992); and Samuel Haber, *Efficiency and Uplift: Scientific Management in the Progressive Era, 1890–1920* (Chicago, 1964), 63. For the bureaucratic revolution in American society, see Wiebe, *The Search for Order.*

2. On the changing conceptions of the self spawned by modern industrial capitalism, see Warren I. Susman, *Culture as History* (New York, 1984), chap. 14; and Lears, *No Place of Grace.* On the way large denominations dealt with divisions, see Primer, *Protestants and American Business Methods*, chap. 8.

3. Samuel Chadwick, "What Is Faith?" (March 25, 1926); W. B. Selbie, "Let Us Christianize Our Theology" (April 1, 1926); C. Rydar Smith, "The Way of the Peacemaker" (April 8, 1926); H. R. Mackintosh, "The Religion of the Centre" (April 15, 1926); W. M. MacGregor, "Fundamentalism: A Friendly Admonition" (May 27, 1926); J. T. Forbes, "Faith and Knowledge" (June 10, 1926); A. B. Macaulay, "Preacher and Controversialist" (July 1, 1926); W. M. Clow, "The Puritan Gospel" (July 8, 1926); letter to the editor (June 3, 1926); and "Dr. Machen's Acknowledgement," *British Weekly* 80 (Sept. 23, 1926), in *What Is Faith?* "Scrapbook," MA. Machen and the *British Weekly*'s editor, Dr. John B. Hutton, had met at the Grove City Bible Conference where Machen had delivered the substance of the book as lectures. See Stonehouse, *J. Gresham Machen*, 397–400.

4. Machen, *The Christian Faith in the Modern World* (New York, 1936); idem, *The Christian View of Man* (New York, 1937). For background on these addresses, see Stonehouse, *J. Gresham Machen*, 505–6.

5. For Protestant cooperative efforts from the 1920s and their rationale, see Frederick Lynch, *The Christian Unity Movement in America* (London, 1923); *The Problem of Christian Unity*, ed. The Christian Unity Foundation (New York, 1921); *Christian Unity*; Primer, *Protestants and American Business Methods*; W. Lloyd Warner, ed., *The Emergent American Society: Large-Scale Organizations*, Vol. 1 (New Haven, 1967), chap. 11; James H. Madison, "Reformers and the Rural Church," *JAH* 73 (1986): 645–68; and Charles E. Harvey, "John D. Rockefeller, Jr., and the Interchurch World Movement of 1919–1920: A Different Angle on the Ecumenical Movement," *Church History* 51 (1982): 198–209. On centralization within the Presbyterian Church, see Loetscher, *Broadening Church*, chap. 11.

6. See Robert Hastings Nichols, "Fundamentalism in the Presbyterian Church," *Journal of Religion* 5 (1925): 14–36; William Pierson Merrill, "The Aims of Liberal Presbyterians," *Christian Work* (May 23, 1925): 652–55; and Henry Sloane Coffin,

"What Liberal Presbyterians Are Standing For," *Christian Work* (May 30, 1925): 684–87.

Theologians and historians have criticized Machen's understanding of the church as a departure from Presbyterian tradition. See, for instance, Loetscher, *Broadening Church*, 117; Edward J. Carnell, *The Case for Orthodox Theology* (Philadelphia, 1959), 114–16; Roark, *J. Gresham Machen*, chap. 5; C. Russell, *Voices of American Fundamentalism*, 158–61; Sandeen, *Roots of Fundamentalism*, 257–60; Clutter, *Reorientation of Princeton*, 226–34; and Mark A. Noll, "Commemorating a Warrior," *Reformed Journal* 37 (1987): 4–6.

7. Historians have often overlooked the legal arguments of fundamentalists. See, for instance, Loetscher, *Broadening Church*, 117; Russell, *Voices of American Fundamentalism*, 158–61; and Sandeen, *Roots of Fundamentalism*, 257–60. For a different perspective, see Kim Ki-Hong, *Presbyterian Conflict in the Early Twentieth Century*.

8. Machen, "The Parting of the Ways," *Presbyterian* 94 (April 1924): 7; and idem, *Christianity and Liberalism*, 163–66.

9. Machen, *Christianity and Liberalism*, 168; idem, "Honesty and Freedom in the Christian Ministry," *Moody Monthly* 24 (1924): 355–57; idem, "Christianity and Liberty: A Challenge to the 'Modern Mind,' " *Forum and Century* 85 (1931): 162–66; and idem, "Relations between Jews and Christians," in *What Is Christianity?* ed. Stonehouse, 113.

10. Machen, *Christianity and Liberalism*, 168–69, 162–63, 170.

11. Ibid., 160, 163.

12. Ibid., 21–23, 168–70; Machen, "Honesty and Freedom in the Christian Ministry," 355–56.

13. Machen, *Christianity and Liberalism*, 167–68; "Does Fundamentalism Obstruct Social Progress?" 249; Machen, *Christianity and Liberalism*, 162–63; "Relations between Jews and Christians," 106, 107; and Walter Lippmann, *American Inquisitors* (New York, 1928), 65–66.

14. Machen, *Christianity and Liberalism*, 160, 167.

15. On evangelical traits, see Mark A. Noll, "The Scandal of Evangelical Political Reflection, 1896–1991," paper presented at the Ethics and Public Policy Center, Washington, D.C., April 1991. On the relationship between corporate developments and personality, see Primer, *Protestants and American Business*, chap. 8; Karen Halttunen, *Confidence Men and Painted Women* (New Haven, 1982), 198–210; and Weeks, "The Incorporation of American Religion," 101–18.

16. Loetscher, *Broadening Church*, chap. 13; Longfield, *Presbyterian Controversy*, chap. 6. Interestingly enough, John Foster Dulles, then a young New York attorney and Presbyterian elder, supplied legal council for the liberals. See, Mark G. Toulouse, *The Transformation of John Foster Dulles* (Macon, Ga., 1985), 15–26.

17. G.A. *Minutes*, 1925, 87, 25; Loetscher, *Broadening Church*, 125–28; Longfield, *Presbyterian Controversy*, chap. 6; and Morgan Phelps Noyes, *Henry Sloane Coffin: The Man and His Ministry* (New York, 1964), 173–76.

On theological traditions of New York Presbyterianism, see Robert Hastings Nichols, *Presbyterianism in New York State*, edited and completed by James Hastings Nichols (Philadelphia, 1963); Smith, *The Presbyterian Ministry in American Culture*; Trinterud, *The Forming of an American Tradition*; Marsden, *The Evangelical Mind and the New School Presbyterian Experience*; idem, "The New School Heritage and Presbyterian Fundamentalism," *WTJ* 32 (1970): 129–47; and Loetscher, *Broadening Church*, chap. 12.

18. *AN AFFIRMATION designed to safeguard the unity and the liberty of the Presbyterian Church . . .* (Auburn, 1924), 6. On the document's origins and its impact, see Charles Evans Quirk, *The Auburn Affirmation: A Critical Narrative of the Document Designed to Safeguard the United and Liberty of the Presbyterian Church U.S.A* (Ann Arbor, Mich., 1967), 78–115, chap. 3. On the tactics of conservatives and liberals, see Delwin G. Nykamp, "A Presbyterian Power Struggle: A Critical History of Communication Strategies Employed in the Struggle for Control of the Presbyterian Church, U.S.A., 1922–1926," Ph.D. diss., Northwestern University, 1974.

19. Machen, "A Counter-Affirmation designed to Safeguard the Corporate Witness of the Presbyterian Church to the Gospel of Jesus Christ" (n.d.), 1, 2, MA.

20. Toulouse, *John Foster Dulles,* 19–22.

21. For Erdman's platform, see "Dr. Erdman Holds to Law of Church," *Philadelphia Public Ledger,* April 30, 1924. For Machen's opposition to Erdman and his reaction to the 1925 Assembly, see Machen, "Dr. Machen Replies to Dr. Erdman," *Presbyterian* 95 (Feb. 5, 1925): 20–21; idem, *Statement by J. Gresham Machen . . . to the Committee Appointed by Action of the General Assembly of 1926 . . .* (1926), 9, 10, 12–13, 21; idem, *Additional Statement Concerning the Personal Relations between the Rev. Professor Charles R. Erdman . . .* (1926); and Machen to Minnie Gresham Machen, June 5, 1925, MA.

22. G.A. *Minutes,* 1926, 68, 65–66, 86–87; and papers related to the Special Commission of 1925 of the General Assembly of the Presbyterian Church in the U.S.A., Presbyterian Historical Society, Philadelphia.

23. G.A. *Minutes,* 1926, 73; Longfield, *Presbyterian Controversy,* 158–61; and Loetscher, *Broadening Church,* 136.

24. G.A. *Minutes,* 1926, 71–72.

25. Ibid., 71–72; and "Written and Verbal Statements of Rev. J. Gresham Machen, D.D., Rev. Henry Sloane Coffin, D.D., Rev. William Adams Brown, D.D., Rev. Clarence E. Macartney, D.D., Presented to the Special Commission of 1925 . . . ," 1–5, MA.

26. "Written and Verbal Statements . . . ," 6, 17; Loetscher, *Broadening Church,* 135, makes the argument that the Special Commission's report signified theological diversity within the church. For a similar perspective, see Longfield, *Presbyterian Controversy* 156–61; and Milton J. Coalter, John M. Mulder, and Louis B. Weeks, *The Re-Forming Tradition: Presbyterians and Mainstream Protestantism* (Louisville, 1992), 119–26.

27. Machen to Macartney, May 29, 1926, and Machen to Maitland Alexander, May 29, 1926, MA; Albert J. McCartney, *Literary Digest* (June 26, 1926): 28, quoted in Longfield, *Presbyterian Controversy,* 160. See also Loetscher, *Broadening Church,* 133; Quirk, *Auburn Affirmation,* 269.

One explanation for conservative compliance at the 1926 assembly was that they had little time to study the report. Despite "Standing Rule 29 of the General Assembly," which stated that all reports of special and other committees be delivered to the stated clerk on or before April 1, the Special Commission only approved its report in late May shortly before the 1926 General Assembly. See "The Minutes of the Special Commission of 1925 . . . , May 24–25, 1926"; and Quirk, *Auburn Affirmation,* 294–95.

28. Loetscher, *Broadening Church,* 141; Clutter, *Reorientation of Princeton,* 166–68; Stonehouse, *J. Gresham Machen,* 383–87.

29. "Statement Regarding the Eighteenth Amendment and the Volstead Act"

(Princeton, 1926), 3–4; Craig to Machen, August 11, 1926, MA; "Presbyterians Deplore Report on Volsteadism," *Baltimore Evening Sun,* June 2, 1926; Longfield, *Presbyterian Controversy,* 163–65. The assembly's prohibitionist stance came in response to a report by the Federal Council of Churches that questioned the wisdom of the Volstead Act.

30. *New York Herald Tribune,* June 3, 1926; G.A. *Minutes,* 1926, 174; "The General Assembly," *Presbyterian* 96 (June 10, 1926): 17.

31. G.A. *Minutes,* 1926, 174–75. On Thompson, see Francis P. Weisenburger, "William Oxley Thompson: Clergyman and Educator," *JPH* 49 (1971): 80–97. Some conservatives argued that according to church law Machen's election was complete because the Assembly had not vetoed his nomination. See Samuel G. Craig, *The Report on the Princeton Seminary Committee, A Criticism* (Philadelphia, 1926), 3–4.

32. "Dr. Henry Van Dyke Returns to His Old Church," *Presbyterian* 95 (Jan. 15, 1925): 12; Machen, *Documents Appended to a Statement by J. Gresham Machen* (Princeton, 1926), 15–103. The best accounts of this episode are Stonehouse, *J. Gresham Machen,* chap. 19; and Clutter, *Reorientation of Princeton,* 133–56.

33. "Transcript of the Hearings by the General Assembly's Special Committee to Visit Princeton Theological Seminary" (hereafter "THPTS"), November 22–24, 1926, and January 5–6, 1927, 211–16, MA; "Dr. Erdman Speaks in Self-Defense," *Presbyterian Advance* 30 (Jan. 22, 1925): 24; "Dr. Machen Replies to Dr. Erdman," *Presbyterian* 95 (Feb. 5, 1925): 20–21; Machen to David S. Kennedy, January 30, 1925, MA; and *Statement by J. Gresham Machen* (Princeton, 1926), 16–23.

34. "THPTS," 1, 48; *Statement by J. Gresham Machen,* 33; and Machen to Donald M. Grant, Dec. 23, 1927, MA.

35. *Statement by J. Gresham Machen,* 21, 9, 10, 12–13. See also F. Harper to Machen, May 4, 1925; Billy Sunday to Machen, May 14, 1925; and S. Earl Orwig to Machen, May 14, 1925, MA.

36. *Statement by J. Gresham Machen,* 21, 22, 27ff.

37. "THPTS," 213.

38. Ibid., 244, 246–47.

39. Ibid., 252–53.

40. Curricular reforms at Princeton in the 1910s are covered well by Clutter, *Reorientation of Princeton.* On the educational philosophy of Bible schools, see Brereton, *Training God's Army.*

41. See D. G. Hart, " 'Dr. Fundamentalis': An Intellectual Biography of J. Gresham Machen, 1881–1937," Ph.D. diss., Johns Hopkins University, 1988, chap. 7.

42. "THPTS," 53–56, 58. Machen, *Christianity and Liberalism,* remains the best summary of this perspective.

43. Charles Erdman, *The Spirit of Christ* (New York, 1926), 11; idem, *Pastoral Epistles of Paul: An Exposition* (Philadelphia, 1923), 40; "The Power of the Holy Spirit," a sermon delivered before the 1926 General Assembly, G.A. *Minutes,* 1926, 34; and Longfield, *Presbyterian Controversy,* chap. 6. For Stevenson's views see "The Presbyterian Church and Unity," in *Christian Unity,* 77–83; and *The Historical Position of Princeton Seminary* (New York, 1928).

44. "THPTS," 62–63, 72, 236, 243. *Historical Position of Princeton Seminary,* 11. For insinuations that Machen's publications were unconstitutional, see "THPTS," 50–52, 200–206. The committee ruled, however, that Machen's writings did not

violate Presbyterian law. For interpretations that regard Machen as a "low church-man" and Stevenson and Erdman as "high churchmen," see Loetscher, *Broadening Church,* 137–47; and Clutter, *Reorientation of Princeton,* 123–24.

45. *Report of the Special Committee to Visit Princeton Theological Seminary . . .* (Philadelphia, 1927), 12–14, 3, 48.

46. Loetscher, *Broadening Church,* 144.

47. William Park Armstrong, *Certain Legal Aspects of the Proposal to Amend the Charter of the Trustees of Princeton Theological Seminary* (Princeton, 1928), 12–15; Craig, *Report on the Princeton Seminary Committee,* 3–5; Machen, *The Attack upon Princeton Seminary: A Plea for Fair Play* (Princeton, 1927), 40–42; and *A Resolution of the Faculty of Princeton Theological Seminary* (Princeton, 1927); Machen, "Statement on Proposed Reorganization of Princeton Seminary," *New York Evening Post,* September 29, 1927; idem, "Dr. Machen's Pamphlet," *Presbyterian Banner* 114 (Jan. 19, 1928): 5–6; idem, "Princeton Seminary Control" (letter to editor), *New York Herald Tribune,* February 12, 1928; and idem, "The Gist of the Princeton Question," *Presbyterian* 98 (May 17, 1928): 16.

The thorny legal question was whether a 1920 New Jersey statute, which allowed the officials of an educational or charitable institution to amend its charter, applied to the Board of Trustees. Arthur Machen argued that the directors, not the trustees, were Princeton's "educational corporation" under state law. See *Legal Opinion of Humes, Buck and Smith* (New York, 1928); and Armstrong, Machen, and Allen, *Legal Opinion on Questions Involved in Proposed Reorganization of Princeton Theological Seminary* (Baltimore, 1928). For the church's appeal to this New Jersey statute, see G.A. *Minutes,* 1928, 170–71; and "The Reorganization of Princeton Seminary," *Princeton Seminary Bulletin* 23 (1929): 2.

48. Longfield, *Presbyterian Controversy,* 168–73; and Loetscher, *Broadening Church,* 143–46.

49. Machen to James M. Gray, June 22, 1927, MA.

50. Machen to Minnie Gresham Machen, June 16, 1929; Machen to Raymond I. Brahams, April 26, 1928, MA; and "Westminster Theological Seminary: Its Purpose and Plan," in *What Is Christianity?* ed. Stonehouse, 232–33.

51. Machen, *Attack upon Princeton,* 33. On Machen's role at Princeton, see Stonehouse, *J. Gresham Machen,* chap. 21; Clutter, *Reorientation of Princeton,* 166–96; John W. Hart, "Princeton Theological Seminary: The Reorganization of 1929," *JPH* 58 (1980): 124–40; George L. Haines, "The Princeton Theological Seminary, 1925–1960," Ph.D. diss., New York University, 1966, 63–64; and Rian, *The Presbyterian Conflict,* chap. 3. Martin Marty (*Irony of It All* and *Noise of Conflict*) provides a helpful overview of these developments within mainstream Protestantism.

52. Sandeen, *Roots of Fundamentalism,* 257; and Robert Moats Miller, "A Compleat (Almost) Guide Through the Forest of Fundamentalism," *Reviews in American History* 9 (1981): 397. See also Ahlstrom, *A Religious History of the American People,* 912; Hudson, *Religion in America,* 3d ed. (New York, 1981), 372–73; Loetscher, *Broadening Church,* 143, 147; Furniss, *The Fundamentalist Controversy,* 35; and Clutter, *Reorientation of Princeton,* 232–33. One exception to this line of analysis is George Marsden, "J. Gresham Machen, History, and Truth," *WTJ* 42 (1979): 172–75, who links Machen's dogmatism to his philosophical outlook.

Leo P. Ribuffo, *The Old Christian Right: The Protestant Far Right from the Great Depression to the Cold War* (Philadelphia, 1983), xiii–xvi, observes a trend among students of extremism to dismiss the far right in psychological categories. Although he focuses on political extremism, Ribuffo's observation may apply equally well to studies of fundamentalism that have attributed religious extremism to various degrees of status anxiety, paranoia, or other temperamental disorders. See for instance, Niebuhr, "Fundamentalism," 6:526–27; Furniss, *The Fundamentalist Controversy;* and Hofstadter, *Anti-Intellectualism in American Life.*

53. For reports about Machen's personality, see testimony throughout "THPTS"; and Paul Hutchinson, "The Battle of Princeton—1925," *Christian Century* (May 25, 1925): 699–701.

54. For a sense of their relationship, see Stonehouse, *J. Gresham Machen,* who provides extensive quotations from this correspondence.

55. Betsy Palmer, interview with the author, May 14, 1988. On Machen's romance, see Stonehouse, *J. Gresham Machen,* 320.

56. See correspondence between Machen and Robinson; and Machen and Armstrong family, MA.

57. See "Personal Reminiscences of J. Gresham Machen," 6–10, 13. On Machen's popularity with seminarians, see "Poll of Princeton Students Mailed to All General Assembly Commissioners," May 6, 1929, MA; and attendance figures, cited in Machen, "The Present Situation in the Presbyterian Church," *Christianity Today* (hereafter *CT*) 1 (May 1930), 7 n. 1.

58. See for example, Machen to Edward P. Holden, January 28, 1925, MA.

59. Machen to Minnie Gresham Machen, June 30, 1915; Machen to Arthur W. Machen, Jr., January 15, 1928; and Arthur W. Machen, Jr., to Machen, January 16, 1928; MA.

60. Contrast Machen, *Attack upon Princeton Seminary,* and "The Reorganization of Princeton Seminary," 2–8.

## Chapter 6. The Responsibility of the Church in the New Age

*Epigraph:* H. Richard Niebuhr, Wilhelm Pauck, and Francis P. Miller, *The Church against the World* (Chicago, 1935), 119.

1. Works that deal insightfully with religion during the 1930s are Marty, *Noise of Conflict;* Alan Brinkley, *Voices of Protest: Huey Long, Father Coughlin and the Great Depression* (New York, 1982); Ribuffo, *The Old Christian Right;* Robert T. Handy, "The American Religious Depression, 1925–1935," *Church History* 29 (1960): 3–16; and Joel Carpenter, "Fundamentalist Institutions and the Rise of Evangelical Protestantism," *Church History* 49 (1980): 62–75.

2. On fundamentalist thought in the 1930s, see Joel A. Carpenter, "From Fundamentalism to the New Evangelical Coalition," in *Evangelicalism and Modern America,* ed. George M. Marsden (Grand Rapids, Mich., 1984), 3–16.

3. Walter Marshall Horton, *Realistic Theology* (New York, 1934), 137; Niebuhr, Pauck, and Miller, *Church against the World,* 32; and H. Richard Niebuhr, *The Kingdom of God in America* (New York, 1937), 193.

4. Financial receipts and statements, MA. On the character of Westminster's education, see *Catalogue of WTS, 1929–1930.* Much of Machen's money in all likelihood came from the Gresham family and from the sale of Machen property in Washington, D.C. On Machen's finances, see Stonehouse, *J. Gresham Machen,* 392–93, 160–66. On Bible schools, see Brereton, *Training God's Army,* 82–84.

5. On Machen's political differences with Princeton colleagues, see Machen to Minnie Gresham Machen, February 3, July 7, and November 10, 1912, August 27, 1916, March 25, 1917, and November 29, 1924, MA.

6. Mencken, "Impregnable Rock," 411, 412; "Presbyterians Deplore Report on Volsteadism"; "Intercepted Letters," *Baltimore Evening Sun*, May 26, 1926. On Machen's voting for Smith, see Machen to Minnie Gresham Machen, November 4, 1928, MA.

7. Allan J. Lichtman, *Prejudice and the Old Politics: The Presidential Election of 1928* (Chapel Hill, N.C., 1979); Marty, *Noise of Conflict*, chap. 6; and Andre Siegfried, *America Comes of Age: A French Analysis*, trans. H. H. Hemming and Doris Hemming (New York, 1927).

8. Machen, *Christianity and Liberalism* (New York, 1923), 11, 13, and 14 n. 2; Machen to Smith, January 4 and April 26, 1923; Smith to Machen, May 3, 1923. On Americanization efforts during and after World War I, see John Higham, *Strangers in the Land* (1963; 2d ed., New York, 1978), chap. 9; and Daniel S. Buczek, "Polish American and the Roman Catholic Church," *Polish Review* 21 (1976): 56–58. Machen, *The Necessity of the Christian School* (Chicago, 1934), 3, gives Smith credit for the repeal of the Lusk Laws.

9. Machen letter to congressmen appears in Stonehouse, *J. Gresham Machen*, 247–48; "Against Alien Enrollment" (letter to editor), *New York Herald Tribune*, December 7, 1925; "Against Fingerprinting" (letter to editor), *New York Times*, September 6, 1933; "Compulsory Registration" (letter to editor), *New York Times*, September 11, 1933; and "Pedestrian Rights," *The Evening Bulletin* (Phila.), January 30, 1933. For helpful nuances in twentieth-century conservative and libertarian thought, see Jerome L. Himmelstein, *To the Right: The Transformation of American Conservatism* (Berkeley, 1990), chap. 2.

10. "Child Labor and Liberty" (letter to editor), *New Republic* 41 (Dec. 31, 1924): 145; "The Christian School the Hope of America," in *The Christian School the Out-Flowering of Faith* (Chicago, 1934), reprinted in Machen, *Education, Christianity and the State*, ed. John W. Robbins (Jefferson, 1987), 130, 129; *Statement of Dr. J. Gresham Machen on the Proposed Department of Education* (Washington, D.C., 1926), 95–108. On traditionalism in twentieth-century American conservative thought, see Himmelstein, *To the Right*, 49–53. On the Sentinels of the Republic, see J. Joseph Huthmacher, *Massachusetts People and Politics* (Cambridge, 1959), 67; and Lynn Dumenil, "'The Insatiable Maw of Bureaucracy': Antistatism and Education Reform in the 1920s," *JAH* 77 (1990): 522.

11. Machen, "Reforming Government Schools," in *Education, Christianity and the State*, 62–64. For Machen's cooperation with Roman Catholics, see his correspondence with James A. Ryan of the National Catholic Welfare Conference, between 1924 and 1926, MA.

12. Machen, "Reforming Government Schools," 64–65.

13. Machen, "The Necessity of the Christian School," in National Union of Christian Schools Yearbook, *Forward in Faith* (Chicago, 1934), reprinted in *Education, Christianity, and the State*, 77, 79. A significant area where nineteenth-century Anglo-American Protestants collapsed religion and national ideals was in their justifications for public schools. See Charles Leslie Glenn, Jr., *The Myth of the Common School* (Amherst, 1987); and Diane Ravitch, *The Great School Wars* (New York, 1974).

14. *Christianity and Liberalism*, 9–10; "Consolations in the Midst of Battle" (1931), in *What Is Christianity?* ed. Stonehouse, 236–37.

15. *Christianity and Liberalism*, 10–11; "Necessity of the Christian School," 138.

16. "Shall We Have a Federal Department of Education?" in *Education, Christianity, and the State*, 87–88; "Compulsory Registration."

17. "Necessity of the Christian School," 139, 138. On Jeffersonian principles, see Lance Banning, *The Jeffersonian Persuasion* (Ithaca, N.Y., 1978).

18. On the ethno-cultural polarities of the 1920s, see Dumenil, "The Insatiable Maw of Bureaucracy," and Lichtman, *Prejudice and Old Politics*. On Machen's Southernness and differences between him and other Presbyterian conservatives, see Longfield, *Presbyterian Controversy*.

Russell, *Voices of American Fundamentalism*, 150, and Marty, *Noise of Conflict*, 176–84, argue that Machen's politics foreshadowed the close identification between right-wing politics and right-wing religion typical of later fundamentalism. For a different perspective, see D. G. Hart, "Mencken and Fundamentalism: Another Perspective," *Menckeniana* 107 (Winter 1988): 1–8.

19. Machen to Minnie Gresham Machen, November 11, 1924, MA; Thomas R. Nevin, *Irving Babbitt* (Chapel Hill, N.C., 1984), 119, 121; Mencken quoted in Ronald Lora, *Conservative Minds in America* (Chicago, 1971), 91; on Nock see, Lora, chap. 6, and Nock, *The State of the Union*, ed. Charles H. Hamilton (Indianapolis, 1991); on the Southern Agrarians, see Lora, chap. 7; and Paul K. Conkin, *The Southern Agrarians* (Knoxville, 1988).

20. "Necessity of the Christian School," 139, 140; and *Christian Faith in the Modern World*, 10. On the fundamentalist Far Right, see Ribuffo, *Old Christian Right*; Brinkley, *Voices of Protest*; and Trollinger, *God's Empire*, chap. 3.

21. On Machen's income, see Stonehouse, *J. Gresham Machen*, 391–92, 148. On the small-business interests of other fundamentalists, see Ribuffo, *Old Christian Right*, passim. Other Machen money came from his mother who pledged $3,000 per year and when she died in 1931 left $15,000 to the seminary in her will. Machen to Frank Stevenson, May 9, 1930, MA.

22. On this relationship, see Stonehouse, *J. Gresham Machen*, 160–66; and correspondence between Machen and Hodges between 1910 and 1933, MA.

23. Machen, *The Responsibility of the Church in Our New Age* (Philadelphia, 1933), 3, originally published in *Annals of the American Academy of Political and Social Science* 165 (1933): 38–47; and "Necessity of the Christian School," 125. On the changing attitudes of intellectuals toward Mencken specifically and social problems more generally, see Charles A. Fecher, *Mencken: A Study of His Thought* (New York, 1978), 161–63, 200–207; Carl Bode, *Mencken* (Carbondale, Ill., 1969), chap. 15; and Richard H. Pells, *Radical Visions and American Dreams* (1973; Middletown, Conn., 1984).

24. FDR to Machen, September 24, 1935; and Machen to FDR, September 28, 1935, printed in the *Herald Tribune*, October 2, 1935.

25. "Words of Christ Are Quoted in Response to Preacher, Who Called Security Laws Inimical to Liberty, Honesty," *New York World-Telegram*, October 4, 1935.

26. Machen to Broun, October 5, 1935, MA; idem, "A Debate about the Child Labor Amendment," *The Banner* 70 (Jan. 4, 1935), 17.

27. Machen, *The Responsibility of the Church in Our New Age*, 9.

28. Ibid., 9–10.

29. Ibid.

30. Machen used this same argument to oppose church support for Prohibition.

See "Statement by J. Gresham Machen [on Prohibition]" (1926), MA. On Southern Presbyterianism, see Ernest Trice Thompson, *The Spirituality of the Church: A Distinctive Doctrine of the Presbyterian Church in the United States* (Richmond, 1961); and James Oscar Farmer, *The Metaphysical Confederacy: James Henley Thornwell and the Synthesis of Southern Values* (Macon, Ga., 1986).

31. Machen to Paul Clelland, October 15, 1931, MA. For a fuller account of Machen's mother's death, see Stonehouse, 465–68. See also correspondence between Machen and the Hodges and Armstrongs, 1930–36, MA.

32. *Re-Thinking Missions: A Laymen's Inquiry after One Hundred Years* (New York, 1932), 22, 59, quoted in William R. Hutchison, *Errand to the World: American Protestant Thought and Foreign Missions* (Chicago, 1987), 159. On the controversy surrounding the "Laymen's Inquiry," see Archibald G. Baker, "Reactions to the Laymen's Report," *Journal of Religion* 13 (Oct. 1933): 379–98; Hutchison, *Errand to the World*, 158–75; and John R. Fitzmier and Randall Balmer, "A Poultice for the Bite of the Cobra: The Hocking Report and Presbyterian Missions in the Middle Decades of the Twentieth Century," in *The Diversity of Discipleship: The Presbyterians and Twentieth-century Christian Witness*, ed. Milton J Coalter, John M. Mulder and Louis B. Weeks (Louisville, 1991), chap. 4.

33. Machen, *Modernism and the Board of Foreign Missions of the Presbyterian Church in the U.S.A.* (Philadelphia, 1933), 5–6; Machen to Maitland Alexander, December 30, 1932, MA; "The Board and the Report," *Presbyterian Magazine* 39 (Jan. 1933): 13–14. *Modernism and the Board*, 8.

34. Pearl Buck, "The Laymen's Mission Report," *Christian Century* 49 (Nov. 23, 1932): 1434; idem, "Is There a Case for Foreign Missions?" *Harper's* (Jan. 1933): 151; and Machen, *Modernism and the Board*, 16–17. See also William R. Hutchison, *Errand to the World*, 166–69; and Nora Stirling, *Pearl Buck: A Woman in Conflict* (Piscataway, N.J., 1983), chap. 8. Some have argued that Buck was no longer under Presbyterian auspices when she made these statements. Although she relinquished her salary in 1933, she retained her status as a regularly appointed missionary, penned her articles as a missionary, and her resignation implied an official connection to the church. See James Alan Patterson, *Robert E. Speer and the Crisis of the American Protestant Missionary Movement, 1920–1937* (Ann Arbor, Mich., 1981), 152–54.

35. Throughout the twenties, Machen had suspected this board of harboring liberalism. Although he had no hard evidence, on a few occasions he made remarks that denominational officials considered inflammatory. In 1926, Robert E. Speer, senior secretary of the board, pressed Machen to substantiate his claims. Knowing that he could not prove his contention, Machen backed down. See Machen, "The Mission of the Church," *Presbyterian* 96 (April 8, 1926): 8–11; Machen to Minnie Gresham Machen, May 1 and October 6, 1926; and Machen to Arthur W. Machen, Jr., October 8, 1926, MA; Patterson, *Robert E. Speer*, 137–45; and Hutchison, *Errand to the World*, 158–59.

36. Machen to Warren H. Allen, October 30, 1929, MA. On Speer's role in the Princeton reorganization, see Hutchison, *Errand to the World*, 172; Patterson, *Robert E. Speer*, 137–38; Longfield, *Presbyterian Controversy*, chap. 8.

37. Machen to Maitland Alexander, February 3, 1933, MA; Machen, *Modernism and the Board*, 1; "Machen-Speer Debate Historic Event in Presbyterian Church," CT 4 (May 1933).

38. Machen, *Modernism and the Board*, 27–64; "A Statement by Mr. Robert E.

Speer to the Presbytery of New Brunswick at Its Meeting in Trenton, N.J., April 11, 1933," in *Brief Submitted to the Standing Committee on Foreign Missions at the General Assembly in 1933* (n.p., n.d.), MA; Machen's other charges concerned the doctrinal views of particular Board members and such small details as the language used on application blanks. On Speer's reasons for avoiding controversy, see Patterson, *Robert E. Speer*, 150–59. For the significance of the debate to conservatives, see Rian, *Presbyterian Conflict*, 135–41; and Stonehouse, *J. Gresham Machen*, 478–80, 19, 22; Longfield, *Presbyterian Controversy*, 205–8.

39. Contrast Speer, *"Re-Thinking Mission" Examined* (New York, 1933); idem, "A Statement by Mr. Robert E. Speer"; and Machen, "Dr. Machen Surveys Dr. Speer's New Book" [review of *Some Living Issues*] CT 1 (Oct. 1930): 9, 25; idem, "Dr. Robert Speer and His Latest Book" [review of *The Finality of Jesus*] CT 4 (May 1933), 11, 16, 23. Despite their differences, in 1928 Machen and Speer conducted a cordial exchange on marriage and divorce. See Machen-Speer correspondence beginning June 29, 1928, MA; and Longfield, *Presbyterian Controversy*, 118–20.

40. H. McAllister Griffiths, "145th Assembly Meets; New Missions Board Announced," CT 4 (June 1933): 12–13; Loetscher, *Broadening Church*, 150; Patterson, *Robert E. Speer*, 155–57; Rian, *Presbyterian Conflict*, 144–46; Stonehouse, *J. Gresham Machen*, 480–81.

41. Charles J. Woodbridge, *The Independent Board for Presbyterian Foreign Missions: A Statement As to its Organization and Program* (Philadelphia, n.d.), 4; Machen, "Why the Presbyterian Guardian?" *Presbyterian Guardian* (hereafter PG) 2 (Sept. 26, 1936): 245–46; Machen to J. S. Luckey, March 11, 1927, MA. For other expressions of Machen's aversion to interdenominationalism: on the fundamentalist side, see Machen to Edwin H. Rian, June 3, 1930; Machen to James M. Gray, July 7, 1929; Machen to Franklin G. Huling, September 6, 1925; on the liberal side, see John Rockefeller, Jr., to Machen, September 20 and November 11, 1926, and September 5 and 14, 1927; Machen to Rockefeller, October 28, 1926, and September 9, 1927; and William Adams Brown to Machen, March 31 and April 2, 1924; Machen to Brown, April 1 and 3, 1924. The correspondence with Brown and Rockefeller concerned Machen's participation in services and projects at the Mount Desert Parish Church in Seal Harbor, Maine, where the Machens worshiped while vacationing.

42. Mudge to A. B. Caldwell, April 1, 1934, MA; "Presbytery of New Brunswick Votes Board Loyalty Test," CT 4 (Oct. 1933): 13; Rian, *Presbyterian Conflict*, 171–72; and Longfield, *Presbyterian Controversy*, 210–13.

43. Machen, "Servants of God or Servants of Men," in *What Is Christianity?* ed. Stonehouse, 241; Stonehouse, *J. Gresham Machen*, 483–84; and "Philadelphia Modernist Attempt Fails: Dr. Machen Received by Presbytery," CT 4 (March 1934): 23–24.

44. "Is the Independent Board 'Constitutional?'" CT 4 (Nov. 1933): 25; Machen, *Statement to the Special Committee of the Presbytery of New Brunswick . . . September 25, 1934* (hereafter *Statement*) (Philadelphia, 1935), 6–7. Behind the scenes, Lewis Mudge, the stated clerk, sent letters to several presbyteries advising action against the new board. See "News of the Church: Foreign Missions—Freedom," CT 5 (May 1934): 20–22. For criticism of Mudge's activities, see Oswald T. Allis, "The Synod of Pennsylvania in 1934: A Study in Present Day Presbyterianism," CT 5 (Aug. 1934): 60–63.

45. *Studies of the Constitution of the Presbyterian Church in the U.S.A.* (Philadelphia, 1934), 4–9, 28–30, 43. On the significance of *Studies*, see Loetscher, *Broadening*

*Church*, 151ff. H. McAllister Griffiths, "Man Versus Machine: The 146th General Assembly," *CT* 5 (July 1934): 41–45.

46. Machen, *Statement*, 22–23, 32–53; "Introduction," *PG* 1 (1936): 4. For conservative reactions, see Maitland Alexander, "The Hierarchy of the Presbyterian Church"; Samuel G. Craig, "Studies of the Constitution"; and Clarence Macartney, "[Statement]," all in *CT* 5 (July 1934): 34, 49, 56.

47. Machen, *Statement*, 27, 64, 60, 39–40; "Why It Is Independent," *Independent Board Bulletin* 1 (Jan. 1935): 4. On the Independent Board's constitutionality, see four articles by Murray Forst Thompson: "Have the Organizers of the Independent Board for Presbyterian Foreign Mission Violated the Law of the Presbyterian Church in the U.S.A.?" *CT* 4 (Dec. 1933): 4, 10–12; "Dr. Pugh v. Dr. Macartney," *CT* 5 (Jan. 1935): 190–94; 5 (Feb. 1935): 213–15; and 5 (March 1935): 237–40.

48. Elmer Walker to Machen, July 16, 1934, MA. "Machen Trial to be Behind Closed Doors, First Appearance, February 14th," *CT* 5 (March 1935): 246; "New Brunswick Commission Refuses to Hear Dr. Machen's Defense," *CT* 5 (April 1935): 265–69; "Dr. Machen 'Guilty'; Penalty Suspension, Notice of Appeal Filed," *CT* 5 (May 1935): 292–94; and "Transcription Notes of Testimony in the Case of the Presbyterian Church in the U.S.A. vs. J. Gresham Machen," 141–203, MA. On the question of jurisdiction, see Oswald T. Allis, "Argument Presented to the Presbytery of Philadelphia in Support of a Memorial to the Synod of New Jersey," *CT* 5 (May 1935): 281–84; Loetscher, *Broadening Church*, 150–52; Rian, *Presbyterian Conflict*, 178–79; and Wayne Headman, "A Critical Evaluation of J. Gresham Machen," Th.M. thesis, Princeton Theological Seminary, 1974, 199–200. On the matter of the hotly disputed stub, it finally surfaced during the trial but the Commission ruled that it was too late, "Transcription," 326–34.

49. "Dr. Machen 'Guilty,'" *New York Times*, March 9, 1935. Even historians not sympathetic to Machen have agreed that Machen's expulsion signified greater theological diversity within the Presbyterian Church. See Longfield, *Presbyterian Conflict*, epilogue; and Loetscher, *Broadening Church*.

50. "Dr. Machen 'Guilty.'"

51. Robert E. Speer, *Some Living Issues* (New York, 1930), 270. On cultural pluralism and assimilation, see John Higham, *Send These to Me* (New York, 1975), chap. 9.

52. "What May Be Learned from the 1935 General Assembly of the Presbyterian Church," *Independent Board Bulletin* 1 (June 1935): 8–9.

53. "Darkness and Light," *Independent Board Bulletin* (September 1936): 7.

54. Loetscher, *Broadening Church*, 151. On the redistricting of conservative strongholds in the Presbyterian Church, see Rian, *Presbyterian Conflict*, chap. 10.

55. "A Statement by Mr. Robert E. Speer," MA.

56. Figures on missionaries come from Joel A. Carpenter, "The Evangelical Missionary Force in the 1930s," in *Earthen Vessels: American Evangelicals and Foreign Missions, 1880–1980*, ed. Joel A. Carpenter and Wilbert R. Shenk (Grand Rapids, Mich., 1990), 335–42. Figures on balloting for moderator come from Loetscher, *Broadening Church*, 150, 151; and Longfield, *Presbyterian Controversy*, 104. On the size of Machen's denomination, see Rian, *Presbyterian Conflict*, 227; and *The Orthodox Presbyterian Church, 1936–1986*, ed. Charles G. Dennison (Philadelphia, 1986), 317. By the second General Assembly, the Orthodox Presbyterian Church consisted of 105 ministers and 26 elders.

57. For membership figures on the Orthodox Presbyterian Church, see Donald A.

Luidens, "Numbering the Presbyterian Branches," in *The Mainstream Protestant "Decline": The Presbyterian Pattern*, ed. Milton J Coalter, John M. Mulder, and Louis B. Weeks (Louisville, 1990), 51–52. Hutchison, *Errand to the World*, 174–75, makes the point that NeoOrthodoxy offered a new and improved variety of conservatism.

58. Machen, "A True Presbyterian Church at Last," *PG* (June 22, 1936): 110. *Minutes* of the First General Assembly of the Presbyterian Church of America, June 1936, 4–5. On the legal disputes surrounding the new church see Rian, *Presbyterian Conflict*, 230–57. On theological controversy in new denomination, see the epilogue below. On the events leading up to Machen's death, see Stonehouse, *J. Gresham Machen*, 506–8. After losing the right to use the name Presbyterian Church of America, Machen's followers eventually adopted in 1939 the designation Orthodox Presbyterian Church.

## Epilogue

*Epigraph:* Ned B. Stonehouse, "Taking Inventory," *PG* 17 (Jan. 10, 1948): 4.

1. Good summaries of Protestant developments during the 1930s may be found in Handy, "The American Religious Depression," 3–16; Carpenter, "Fundamentalist Institutions and the Rise of Evangelical Protestantism," 62–75; and Marty, *Noise of Conflict*.

2. On the resurgence of evangelicalism in the 1940s, see Joel Carpenter, "The Fundamentalist Leaven and the Rise of an Evangelical United Front," in *The Evangelical Tradition in America*, ed. Leonard J. Sweet (Macon, Ga., 1984), 257–88; idem, "From Fundamentalism to the New Evangelical Coalition," 3–16; and George Marsden, *Reforming Fundamentalism: Fuller Seminary and the New Evangelicalism* (Grand Rapids, Mich., 1987).

3. For Machen's influence upon the evangelical intelligentsia, see Marsden, *Reforming Fundamentalism*, 32–34, 41–42, 49, 61; Noll, *Between Faith and Criticism*, 209–14; and Hart, "Doctor Fundamentalis," 341–42.

4. See D. G. Hart, "The Legacy of J. Gresham Machen and the Identity of the Orthodox Presbyterian Church," *WTJ* 53 (1991): 209–25; and Michael A. Hakkenberg, "The Battle over the Ordination of Gordon H. Clark, 1943–1948," in *Pressing Toward the Mark: Essays Commemorating Fifty Years of the Orthodox Presbyterian Church*, ed. Charles G. Dennison and Richard C. Gamble (Philadelphia, 1986), 329–50.

5. *The Southern Methodist, The Banner*, and Hodge, quoted in "Recent Tributes to Dr. Machen," *PG* 3 (Feb. 13, 1937): 189. Dieffenbach quoted in Rian, *Presbyterian Conflict*, 215.

6. On the appeal of the Independent Board to Presbyterian dispensationalists and on dispensationalist attitudes to the visible church, see Marsden, *Reforming Fundamentalism*, 41–44; and Norman Kraus, *Dispensationalism in America* (Richmond, 1956), chaps. 1–3.

7. Frank H. Stevenson to Machen, February 7, 1931, MA. Harold Ockenga, writing for *The Essentialist* (November 1929), estimated that one-quarter of Westminster's students were Methodists. He explained that Arminian students were attracted to the Calvinist seminary because the issues of the day were "Christ vs. Paganism," and whether the Bible was true. Reprint in MA. On other sources of

frictions between faculty and students, see Machen to R. B. Kuiper, March 16, 1931; Kuiper to Machen, March 26, 1931; Machen to Frank H. Stevenson, February 9, 11, March 1, April 6, and July 9, 1931; and Stevenson to Machen, February 10, April 2, and July 7, 1931, MA.

8. See George M. Marsden, "Perspective on the Division of 1937," in *Pressing Toward the Mark*, ed. Dennison and Gamble, 295–328; and Hart, "Doctor Fundamentalis," chap 9.

9. Machen to Buswell, November 27, 1936, MA; Affidavit of Helen Woods Machen, October 6, 1937, MA; Marsden, "Perspective on the Division of 1937," 310–11; Woolley, *Significance of J. Gresham Machen*, 43.

10. Buswell to Machen, December 4, 1936, MA. On Machen's fondness for movies, see, for example, his letters to his mother, May 14, 1913, March 11 and August 23, 1914, MA.

11. "Third General Assembly," *PG* 4 (June 26, 1937): 92–94; and Marsden, "Perspective on the Division of 1937," 318–21.

12. Marsden, "Perspective on the Division of 1937," 321–23; Mark A. Noll, "The Pea Beneath the Mattress—Orthodox Presbyterians in America," *Reformed Journal* 36 (1985): 11–16.

13. This is also the point of Mark A. Noll, "The Spirit of Old Princeton and the Spirit of the OPC," in *Pressing Toward the Mark*, ed. Dennison and Gamble, 235–46.

14. See Carpenter, "Fundamentalist Leaven"; and Hart, "Legacy of J. Gresham Machen."

15. See Carpenter, "New Evangelical Coalition"; Marsden, *Reforming Fundamentalism*, Introduction and chap. 1; and Hart, "Legacy of J. Gresham Machen."

16. Paul Woolley, "Discontent!" *PG* 13 (July 25, 1944): 214; and Hart, "Legacy of J. Gresham Machen." On the Americanism of nineteenth- and twentieth-century evangelicalism, see Daniel Walker Howe, "The Evangelical Movement and Political Culture in the North during the Second Party System," *JAH* 77 (1991): 1216–39; Marsden, *The Evangelical Mind and the New School Presbyterian Experience*, chaps. 9–10; idem, *Reforming Fundamentalism*, chap. 3; and the founding documents of the National Association of Evangelicals collected in *A New Evangelical Coalition*, ed. Joel A. Carpenter (New York, 1988). The OPC's attitude toward American culture should be compared to that of Dutch Calvinists. See James D. Bratt, *Dutch Calvinism in Modern America: A History of a Conservative Subculture*, chaps. 3–4.

17. See Howe, "Evangelical Movement," 1222–32.

18. Ibid., 1216–39; and Robert P. Swierenga, "Ethnoreligious Political Behavior in the Mid-Nineteenth Century: Voting, Values, Cultures," in *Religion and American Politics*, ed. Noll, chap. 7.

19. See Hart, "Legacy of J. Gresham Machen," 219–25; Noll, "Spirit of the OPC"; Marsden, *Reforming Fundamentalism*, chap. 3; Nathan O. Hatch et al., *The Gospel in America* (Grand Rapids, Mich., 1979), chaps. 8–9; and contrast *New Evangelical Coalition*, ed. Carpenter, with Woolley, *Significance of J. Gresham Machen*.

20. Howe, "Evangelical Movement," 1229, makes this point. The issue of religion in public schools provides another example of libertarian views in Old School Presbyterianism. See Robert Michaelsen, "Common School, Common Religion? A Case Study in Church-State Relations, Cincinnati, 1869–70," *Church History* 38 (1969): 201–17; and Glenn, *The Myth of the Common School*, chap. 6.

21. See Milton L. Rudnick, *Fundamentalism and the Missouri Synod: A Historical*

*Study of Their Interaction and Mutual Influence* (St. Louis, 1966); and Joseph H. Hall, "The Controversy over Fundamentalism in the Christian Reformed Church, 1915–1966," Th.D. diss., Concordia Seminary, 1974.

22. For recent assessments of the culture wars, see James Davison Hunter, *Culture Wars: The Struggle to Define America* (New York, 1991); and *Fundamentalisms Observed*, ed. Martin E. Marty and R. Scott Appleby (Chicago, 1992).

Practically all of Machen's correspondence and manuscripts are held in the Montgomery Library, Westminster Theological Seminary, Philadelphia. The archives of the Presbyterian Historical Society have papers related to his trial. A comprehensive chronological bibliography of Machen's published and unpublished writings can be found in Charles G. Dennison and Richard C. Gamble, eds., *Pressing toward the Mark: Essays Commemorating Fifty Years of the Orthodox Presbyterian Church* (Philadelphia, 1986), 461–85. The bibliography in D. G. Hart, "'Dr. Fundamentalis': An Intellectual Biography of J. Gresham Machen, 1881–1937," Ph.D. diss., Johns Hopkins University, 1988, also lists all of Machen's published writings as well as most of the primary sources used in writing this book.

Almost all of Machen's books remain in print. His scholarly works, *The Origin of Paul's Religion* (New York: Macmillan, 1921) and *The Virgin Birth of Christ* (New York: Harper and Brothers, 1930) are still the most thorough treatments of these subjects by conservative Protestants. Among Machen's semipopular books, *Christianity and Liberalism* (New York: Macmillan, 1923) and *What Is Faith?* (New York: Macmillan, 1925) provide the best index to his thought at the height of the fundamentalist controversy. The collections of radio addresses, *The Christian Faith in the Modern World* (New York: Macmillan, 1936) and *The Christian View of Man* (New York: Macmillan, 1937), published posthumously, are further evidence of Machen's theological interests and institutional commitments at the end of his life. His *New Testament Greek for Beginners* (New York: Macmillan, 1923) is still used widely at mainline and evangelical Protestant seminaries.

Machen also wrote extensively about the controversies within the Presbyterian Church and Princeton Seminary. In addition to the articles in such periodicals as the *Presbyterian, Christianity Today,* and the *Presbyterian Guardian* (all of which are listed in the comprehensive bibliography mentioned above), he also wrote and published at his own expense several pamphlets that allowed for a fuller presentation of his arguments. For the disputes at Princeton Seminary Machen produced the following: *Statement by J. Gresham Machen Submitted to the Committee Appointed by Action of the General Assembly of 1926* . . . (Privately printed, 1926); *Documents Appended to a Statement by J. Gresham Machen Submitted to the Committee Appointed by Action of the General Assembly of 1926* . . . (Privately printed, 1926); *Additional Statement Concerning the Personal Relations Between the Rev. Professor Charles R. Erdman, D.D., LL.D., and J. Gresham Machen* (Privately printed, 1926); and *The Attack upon Princeton Seminary: A Plea for Fair Play* (Princeton: J. Gresham Machen, 1927). For the missions controversy of the 1930s Machen prepared the following: *What Bible-Believing Christians Should Do at the General Assembly of 1933: Informal Memorandum* (Privately printed, 1933); *Statement to the Special Committee of the Presbytery of New Brunswick in the Presbyterian Church in the U.S.A. which as Appointed by the Presbytery* . . . (Philadelphia: J. Gresham Machen, 1935); and *Modernism and the Board of Foreign Missions of the Presbyterian Church in the U.S.A.* (Philadelphia: J. Gresham Machen, 1933), which has also been reprinted in Joel A. Carpenter, ed., *Modernism and Foreign Missions: Two Fundamentalist Protests* (New York: Garland, 1988).

Machen also wrote for nonreligious periodicals both about the fundamentalist controversy and about various political matters, from the creation of a federal department of education to Philadelphia city ordinances regulating jaywalking. Some of these efforts were solicited by editors, others appeared as letters to the editor. For a virtually complete list of these articles and letters, see the bibliography in *Pressing toward the Mark*.

Despite Machen's notoriety he has received little attention from historians outside Presbyterian circles. The only sustained biographical studies are Ned B. Stonehouse, *J. Gresham Machen: A Biographical Memoir* (Grand Rapids, Mich.: Eerdmans, 1954); and my "'Doctor Fundamentalis.'" Bradley J. Longfield, *The Presbyterian Controversy: Fundamentalists, Modernists, and Moderates* (New York: Oxford University Press, 1991), and C. Allyn Russell, *Voices of American Fundamentalism: Seven Biographical Studies* (Philadelphia: Westminster Press, 1976), devote separate chapters to Machen's thought and career. Several articles deal with Machen's abilities as a defender of historic Christianity: Cullen I. K. Story, "J. Gresham Machen: Apologist and Exegete," *Princeton Seminary Bulletin* 72 (1978): 91–103; George M. Marsden, "J. Gresham Machen, History, and Truth," *Westminster Theological Journal* 42 (1979): 157–75; and Darryl G. Hart, "The Princeton Mind in the Modern World and the Common Sense of J. Gresham Machen," *Westminster Theological Journal* 46 (1984): 1–25. Machen is also the subject of several dissertations, most of which evaluate him for theological purposes: William Masselink, "Professor J. Gresham Machen: His Life and Defence of the Bible," Th.D. diss., Free University of Amsterdam, 1938; Charles William McNutt, "The Fundamentalism of J. Gresham Machen," Th.D. diss., Union Theological Seminary, Richmond, 1952; Dallas M. Roark, "J. Gresham Machen and His Desire to Maintain a Doctrinally True Presbyterian Church," Ph.D. diss., University of Iowa, 1963; Wayne Headman, "A

Critical Evaluation of J. Gresham Machen," Th.M. thesis, Princeton Theological Seminary, 1974; and Terry A. Chrisope, "The Bible and Historical Scholarship in the Early Life and Thought of J. Gresham Machen, 1881–1915," Ph.D. diss., Kansas State University, 1988.

Several themes in American cultural and intellectual history are crucial for understanding Machen's significance and influence. One of these concerns his identity as a conservative Southerner. Figuring out the ramifications of this identity is complicated both by Machen's growing up in Baltimore, an industrial city that was not overtly Southern, and the relationship between the Victorian outlook of the New South and the classicism of the Old South. On southern intellectual developments I have relied upon Edwin A. Miles, "The Old South and the Classical World," *North Carolina Historical Review* 48 (1971): 258–75; Daniel J. Singal, *The War Within: From Victorian to Modernist Thought in the South, 1919–1945* (Chapel Hill: University of North Carolina Press, 1982); Michael O'Brien, *The Idea of the American South, 1920–1941* (Baltimore: Johns Hopkins University Press, 1979); Robert A. Ferguson, *Law and Letters in American Culture* (Cambridge: Harvard University Press, 1984); Ronald Lora, *Conservative Minds in America* (Chicago: Rand McNally, 1971); and Paul Conkin, *The Southern Agrarians* (Knoxville: University of Tennessee Press, 1988).

Striking parallels exist between Machen and other conservative intellectuals which suggest that factors other than region were responsible for Machen's conservative outlook. Works that provide material for making connections between Machen and nonreligious conservatives on both literary and political grounds are Fred C. Hobson, Jr., *The Serpent in Eden: H. L. Mencken and the South* (Chapel Hill: University of North Carolina Press, 1974); Joseph L. Morison, "Colonel H. L. Mencken, C.S.A.," *Southern Literary Journal* 1 (1968): 41–53; J. David Hoeveler, Jr., *The New Humanism: A Critique of Modern America, 1900–1940* (Charlottesville: University of Virginia Press, 1977); Thomas R. Nevin, *Irving Babbitt: An Intellectual Study* (Chapel Hill: University of North Carolina Press, 1984); Edwin Harrison Cady, *The Gentleman in America* (Syracuse: Syracuse University Press, 1949); Stow Persons, *The Decline of American Gentility* (New York: Columbia University Press, 1973); D. G. Hart, "Mencken and Fundamentalism: A Reconsideration," *Menckeniana* 107 (Fall 1989): 1–8; idem, "A Connoisseur of Rabble-Rousing, Human Folly and Theological Pathology: H. L. Mencken on American Presbyterians," *American Presbyterians* 66 (1988): 195–204; and the works on Southern Agrarians above.

Machen's classical training and his views on the purpose and nature of education placed him on the conservative side of debates within the academy about the curriculum and the study of ancient texts. The best studies of the changes within higher education during Machen's lifetime, some of which he resisted, others which he encouraged, are Laurence Veysey, *The Emergence of the American University* (Chicago: University of Chicago Press, 1965); Hugh Hawkins, *Pioneer: A History of The Johns Hopkins University* (Baltimore: Johns Hopkins University Press, 1960); Burton J. Bledstein, *The Culture of Professionalism: The Middle Class and the Development of Higher Education in America* (New

York: Oxford University Press, 1978); Thomas Bender, *Intellect and Public Life: Essays on the Social History of Academic Intellectuals in the United States* (Baltimore: Johns Hopkins University Press, 1993); Thomas L. Haskell, ed., *The Authority of Experts* (Bloomington: Indiana University Press, 1984); idem, *The Emergence of Professional Social Science: The American Social Science Association and the Nineteenth Century Crisis of Authority* (Chicago: University of Chicago Press, 1977); and Alexandra Oleson and John Voss, eds., *The Organization of Knowledge in Modern America, 1860–1920* (Baltimore: Johns Hopkins University Press, 1979).

On the implications of these developments for Machen's scholarship, see Henry Warner Bowden, *Church History in an Age of Science* (Chapel Hill: University of North Carolina Press, 1971); Robert W. Funk, "The Watershed of American Biblical Tradition: The Chicago School, First Phase, 1892–1920," *Journal of Biblical Literature* 95 (1976): 4–22; Mark S. Massa, *Charles Augustus Briggs and the Crisis of Historical Criticism* (Minneapolis: Fortress Press, 1990); Mark A. Noll, *Between Faith and Criticism: Evangelical, Scholarship, and the Bible in America* (San Francisco: Harper and Row, 1986); James P. Wind, *The Bible and the University: The Messianic Vision of William Rainey Harper* (Atlanta: Scholars Press, 1987); and Nathan O. Hatch and Mark A. Noll, eds., *The Bible in America: Essays in Cultural History* (New York: Oxford University Press, 1982). On the effects of academic professionalization upon religion and higher education see the essays in George M. Marsden and Bradley J. Longfield, eds., *The Secularization of the Academy* (New York: Oxford University Press, 1992).

Ideas about history and the meaning of texts were as important for shaping Machen's biblical scholarship as were theological convictions. In order to compare his research and assumptions with that of contemporaries in humanistic and historical disciplines I have relied upon Oleson and Voss, ed., *The Organization of Knowledge;* Hoeveler, *The New Humanism;* Persons, *The Decline of American Gentility;* Gerald Graff, *Professing Literature: An Institutional History* (Chicago: University of Chicago Press, 1987); Frederick J. Hoffman, *The Twenties: American Writing in the Postwar Decade* (New York: Viking Press, 1955); William Riley Parker, "The MLA, 1883–1953," *Proceedings of the Modern Language Association* 68 (1953): 3–39; John Higham, *History: Professional Scholarship in America* (1965; rev. ed., Baltimore: Johns Hopkins University Press, 1983); David A. Hollinger, *In the American Province: Studies in the History and Historiography of Ideas* (Bloomington: Indiana University Press, 1985); David W. Noble, *The Paradox of Progressive Thought* (Minneapolis: University of Minnesota Press, 1958); Allen Skotheim, *American Intellectual Histories and Historians* (Princeton: Princeton University Press, 1966); and Morton White, *Social Thought in America: The Revolt against Formalism* (1947; rev. ed., New York: Oxford University Press, 1976).

Another important source of Machen's conservatism was Calvinism. The literature on Calvinist theology in American intellectual life is dominated by studies of Puritanism. More germane for understanding Machen and the Presbyterian controversies in which he was involved is the work on nineteenth- and twentieth-century Presbyterianism. Most of this work centers on Princeton Seminary and evaluates the institution's teaching about the Bible. These works include Mark A. Noll, ed., *The Princeton Theology, 1812–1921: Scripture, Science, and Theological Method from Archibald Alexander to Benjamin Warfield* (Grand Rapids, Mich.: Baker Book House, 1983); W. Andrew Hoffecker, *Piety and the Princeton Theologians: Archibald Alexander, Charles Hodge, and Benjamin Warfield* (Phillipsburg, N.J.: Presbyterian and Reformed Publishing Co., 1981); Jack B. Rogers and Donald K. McKim, *The Authority and Interpretation of the Bible: An Historical Approach* (San Francisco: Harper and Row, 1979); John C. Vander Stelt, *Philosophy and Scripture: A Study in Old Princeton and Westminster Theology* (Marlton, N.J.: Mack Publishing, 1978); Randall H. Balmer, "The Princetonians and Scripture: A Reconsideration," *Westminster Theological Journal* 44 (1982): 352–65; and Ernest R. Sandeen, "The Princeton Theology: One Source of Biblical Literalism in American Protestantism," *Church History* 31 (1962): 307–21.

An important theme in the literature on Old Princeton has been the influence of Scottish Common Sense Philosophy. In addition to the works cited above, the following explore the relationship between Enlightenment philosophy and Presbyterian theology: Theodore Dwight Bozeman, *Protestants in an Age of Science: The Baconian Ideal and Antebellum American Religious Thought* (Chapel Hill: University of North Carolina Press, 1977); J. David Hoeveler, Jr., *James McCosh and the Scottish Intellectual Tradition* (Princeton: Princeton University Press, 1981); Herbert Hovenkamp, *Science and Religion in America, 1800–1860* (Philadelphia: University of Pennsylvania Press, 1978); Bruce Kuklick, *Churchmen and Philosophers: From Jonathan Edwards to John Dewey* (New Haven: Yale University Press, 1985); George M. Marsden, "The Collapse of American Evangelical Academia," in *Faith and Rationality: Reason and Belief in God*, ed. Alvin Plantinga and Nicholas Wolterstorff (Notre Dame: University of Notre Dame Press, 1983), 219–64; Mark A. Noll, "Common Sense Traditions and American Evangelical Thought," *American Quarterly* 37 (1985): 216–38; idem, *Princeton and the Republic, 1768–1822* (Princeton: Princeton University Press, 1989); and Sydney E. Ahlstrom, "The Scottish Philosophy and American Theology," *Church History* 24 (1955): 257–72.

Debates about the influence of Common Sense Realism on Machen can be found in George M. Marsden, "J. Gresham Machen, History, and Truth"; Darryl G. Hart, "The Princeton Mind in the Modern World"; and idem, "A Reconsideration of Biblical Inerrancy and the Princeton Theology's Alliance with Fundamentalism," *Christian Scholar's Review* 20 (1991): 362–75.

Unfortunately, the work on the Princeton theology has rarely moved beyond questions about Common Sense Philosophy and biblical inerrancy. Fuller treatments of Northern Presbyterian thought and culture have not been attempted but the following on southern Presbyterianism serve as excellent models: James Oscar Farmer, Jr., *The Metaphysical Confederacy: James Henley Thornwell and the Synthesis of Southern Values* (Macon, Ga., Mercer University Press, 1986); E. Brooks Holifield, *The Gentlemen Theologians: American Theology in Southern Culture, 1795–1860* (Durham: Duke University Press, 1978); Eugene D. Genovese, *"Slavery Ordained of God": The Southern Slaveholders' View of Biblical History and Modern Politics* (Gettysburg, Pa.: Gettysburg College, 1985); Eugene D. Genovese and Elizabeth Fox-Genovese, "The Divine Sanction of Social Order: Religious Foundations of the Slaveholders' World View," *Journal of the American Academy of Religion* 55 (1987): 211–33; Ernest Trice Thompson, *Presbyterians in the South,* 3 vols. (Richmond: John Knox Press, 1973); and idem, *The Spirituality of the Church: A Distinctive Doctrine of the Presbyterian Church in the United States* (Richmond: John Knox Press, 1961). Also useful on broader Presbyterian developments are George M. Marsden, *The Evangelical Mind and the New School Presbyterian Experience: A Case Study of Thought and Theology in Nineteenth-century America* (New Haven: Yale University Press, 1970); Elwyn Smith, *The Presbyterian Ministry in American Culture* (Philadelphia: Westminster Press, 1962); Leonard J. Trinterud, *The Forming of an American Tradition: A Re-examination of Colonial Presbyterianism* (Philadelphia: Westminster Press, 1949); and the essays in Dennison and Gamble, *Pressing toward the Mark.*

The literature on fundamentalism is large and growing. The old image of fundamentalists as rural, Southern, and anti-intellectual dominated standard historical accounts. This impression was created chiefly by Stewart G. Cole, *The History of Fundamentalism* (New York: Richard R. Smith, 1931); Norman Furniss, *The Fundamentalist Controversy, 1918–1931* (New Haven: Yale University Press, 1954); Ray Ginger, *Six Days or Forever? Tennessee v. John Thomas Scopes* (Chicago: Quadrangle Books, 1968); and Richard Hofstadter, *Anti-intellectualism in American Life* (New York: Vintage Books, 1962). Recent revisionist studies have treated fundamentalism more sympathetically as a robust theological tradition that became marginal to academic life. The following works are responsible for this historiographical shift: Paul A. Carter, "The Fundamentalist Defense of the Faith," in *Change and Continuity in Twentieth-century America: The 1920s,* ed. John Braeman, Robert Bremmer, and David Brody (Columbus: Ohio State University Press, 1968), 179–214; Ernest R. Sandeen, *The Roots of Fundamentalism: British and American Millenarianism, 1800–1930* (Chicago: University of Chicago Press, 1970); and George M. Marsden, *Fundamentalism and American Culture: The Shaping of Twentieth-century Evangelicalism, 1870–1925* (New York: Oxford University Press, 1980). Two recent books that carry forward this revised understanding of fundamentalism are Virginia Lieson Brereton, *Training God's Army: The American Bible School, 1880–1940* (Bloomington: Indiana University Press, 1990); and William Vance Trollinger, Jr., *God's Empire: William Bell Riley and Midwestern Fundamentalism* (Madison: Wisconsin University Press, 1990).

The newer interpretation of fundamentalism as a distinct intellectual tradition has made it easier to explain Machen's involvement in the controversy, although the links between him and fundamentalism have focused too much upon science and Common Sense Philosophy. More important for understanding Machen's religious conservatism were the peculiar tensions within American Presbyterianism over the meaning of the Westminster Confession and church polity. Works that explore some of these dynamics are Lefferts A. Loetscher, *The Broadening Church: A Study of Theological Issues in the Presbyterian*

*Church since 1869* (Philadelphia: University of Pennsylvania Press, 1954); Longfield, *The Presbyterian Controversy;* Ronald Thomas Clutter, "The Reorientation of Princeton Theological Seminary," Th.D. diss., Dallas Theological Seminary, 1982; George L. Haines, "The Princeton Theological Seminary, 1925–1960," Ph.D. diss., New York University, 1966; Kim Ki-Hong, "Presbyterian Conflict in the Early Twentieth Century: Ecclesiology in the Princeton Tradition and the Emergence of Presbyterian Fundamentalism," Ph.D. diss., Drew University, 1983; and John W. Hart, "Princeton Theological Seminary: The Reorganization of 1929," *Journal of Presbyterian History* 58 (1980): 124–40.

The modernist-fundamentalist controversy was contemporaneous with the shift in American culture from Victorianism to modernism. The literature on this cultural transformation is immense but few attempts have been made to link Protestant controversies to cultural change. For insights into this relationship I have relied especially upon Daniel Joseph Singal, "Towards a Definition of American Modernism," and David A. Hollinger, "The Knower and the Artificer," in *Modernist Culture in America*, ed. Daniel Joseph Singal (Belmont, Calif.: Wadsworth Publishing, 1991), 1–27, 42–69; Singal, *The War Within;* Henry F. May, *The End of American Innocence: The First Years of Our Time, 1912–1917* (New York: Alfred A. Knopf, 1959); Hollinger, *In the American Province;* Daniel Walker Howe, ed., *Victorian America* (Philadelphia: University of Pennsylvania Press, 1976); James T. Kloppenberg, *Uncertain Victory: Social Democracy and Progressivism* (New York: Oxford University Press, 1986); White, *Social Thought in America;* Robert H. Wiebe, *The Search for Order, 1877–1920* (New York: Hill and Wang, 1967); T. J. Jackson Lears, *No Place of Grace: Antimodernism and the Transformation of American Culture, 1880–1920* (New York: Pantheon, 1981); and Stanley Coben, *Rebellion against Victorianism: The Impetus for Cultural Change in 1920s America* (New York: Oxford University Press, 1991).

Histories of fundamentalism and theological modernism have primarily interpreted the controversy as a struggle over epistemologies, that is, between fundamentalist realism and modernist historicism. This has led to the conclusion that theological modernists implicitly supported cultural modernism while fundamentalists defended Victorian culture. Yet this perspective has obscured the degree to which mainstream Protestantism perpetuated a Victorian outlook throughout the first half of the twentieth century. The best guides to the intellectual dimensions of the fundamentalist-modernist controversy are Marsden, *Fundamentalism and American Culture;* Carter, "The Fundamentalist Defense of the Faith"; William R. Hutchison, *The Modernist Impulse in American Protestantism* (Cambridge: Harvard University Press, 1976); Grant Wacker, *Augustus H. Strong and the Dilemma of Historical Consciousness* (Macon, Ga.: Mercer University Press, 1985); and Rudolph Nelson, *The Making and Unmaking of an Evangelical Mind: The Case of Edward Carnell* (New York: Cambridge University Press, 1987). On the cultural consequences of the fundamentalist controversy for mainstream Protestantism, see William R. Hutchison, ed., *Between the Times: The Travail of the Protestant Establishment, 1900–1960* (New York: Cambridge University Press, 1989); idem, "Cultural Strain and Protestant Liberalism," *American Historical Review* 76 (1971): 386–411; idem, *Errand to the World: American Protestant Thought and Foreign Missions* (Chicago: University of Chicago Press, 1987); Martin A. Marty, *Modern American Religion*, Vol. 2: *The Noise of Conflict, 1919–1941* (Chicago: University of Chicago Press, 1991); Joel A. Carpenter, "The Renewal of American Fundamentalism, 1930–1945," Ph.D. diss., Johns Hopkins University, 1984; George M. Marsden, *Reforming Fundamentalism: Fuller Seminary and the New Evangelicalism* (Grand Rapids, Mich.: Eerdmans, 1987); and George M. Marsden, ed., *Evangelicalism and Modern America* (Grand Rapids, Mich.: Eerdmans, 1984).

An issue particularly relevant to mainstream Protestantism's influence upon American culture is politics. Beyond studies of fundamentalism's anti-evolution campaign and the social gospel's ties to Progressivism the relationship between religion and politics in Machen's lifetime has not been adequately addressed. Because Machen's politics differed greatly from those of both fundamentalist and mainstream Protestants, interpreting his political views in light of his beliefs is particularly difficult. Nevertheless, a number of works were very helpful for locating Machen's voice in the political discourse of the early twentieth century. For general overviews of progressivism see Wiebe, *Search for Order*; Daniel T. Rodgers, "In Search of Progressivism," in *The Promise of American History*, ed. Stanley I. Kutler and Stanley N. Katz (Baltimore: Johns Hopkins University Press, 1982), 113–32; and John Higham, "Hanging Together: Divergent Unities in American History," *Journal of American History* 61 (1974): 5–28. On the links between reform and the ethical concerns of mainstream Protestantism see Robert M. Crunden, *Ministers of Reform: The Progressives' Achievement in American Civilization, 1889–1920* (New York: Basic Books, 1982); David B. Danbom, *"The World of Hope": Progressives and the Struggle for an Ethical Public Life* (Philadelphia: Temple University Press, 1987); and Donald K. Gorrell, *The Age of Social Responsibility: The Social Gospel in the Progressive Era, 1900–1920* (Macon, Ga.: Mercer University Press, 1988). On the politics of fundamentalists see Leo P. Ribuffo, *The Old Christian Right: The Protestant Far Right from the Great Depression to the Cold War* (Philadelphia: Temple University Press, 1983); Lawrence Levine, *Defender of the Faith: William Jennings Bryan, 1915–1925* (New York: Oxford University Press, 1965); and Alan Brinkley, *Voices of Protest: Huey Long, Father Coughlin and the Great Depression* (New York: Vintage Books, 1982). In order to gain some perspective on Machen's antistatist libertarianism I have relied upon Lynn Dumenil, " 'The Insatiable Maw of Bureaucracy': Antistatism and Education Reform in the 1920s," *Journal of American History* 77 (1990): 499–524; Jerome L. Himmelstein, *To the Right: The Transformation of American Conservatism* (Berkeley: University of California Press, 1990); and Paul L. Murphy, *World War I and the Origin of Civil Liberties in the United States* (New York: W. W. Norton, 1979). Also helpful for understanding the political implications of Machen's Presbyterian confessionalism has been the ethnocultural interpretations offered by Allan J. Lichtman, *Prejudice and the Old Politics: The Presidential Election of 1928* (Chapel Hill: University of North Carolina Press, 1979); Robert P. Swierenga, "Ethnoreligious

Political Behavior in the Mid-nineteenth Century: Voting, Values, Cultures," in *Religion and American Politics*, ed. Mark A. Noll (New York: Oxford University Press, 1990); and Daniel Walker Howe, "The Evangelical Movement and Political Culture in the North during the Second Party System," *Journal of American History* 77 (1991): 1216–39.

# INDEX